Language, Sexuality, and Power

STUDIES IN LANGUAGE, GENDER, AND SEXUALITY
Lal Zimman, *General Editor*

Advisory Board
Deborah Cameron, University of Oxford
Marjorie Goodwin, University of California, Los Angeles
Michelle Lazar, National University of Singapore
William Leap, American University
Bonnie McElhinny, University of Toronto
Tommaso Milani, University of the Witwatersrand
Norma Mendoza-Denton, University of Arizona
Pia Pichler, Goldsmiths University of London

Reinventing Identities: The Gendered Self in Discourse
Edited by Mary Bucholtz, A.C. Liang, and Laurel A. Sutton

Pronoun Envy: Literacy Uses of Linguistic Gender
Anna Livia

Japanese Language, Gender and Ideology: Cultural Models and Real People
Edited by Shigeko Okamoto and Janet S. Shibamoto Smith

Language and Women's Place: Text and Commentaries
Revised and Expanded Edition
By Robin Tolmach Lakoff
Edited by Mary Bucholtz

From the Kitchen to the Parlor: Language and Becoming in African American Women's Hair Care
Lanita Jacobs-Huey

Gender, Sexuality, and Meaning: Linguistic Practice and Politics
Sally McConnell-Ginet

Queer Excursions: Retheorizing Binaries in Language, Gender, and Sexuality
Edited by Lal Zimman, Jenny Davis, and Joshua Raclaw

Language, Sexuality, and Power: Studies in Intersectional Sociolinguistics
Edited by Erez Levon and Ronald Beline Mendes

Language, Sexuality, and Power

STUDIES IN INTERSECTIONAL SOCIOLINGUISTICS

Edited by Erez Levon
and
Ronald Beline Mendes

OXFORD
UNIVERSITY PRESS

OXFORD
UNIVERSITY PRESS

Oxford University Press is a department of the University of
Oxford. It furthers the University's objective of excellence in research,
scholarship, and education by publishing worldwide.

Oxford   New York
Auckland   Cape Town   Dar es Salaam   Hong Kong   Karachi
Kuala Lumpur   Madrid   Melbourne   Mexico City   Nairobi
New Delhi   Shanghai   Taipei   Toronto

With offices in
Argentina   Austria   Brazil   Chile   Czech Republic   France   Greece
Guatemala   Hungary   Italy   Japan   Poland   Portugal   Singapore
South Korea   Switzerland   Thailand   Turkey   Ukraine   Vietnam

Oxford is a registered trademark of Oxford University Press
in the UK and certain other countries.

Published in the United States of America by
Oxford University Press
198 Madison Avenue, New York, NY 10016

Cataloging-in-Publication data is on file at the Library of Congress
ISBN 978-0-19-021036-6 (hbk.); 978-0-19-021037-3 (pbk.)

9 8 7 6 5 4 3 2
Printed in the United States of America
on acid-free paper

CONTENTS

SERIES FOREWORD

Oxford's series Studies in Language, Gender, and Sexuality provides a broad-based interdisciplinary forum for the best new scholarship on language, gender, and sexuality. The mandate of the series is to encourage innovative work in the field, a goal that may be achieved through the revisitation of familiar topics from fresh vantage points, through the introduction of new avenues of research, or through new theoretical or methodological frameworks. The series is interdisciplinary in its scope: Volumes may be authored by scholars in such disciplines as anthropology, communication, education, feminist and gender studies, linguistics, literary studies, psychology, queer studies, race and ethnic studies, and sociology, and other fields.

EDITOR'S PREFACE

The publication of *Language, Sexuality, and Power* marks the beginning of a new phase—with a new name—for Oxford University Press's Studies in Language, Gender, and Sexuality. Founded by Mary Bucholtz with the publication of *Reinvented Identities: The Gendered Self in Discourse* (edited by Mary Bucholtz, A. C. Liang, & Laurel A. Sutton, 1999), the series has played a vital role in shaping the field of language, gender, and sexuality, and to take on the mantle of Series Editor is nothing short of an honor.

Language, Sexuality, and Power offers, in many ways, an ideal starting point for the series' new phases. Most simply, its specific focus on sexuality highlights the shift from the name *Studies in Language and Gender* to the more inclusive *Studies in Language, Gender, and Sexuality*. Sexuality has always been an important part of the books published in the series, but this change offers a more overt recognition of sexuality as a realm of human experience that is intimately connected with, but not wholly subsumable under, gender. Beyond this focus, however, Levon & Mendes' volume represents a marriage of sorts between the closely connected fields of sociolinguistics and linguistic anthropology. For decades, one of the central disciplinary questions for scholars of language, culture, and society has been the relative positioning of these two academic traditions, which have sometimes been referred to as "twin fields." Despite a shared concern for the variable, multifaceted, and inherently social nature of language, the two disciplines grew in different directions during the latter half of the twentieth century, resulting in different theoretical frameworks, methodological priorities, and analytic tools. Though much can be (and has been) said about the relationship between sociolinguistics and linguistic anthropology, one of the differences most often highlighted is their differing orientations to quantitative and qualitative analysis. These varying alignments seem particularly salient in the study of language and sexuality, which at times has seemed like two parallel areas of research: the qualitative, discourse-focused queer linguistics that was birthed in the early days of 1990s queer theory and the quantitative, often phonetically oriented, research on sexuality as an important variable driving sociolinguistic variation, which has become an increasingly vibrant topic over the past fifteen years.

For those of us who hope for a more closely united future for sociolinguistics and linguistic anthropology, *Language, Sexuality, and Power* is an extremely promising example of the ways quantitative analysis of the distribution of linguistic forms can be brought together with a deep sensitivity to sociocultural context and the insights of social theory. While employing methods common in variationist studies, such as acoustic and statistical analysis, the authors featured in this volume also offer discussions of social and interactional context that go beyond typical variationist fare. One clear reason for this depth is the variety of cultural locales in which the authors situate their investigations. This diversity inhibits the possibility of implicitly relying on the reader's social knowledge as a (presumed) member of the social groups most typically studied in sociolinguistics—namely, factions of dominant Anglophone cultural systems in North America and the United Kingdom. In this sense, contributors place themselves within an anthropological framework of cultural description that also reflects the ongoing internationalization of the field of language, gender, and sexuality—and sociolinguistics more broadly—in this age of globalization.

Finally, *Language, Sexuality, and Power* takes on one of the most central issues in the study of language, culture, and society: the locus for the production of social meaning. As the editors' introduction notes, one major challenge in sociolinguistics has been to move away from a correlational model of meaning, in which social characteristics statistically linked to particular linguistic features are assumed to be the cause of those features' use. The analysis of stance provides an alternative to this model with several advantages. To begin, it avoids the essentialism of claims that groups like "women" and "men" or "lesbians/gays" and "straights," as a whole, engage in a particular linguistic practices without respect for the way gender intersects with race, nationality, sexuality, class, and myriad other forms of social subjectivity. Incorporating stance into quantitative analysis provides a means for understanding why not all individuals participate in trends associated with their demographic characteristics. Most important, stance grounds the production of social meaning in the discourse that speakers produce in interaction. In other words, a consideration of stance demands that we go beyond counting the occurrence of linguistic variables in an interview or other speech event, and instead requires a deeper look at the discursive and interactional context in which those variants are deployed. A focus on stance reminds us that socioindexical meaning is always produced in concert with referential and interactional meaning, and that a focus on sociolinguistic variables without regard for what a speaker is saying or doing when that variable occurs provides, at best, a limited understanding of how social meaning emerges.

In these ways, *Language, Sexuality, and Power* pushes forward the study of language, gender, and sexuality, and it is with these strengths in mind that I am delighted to present this volume with the hope that it marks a new chapter not only for the series but for the field itself.

Lal Zimman
Series Editor

LIST OF CONTRIBUTORS

Erez Levon is Senior Lecturer in Linguistics at Queen Mary University of London. His work uses quantitative, qualitative, and experimental methods to examine socially meaningful patterns of variation in language, particularly those related to gender and sexuality. He is the author of *Language and the Politics of Sexuality: Lesbians and Gays in Israel* (Palgrave, 2010).

Marie Maegaard is Associate Professor in the Department of Nordic Research and the LANCHART Center at the University of Copenhagen. She is a sociolinguist and her work focuses on language variation and social meaning.

Claire Maree is Senior Lecturer in Japanese at the Asia Institute, University of Melbourne. Her research explores the linguistic negotiation of gender and sexuality in spoken discourse and the dynamics of language, gender, and sexuality in the media.

Sara Mack (PhD, University of Minnesota) is Lecturer in the Department of Spanish and Portuguese at the University of Minnesota. Her current research investigates sociophonetics and psychosocial aspects of language learning at the university level. Other research interests include mobile applications in language teaching, bilingual cognition, and learning and memory.

Ronald Beline Mendes is an Associate Professor of Linguistics at the University of São Paulo. His work focuses on qualitative and quantitative sociolinguistics of the Portuguese spoken in São Paulo, with a particular interest in social meanings of linguistic variation related to social class, gender, and sexuality.

Thabo Msibi is Senior Lecturer in the School of Education at the University of KwaZulu-Natal, South Africa, where he teaches in the Discipline of Curriculum and Education Studies. His research focuses on "non-normative" gender and sexual diversities and schooling.

Viktória Papp is Lecturer at the University of Canterbury, New Zealand. Her main areas of interest are language and sexuality, phonetics, and forensic linguistics.

Nicolai Pharao is Associate Professor in the Department of Scandinavian Studies and Linguistics and the LANCHART Center at the University of Copenhagen. His work focuses on segmental variation and the interplay between features in speech production and perception.

Robert J. Podesva is Assistant Professor of Linguistics at Stanford University, where he directs the Interactional Sociophonetics Laboratory and participates in the Voices of California project. His research investigates the social significance of phonetic variation, with a focus on gender/sexuality.

Péter Rácz is a postdoctoral research fellow at the New Zealand Institute of Language Brain and Behaviour at the University of Canterbury, New Zealand. His main areas of interest are sociolinguistic variation and change.

Stephanie Rudwick holds a research position at the Afrikanistik Institute at Leipzig University, Germany, funded by the DFG (German Research Foundation). Her main interest is language and gender, identity and ethnicity, and, more recently, language policy and planning.

Pavadee Saisuwan is Lecturer in the Linguistics department at Chulalongkorn University, and a PhD candidate in Linguistics at Queen Mary University of London. Her research focuses on linguistic variation and male femininity among men who identify with non-normative male roles in Thailand.

Janneke Van Hofwegen is a PhD candidate in Linguistics at Stanford University and also holds an MA in English Linguistics from North Carolina State University. She studies regional and ethnic dialectology and stylistic variation from both sociophonetic and morphosyntactic perspectives.

Andrew D. Wong is Associate Professor of Anthropology at California State University, East Bay. His publications on language and sexuality have appeared in *Pragmatics, Language in Society, Journal of Sociolinguistics*, and *Journal of Linguistic Anthropology*.

1

Introduction

LOCATING SEXUALITY IN LANGUAGE

Erez Levon and Ronald Beline Mendes

Research on language and sexuality has come a long way since the inception of the field some thirty-five years ago. Even our choice of the title for this introductory chapter can be taken as evidence of how work in this area has developed from one focused primarily on the linguistic behavior of specific groups of speakers (lesbians, gay men, etc.) to one that focuses instead on how sexuality (in all of its guises) emerges through linguistic practice. As Queen (2014) notes, this change in how the field conceptualizes its object of study is due in large part to the increased integration within sociolinguistics of theoretical models of self and society drawn from related disciplines, including cultural studies and anthropology. At the same time, research on language and sexuality has also grown increasingly prominent in areas outside sociolinguistics, notably in laboratory phonology (see Munson & Babel 2007; Eckert & Podesva 2011), where critical social theory has less of a foothold. This expansion of disciplinary approaches to the topic is a welcome development and has helped to solidify the empirical foundation of research in this area. Yet we would argue that it has also had the effect of making it at times more difficult to see how all the research conducted under the rubric of language and sexuality studies contributes to a common scholarly endeavor. One of the goals of this book is to demonstrate that it does, and to illustrate how studies emanating from various methodological perspectives all contribute to a broader understanding of the relationship between sexuality and language. For this reason, we aim in this chapter to take stock of where we currently stand, both theoretically and empirically, in relation to the study of language and sexuality. We do so not to establish prescriptive boundaries around this particular field of inquiry but rather to situate the different strands of existing research in a comprehensive and inclusive analytical framework. Put somewhat more simply, our goal is to demonstrate how all the different pieces fit together, and, as a result, to high-light fruitful avenues for taking language and sexuality research forward.

The framework we propose, which we describe in detail in this chapter, is grounded within an approach to the study of language that focuses on examining how the distribution of discrete linguistic features—be they phonological, morphosyntactic, lexical, or discursive—participates in the construction and perception of social meaning. Aware of the extent to which the naming of a methodology is itself a meaning-making practice (Wong, Roberts, & Campbell-Kibler 2002), we choose to avoid using a label like "variationist" to describe this approach in order to highlight that the framework we have in mind involves bringing together quantitative, qualitative, and experimental methods. We simultaneously wish to emphasize, however, our belief that it is only by investigating the systematic distribution of socially meaningful linguistic forms that we can come to understand the relationship between social structure and individual subjectivity and the ways in which language mediates between the two. In other words, we maintain that a distributional focus on linguistic form provides us with the most robust and empirically reliable means for uncovering the linguistic processes through which sexuality is socially materialized. This is not to say that (critical) discourse analytic approaches are unimportant. Past research has shown that they are immensely useful in teasing apart the sociocultural intricacies of interaction and in identifying the ideologies that constrain and inform how sexualities are experienced. Yet, we nevertheless wish to reaffirm the importance of "sociolinguistic empiricism" (Woolard 1985) to this endeavor—not just in providing a complementary perspective but also in tying down our interpretations (Rampton 2007) and making them accountable to systematic patterns of language-in-use.

In the remainder of this chapter, we describe the basic contours of our theoretical and methodological approach. We begin with a brief review of the major developments in the field of language and sexuality over the past thirty-five years (for more extensive reviews, see Cameron & Kulick 2003; Queen 2007, 2014). Through this review, we identify two inter-related areas that we believe require further critical attention. The first involves the relationship between structure and agency in constraining sociolinguistic practice, or, put another way, the central role of power in shaping linguistic behavior. This is by no means a new concern in language and sexuality research (Bucholtz & Hall 2004; Cameron 2011), and we offer suggestions for how to re-center this issue in our work via the adoption of a multilevel framework for conceptualizing social practice (Bourdieu & Wacquant 1992). The second area that we identify involves the imbrication of sexuality with other dimensions of lived experience, including those shaped by gender, nation, race, and social class. While, once again, this is not an entirely new critique (e.g., Cameron & Kulick 2003), we claim that language and sexuality research needs to adopt a more sophisticated approach to the ways in which these different dimensions interact. We argue here that *intersectionality theory* (Crenshaw 1989; McCall 2005; Yuval-Davis 2011b) provides us with an analytical framework for doing so. We describe how, because of its insistence on the mutual constitution of socially relevant categories, intersectionality prevents us from considering sexuality in isolation. Instead, it pushes us to critically examine how both the positioning of sexualities in particular social and historical contexts (i.e., structure) and the ways in which individuals negotiate these positionings (i.e., agency) are the product of multiple and intersecting systems of social classification (Choo & Ferree 2010). Our use of intersectionality theory thus complements our arguments with respect to the structure/agency divide, and enables us to illustrate a method for examining the "total linguistic fact" (Silverstein 1985) of sexuality. Finally, we close the chapter with a brief outline of how the various contributions to the volume serve to illustrate the theoretical arguments we make here.

Mapping the Field of Inquiry

It is difficult to pinpoint an exact date when the field of language and sexuality began. For our purposes, we identify the publication of Chesebro's (1981a) volume titled *Gayspeak: Gay Male and Lesbian Communication* as the first major publication in which the issue of lesbian and gay language was situated within a broader theoretical framework. Prior to this, scholarly work on language and sexuality was restricted primarily to the compilation of lists of lexical items or phrases that could be said to comprise a gay or lesbian "argot" (e.g., Legman 1941; Stanley 1970), though a handful of studies also examined certain discursive and/or interactional phenomena (see Livia & Hall 1997 for a review). Building on this earlier work, Chesebro (1981b) sets out to initiate "a new research approach to an old topic . . . [by providing] a framework . . . for viewing homosexuality as a communication phenomenon and as a communication system" (xiii–xiv). To that end, Chesebro enumerates six questions that the field of language and sexuality should address, the second of which is relevant to us here: "What constitutes the intersubjective reality of those who label themselves gay or lesbian?" (xiv).[1] In Chesebro's formulation, this intersubjective reality is itself reflected in shared linguistic practice. Identifying how lesbians and gays use language would thus allow research to understand what it means to *be* lesbian or gay. While Chesebro's framework allows for variation among lesbians and gays, such that there may be varying levels of the use of so-called Gayspeak, this variation is conceptualized as resulting from differential levels of integration in the lesbian and/or gay community, or, as Hayes (1981) puts it, "subculture."

The theoretical framework that Chesebro describes relies on two foundational assumptions. The first is that there exists a lesbian/gay community or subculture, and that it is membership in this community and the shared experiences therein that define lesbian/gay "identity." The second assumption is then that this shared identity gives rise to a set of distinctive social and linguistic practices. In this respect, Chesebro's framework is *correlational* in nature (cf. Eckert 2012). It assumes that an underlying social structure is the cause of distinctive linguistic practice, meaning that we as researchers can account for any practices observed by correlating them with the social structure from which they purportedly emerge. This correlational approach predominated in language and sexuality research throughout the 1980s and early 1990s (as it did in much sociolinguistic work of the period more generally). During that time, a series of influential studies appeared that examined both the phonological (Moonwomon 1985; Fai 1988; Avery & Liss 1996; Taylor 1996) and the discursive (Day & Morse 1981; Hayes 1981; Leap 1993, 1996) characteristics that could arguably constitute a "lesbian" or "gay" way of speaking. This work on language production was coupled with a growing body of research on perception, in which scholars employed experimental methods in an attempt to correlate listeners' abilities to (correctly) identify the sexual orientation of a speaker with the presence of specific features in the speech signal (e.g., Moonwomon 1985; Gaudio 1994).

Beginning in the 1990s, a confluence of developments in both linguistic and social theory challenged the theoretical underpinnings of the correlational model. The most prominent of these was the advent of *queer theory* (Butler 1990, 1993), which destabilized the very notion of identity and its connection to group membership. Inverting the causal relationship between identity and social practice, the queer theoretic approach argued that individuals draw on socially meaningful symbolic resources (including language) in the performative enactment of identity. In other words, identity is not the cause of observed behavior but rather its result. This process is enabled by the fact that practices are already linked to identifiable social categories and positions, making them available to speakers in the active construction of identity. The *constructionist* approach advocated by queer theory was further extended within linguistics by a reconceptualization of the relationship between language and social meaning. With her theory of indexicality, Ochs (1992) popularized the notion that the link between language and a social category is rarely, if ever, a direct one. Rather, Ochs argues that linguistic forms serve to index particular stances, acts, and activities that are then ideologically linked to salient social categories. According to this approach, tag questions, for example, do not directly index the category *woman*. Instead, they are taken to signal a stance of "uncertainty," which is itself linked to stereotypes of womanhood. Together then, queer theory and Ochsian indexicality undermined the basic premise of Chesebro's correlational approach, arguing that we cannot view practice as emerging from identity just as we cannot interpret patterns of linguistic variation without situating them in relation to the normative forces that frame how social practice gets interpreted and assigned meaning.

This constructionist approach to language and sexuality spawned a new type of sociolinguistic research on sexuality (and in many ways drove a shift in sociolinguistics more broadly). Rather than attempting to catalogue a characteristic lesbian or gay way of speaking, research in this paradigm sought to identify the ways in which people use language to construct sexual personae. In other words, these works sought to map out a field of social and linguistic behavior in order to understand how certain linguistic practices come to be identified with certain identities, and to demonstrate the ways in which individuals make use of these salient links in their daily lives (Livia & Hall 1997). Barrett (1995, 1997), for example, describes how African American drag queens in Texas juxtapose features that are stereotypically linked to both white women in the US South and African American men in order to variably construct themselves as gay men, as African Americans, and as drag queens. In a similar vein, Hall (1995) details how "fantasy makers" (telephone sex workers) strategically adopt linguistic forms associated with various racial and gender categories in order to present selves that match their customers' sexual desires. Finally, the constructionist model also gave rise to burgeoning research on perceptions of sexuality. Unlike previous work in this area, which sought to determine how listeners succeeded in identifying speakers' sexual orientations, newer studies aimed instead to isolate those features that are indexically linked to sexuality regardless of the sexual orientations of the speakers themselves (e.g., Crist 1997; Smyth, Jacobs, & Rogers 2003; Levon 2006).[2]

The move from a correlational to a constructionist model notwithstanding, language and sexuality research continued to come under critical scrutiny. In their book *Language and Sexuality*, Cameron & Kulick (2003) argue that research in the field to that point was beholden to a reified understanding of sexuality that equates it with sexual identity (see also Kulick 2000). In other words, Cameron & Kulick claim that while sexual identity implies a stable (self-)categorization, sexuality describes a field of desires, contradictions, and repressions, and that research on sexuality should not ignore these aspects. Put more succinctly, Cameron & Kulick claim that sexuality is about more than sexual identity because it is a phenomenon that exceeds conscious control (Kulick 2005). In order to model what they mean by this, Cameron & Kulick introduce the concept of *identifications*. Unlike identities, which represent a conscious claiming or rejection of a particular category or position (though cf. Bucholtz & Hall 2005), identifications denote all the different social and cultural affiliations, both recognized and repressed, that an individual maintains. As described by Laplanche & Pontalis (1973), individual identifications are not by themselves determinative; they contribute one piece to the puzzle. Because of this, individuals can maintain conflicting identifications, all of which (including those which are repudiated or repressed) come together to shape social practice. For Cameron & Kulick, capturing the underlying complexity of sexual subjectivity and how that complexity is materialized linguistically requires looking beyond the confines of "identity" (for further discussion of these arguments, see Eckert 2002; Bucholtz & Hall 2004; Cameron & Kulick 2005; see also Brubaker & Cooper 2000; Bucholtz & Hall 2005 for further discussion and alternative conceptualizations of "identity").

At about the same time that Cameron & Kulick's critique appeared, developments elsewhere in sociolinguistics also began to challenge some of the theoretical foundations of the constructionist approach. These developments focused primarily on the assumptions that constructionism makes about the relationship between language and social meaning, arguing that while constructionism had succeeded in inverting the causal relationship between identity and linguistic practice (such that identity was seen as the result of practice rather than its cause), the social meaning of variable forms was very often still reduced to the cultural formations it was used to construct. "Gay language," for example, though not necessarily viewed as the inherent correlate of gay identity, was nevertheless understood as that set of linguistic features used to construct a gay "self." In practice, this understanding of the social meaning of linguistic forms is not that different from the correlation view, since both see the "meaning of variation as incidental fallout from social space" (Eckert 2012: 94). To overcome this, Eckert (2008, 2012) proposes a renewed emphasis on Ochs's (1992) argument (introduced briefly earlier) that language indexes identities indirectly and through the mediating level of stance. Moreover, Eckert adds to this framework the claim that the indexical links between language and stance are themselves indeterminate and only fully emerge in the context of styles that are relevant to the current interaction. This means that a feature like /t/ release, for example, can potentially be linked to a number of different stance-level meanings (e.g., "emphatic," "articulate," and "exasperated") and that its particular meaning in a given interactional moment (and hence the *persona*, or situationally relevant social type, that the feature serves to index) will depend on other social and linguistic factors in the immediate context.[3] In formulating her framework in this way, Eckert manages to bypass the mechanistic assumption that speakers use language to "do" identity, and instead provides us with a mechanism for modeling how identities can emerge in interaction (see also, e.g., Bucholtz 2009; Kiesling 2009).

Though developed from somewhat different theoretical perspectives, both Cameron & Kulick's and Eckert's interventions opened up a space for what we term an *emergentist* approach to language and sexuality. Rather than taking the construction of sexual identity as its analytical point of departure, work in this framework examines how speakers recruit the meaning potentials of variable forms in order to adopt locally meaningful stances. In certain cases, speakers do this kind of stance-taking as a means of constructing contextually relevant personae. Podesva (2007, 2008), for example, discusses how a man he calls Heath draws on the ability of falsetto voice to index "expressive-ness" to construct distinct personae in different settings. When at a barbecue with his friends, Heath uses falsetto to help adopt an expressive stance that, in conjunction with other relevant features, results in the creation of a "diva" style. At the medical clinic where he works, in contrast, Heath's use of falsetto serves instead to index expressivity as part of the creation of a "caring doc-tor" persona. Crucially, while the same linguistic feature is deployed in both contexts, the ultimate meaning of the feature, in terms of the persona it helps to construct, is context-dependent. Moreover, while he acknowledges that the perception of "gay identity" may emerge from Heath's use of falsetto, Podesva argues that this is in a sense a potential by-product of Heath's use of the feature and that the primary motivation behind Heath's observed practice is the con-struction of situational-relevant personae.

Jones (2011, 2012) makes a similar point in her examination of language and self-positioning among women in a lesbian hiking group in the north of England. In that work, Jones demonstrates how the women use a variety of interactional strategies to adopt specific evaluative stances with respect to dif-ferent behaviors and physical characteristics (including dress, hairstyle, sexual activity, and even finger length) as a way of disaligning themselves from nor-mative, heterosexual models of femininity. Jones argues that in doing so, the women are able to construct a "dyke" persona that they then subsequently position as the true and "authentic" articulation of lesbian sexuality. Like Podesva, Jones's analysis illustrates how individuals use stance-taking to create locally relevant personae. Jones also extends these arguments a step further, and delineates the ways in which the local personae that the women construct (like "dyke" and "girl") are explicitly cast by the women in relation to broader macro-categories of sexual identity (like "lesbian").

While both Podesva's and Jones's analyses treat stance as a means to con-struct a persona, other work in this paradigm sees the adoption of interac-tional stance as an end in itself. Levon (Chapter 11, this volume), for example, examines the use of "creaky voice" by a speaker he calls Igal, an Orthodox Jewish man who has sexual and romantic relationships with other men. Levon argues that Igal deploys creaky voice in conversation as a means of suppressing an expression of affect when discussing same-sex desires. In doing so, Levon claims, Igal is able to adopt a deontic stance (Shoaps 2004) that conforms to the dominant valuative framework of Orthodox Judaism while recognizing that he engages in (same-sex) practices that transgress this framework. Creaky voice therefore acts as the linguistic materialization of the conflict between Igal's identification with both Orthodox Judaism and same-sex desire but, as Levon argues, is not used to construct a persona that is directly linked to either.

Finally, as in the previous approaches described, work on the emergence of sexuality in linguistic production has also been accompanied by work on its emergence in perception. This research has focused on understanding the mechanisms underlying the attribution of meaning to variable forms from a range of underspecified possibilities, and, as a result, has paid special attention to how listeners process multiple and potentially contradictory sociolinguistic cues. Campbell-Kibler (2011), for instance, describes how the phonetic fronting of /s/ in US English serves to signal sexuality in men's voices, but only when combined with other phonetic features that themselves signal stereotypically compatible traits. Similarly, Pharao et al. (2014; see also Maegaard & Pharao, Chapter 5, this volume) demonstrate how perceptions of male sexuality in Danish are tightly linked to the simultaneous perception of both ethnicity and social class, such that variables that have a significant effect on listener judgments in one context have no such effect in another. Levon (2014) identifies a parallel pattern for perceptions of sexuality and social class in the United Kingdom, which leads him to argue that stereotypes play a central role in the emergence of sociolinguistic meaning.

The Bigger Picture

Eckert & Podesva (2011) state that the ultimate goal of research on language and sexuality is to understand "the nature of the relationship between linguistic features and the dimensions of the social world they evoke" (9). We argue that their use of the term *dimensions* here is crucial, since the world in which sociolinguistic practice takes place is itself multifaceted and complex. Analyzing that complexity requires the adoption of multiple approaches, including aspects of all three of the paradigms for language and sexuality research that we described previously (i.e., correlational, constructionist, and emergentist). In other words, though we structure it chronologically for expositional reasons, our review of the field is not intended to function as a teleological narrative or to be taken as advocating the wholesale replacement of one approach by another. Rather, we believe that what is needed is a holistic theoretical framework within which components of each of these approaches have their place. We argue that it is by adopting such a holistic approach that we can address the issues of structure, agency, and power introduced earlier. We suggest, moreover, that Bourdieu's theory of social practice (e.g., Bourdieu 1979, 1991) provides the right kind of holistic framework for doing this.

The basic principles of Bourdieu's work, and particularly his conceptualization of symbolic capital and the linguistic marketplace, are fairly well known in sociolinguistics and have been successfully applied in much previous research (e.g., Eckert 2000; see also Ahearn 2001; Hanks 2005 for reviews). For this reason, we only provide a brief overview of the main building blocks of Bourdieu's theory, before describing how it applies to the study of language and sexuality. Bourdieu's central argument is that social practice emerges from the relationship between three factors: what he terms the *field*, *capital*, and *habitus.* In its most general sense, the field refers to the social space in which interactions take place. This space is itself characterized by a "logic," or a set of historically contingent rules that govern the configuration of social roles and positionings within the field. The rules also function to assign value to the various "assets" that circulate within the field. These value-laden assets are what Bourdieu terms *capital.* Bourdieu identifies two main forms of capital: economic capital, which essentially refers to money and other monetized assets, and symbolic capital, which refers to a range of activities, relationships (e.g., friendship), and other products that while not normally thought of as "money" are nevertheless associated with value in a given field. The concept of capital is crucial for Bourdieu since he argues it is via the consumption of capital (e.g., eating a particular food or speaking in a particular way) that individuals navigate the field and adopt social roles and positions. It is not the case, however, that individuals consume capital freely or haphazardly. Rather, Bourdieu argues that consumption (i.e., *practice*) is partially structured by *habitus,* or a set of durable dispositions that shape the choices we make. These dispositions represent our internalization of the rules of the field based on our position within the field and our experiences in the other fields in which we have also interacted. In other words, Bourdieu argues that our position in the social world together with the totality of our previous experiences lead us to have certain dispositions to act in a particular way, and this is what he terms the *habitus.*

The concept of habitus, or, more precisely, the theorized relationship between habitus and the field, is what distinguishes Bourdieu's framework from other theories of social action (Hanks 2005). In arguing that practice results from the relationship between field, capital, and habitus, Bourdieu aims to transcend the dichotomy between social structure and individual agency that he believes characterizes prior research (Maton 2012). His idea is that social practice is not simply a result of either an agentive search for capital or an individual's social position or past experiences. Instead, it results from the interaction of all three in what Bourdieu (1977) describes as the "dialectic of the internalization of externality and the externalization of internality" (72). To make this argument more concrete, Bourdieu (1990) offers the metaphor of a game. In any game (i.e., *field*), there are rules that determine the positions of the different players, the "regular" way of playing, and the assignment of value (i.e., *capital*) to certain actions and not to others. The choices that players make while in the game (i.e., their *practices*) are then based on a number of factors. First is the player's position in the game. Just as a football player cannot necessarily see the entire football field and must instead make choices based on her own perspective and the options available to her from that position, Bourdieu argues that an individual's possibilities for action are in part structurally determined by the individual's social position. Next are the rules of the game, which are reflected in the regularities of play. For Bourdieu, these regularities are internalized and form part of a player's disposition to act in a particular way (i.e., *habitus*). Third are the player's previous experiences playing this particular game as well as other games in other fields. These experiences also form part of a player's dispositions. Finally, there is a player's own subjective agency—her desires, personality, and beliefs. Bourdieu argues that only by taking into consideration the relationship between all four of these components can we adequately model meaningful social practice.[4]

In order to describe how to apply his theory to research on language and sexuality, it is useful to consider Bourdieu's own suggestion for a three-level analytical method (Bourdieu & Wacquant 1992; see also Grenfell 2014):

(1) Analyze the position of the field in relation to other fields, particularly the field of power;

(2) Examine the structural topography of the field, including the positioning of actors, the regularities of practice, and the distribution of capital;

(3) Analyze the habitus of individuals within the field, with a focus on the relationships individuals establish with one another and on the correspondence between individual habitus and the structures of the field.

The first level of Bourdieu's suggested method involves understanding how a particular field of interaction (e.g., the "family") is positioned in relation to the dominant structuring principles of society, the so-called field of power. Research on the family at this level, for example, might examine how notions of kinship and familial obligation are structured by constructs such as patriarchy. At the second level, research identifies the value associated with specific practices in a given field, and examines the regular distribution of those practices in order to understand how the different roles in the field are positioned. Continuing with the example of the family, research at this level would identify particular acts and activities associated with various family roles (e.g., "mothering") and consider how those activity-role relationships serve to position actors in relation to one another. Finally, the third level of analysis focuses on the individual actor, exploring both the complex motivations that underlie observed practice and the positionings of self that result from behaving in this way.

We believe that Bourdieu's three-level method provides us with a straightforward way to unify the different strands of language and sexuality research into a single overarching program. At the first level, work on language and sexuality considers how the local organization of gender and sexuality is linked to larger societal forces, including patriarchy (e.g., Kulick 1998; Rudwick & Msibi, Chapter 3, this volume), hetero- and homonormativity (Valentine 2003; Kiesling 2004; Hall 2009), and nationalism (Besnier 2002; Boellstorff 2004; Levon 2010). It is then at the second level that language and sexuality research uncovers how these larger social forces are inscribed in local fields of practice. Perception research, for example, identifies the capital associated with distinct linguistic features (e.g., which forms sound "masculine" and which do not), while correlational analyses explore the regular distribution of practices across the social space. These two endeavors are related since the value of a linguistic form is in part based on the social positioning of those who normally use it (or at least are imagined to use it; Johnstone & Kiesling 2008). They are also both important since it is only in relation to the regular distribution of capital in the field that we can ultimately understand meaningful social practice. Finally, language and sexuality research at the third level is where the focus is most squarely on individual action. By framing this focus in terms of habitus, however, research at this level does not lose sight of the structuring properties of the field and of the limits imposed by both experience and perspective. Stance-taking and/or persona construction are thus necessarily understood as "constrained by the resources available to do [them], which in turn are shaped by material conditions—those of the past as well as the present" (Cameron 2011: 103). Overall then, Bourdieu's three-level method provides the framework for an inclusive approach to the study of language and sexuality, one that recognizes the crucial and interrelated importance of structure, agency, and power.

This Book: Intersectional Sociolinguistics

Our ultimate objective in this book is to illustrate the utility of examining how structure, agency, and power together shape sexuality-linked linguistic practice. Bourdieu's multilevel model provides an invaluable tool for achieving this. Yet, as we note previously, we also argue that a full examination of the topic requires us to recognize that sexuality—whether in terms of individual subjectivity or social structure—never exists in isolation. It is instead always cross-cut, contested, and transfigured by other vectors of social organization, including gender, race, nation, and socioeconomic status. For this reason, we have collected contributions for the volume that place the *intersectionality* (Crenshaw 1989; Yuval-Davis 2011b) of sexuality at the center of their analyses.

The term *intersectionality* has become something of a "buzzword" in the humanities and social sciences over the past twenty years (Davis 2008). Originating within black feminist theorizing as a way to conceptualize race, class, and gender as a "trilogy of oppression and discrimination" (Knapp 2005: 255), intersectionality has since been put to use in a wide variety of disciplinary and methodological traditions. In the process, the concept has come to mean a number of different things to different scholars (see, e.g., McCall 2005; Choo & Ferree 2010). In this book, we understand intersectionality to refer to the ways in which dynamic systems of social organization mutually constitute one another. In other words, we do not subscribe to the view of intersections as simple crossings or "street corners" (Crenshaw 1991) where static categories like "gay" and "working class" meet on a Cartesian plane. Instead, we adopt a process-centered approach (Weldon 2008) that views the production of sexuality at both the individual and the structural levels as inextricably linked to the production of other relevant social systems. A useful heuristic for engaging in this type of intersectional investigation is what Matsuda (1991) describes as "asking the other question"—that is, constantly and continually exploring how a practice related to sexuality may also be related to gender, race/ethnicity, social class, and so on, and critically interrogating why it is that these categories are linked in this way. We argue that it is only by exploring the dynamic relations between systems that we can adequately model the lived experience of sexuality, and hence the ways in which language participates in its materialization (Cameron & Kulick 2003). For us, the inclusion of an intersectional perspective does not supplant the importance of Bourdieu's multilevel approach. Rather, we see the two frameworks as complementary and mutually reinforcing (Yuval-Davis 2011a). Methodologically, intersectionality prompts us to "ask the other question" at each level of Bourdieu's model. In other words, whether we are looking at the position of the field in relation to the field of power (level 1), the structural topography of the field and the distribution of capital within it (level 2), or the relationship between habitus and individual practice (level 3), an intersectional perspective encourages us to expand our analytical gaze beyond the specific confines of sexuality and to explore the *relationships* between categories at all levels of social organization.

The following ten chapters thus all focus on sexuality as one component of a broader sociolinguistic space. In an effort to highlight the links between sexuality and the other dimensions of lived experience, we have chosen to focus primarily on studies of language and sexuality outside English-speaking contexts (with the sole exception of Podesva & von Hofwegen, Chapter 9, this volume). We do so not because we feel that intersectionality as a concept is not relevant to research in the English-speaking world. This is obviously not the case. Yet, we believe that concentrating on issues of language and sexuality in languages other than English and in cultures other than the United Kingdom and North America serves to foreground the socially and historically contingent nature of sexuality, and hence underscores the importance of an intersectional perspective. We nevertheless recognize that by juxtaposing a call for an intersectional perspective with studies mostly from outside North America and Northern Europe, we risk re-inscribing a North Atlantic norm (Boellstorff & Leap 2004) and implicitly positioning other cultures as somehow intersectionally "deviant." This is emphatically not our intention, and we strongly encourage research on sexuality as an intersectional phenomenon in a wide variety of cultural and linguistic contexts, including those that have received the most attention in the literature to date, like the United States.

While each of the chapters in the volume offers a self-contained analysis of sexuality as an intersectional phenomenon in a given cultural and linguistic context, the organization of the book overall is designed to emulate Bourdieu's multilevel analytical method. The contributions to the volume are thus organized according to level. The first three chapters (2, 3, and 4) are situated at the first level, and all examine how sexuality is positioned in relation to the local fields of power in Hong Kong (Wong), Zulu-speaking South Africa (Rudwick & Msibi), and Japan (Maree), respectively. The next four chapters (5, 6, 7, and 8) all involve the second level of analysis. As such, they each consider the topography of the social fields in question by examining the perception of sexuality-linked features in Denmark (Maegaard & Pharao), Brazil (Mendes), Puerto Rico (Mack), and Hungary (Rácz & Papp). Finally, the remaining three chapters (9, 10, and 11) are situated at the third level of analysis, and all explore how individuals in rural California (Podesva & von Hofwegen), Thailand (Saisuwan), and Israel (Levon) use language to negotiate conflicting pressures and identifications as they relate to gender, sexuality, and same-sex desire. In structuring the volume in this way, we aim to illustrate how these three different levels of analysis inform one another, as well as how an intersectional perspective can be productively applied at each level. Ultimately, it is our hope that the structure and organization of this book as a whole serve as a demonstration of the theoretical proposals we make in this introductory chapter—proposals that we believe will allow the field to develop a more complete understanding of the relationship between sexuality and language.

Acknowledgments

Very special thanks to Robin Queen and Penelope Eckert for their detailed comments on an earlier version of this chapter. We alone are responsible for any errors or shortcomings.

Notes

1. The majority of Chesebro's questions are not "linguistic" questions, as such, given the volume's grounding in communication and rhetoric studies (Livia & Hall 1997; Queen 2014). Chesebro's question 2 is the only one to speak to issues directly relevant to distributional sociolinguistics.

2. Though beyond the scope of this brief review, it is important to note that the constructionist model has also long had a foothold in linguistic anthropological work on sexuality. See, e.g., Hall & O'Donovan (1996); Hall (1997, 2005); Kulick (1998); Gaudio (1997, 2009); Besnier (2002, 2004); Boellstorff (2004, 2005); Leap & Boellstorff (2004).

3. Eckert uses the concept of *personae* as a more locally relevant alternative to "identity," which she argues tends to refer to a "reified locus of iterability" (Eckert 2002: 102). In

other words, "identity" and "identity categories" are ideological constructs that circulate in the social space (e.g., "woman," "gay," and "Buddhist"). Personae, in contrast, represent somewhat more holistic presentations of self that, while they may certainly draw on a number of different identity-linked stereotypical associations, cannot be reduced to any one "identity" (see also Podesva 2007).

4. There is a great deal of discussion in the literature about the extent to which Bourdieu's framework actually allows for agency and, subsequently, for social change. These arguments are beyond the scope of our discussion here, though see Ahearn (2001) and Crossley (2003) for details. We assume an interpretation of Bourdieu's theory that allows for the operation of individual agency.

References

Ahearn, Laura. 2001. Language and agency. *Annual Review of Anthropology* 30. 109–137.

Avery, Jack & Julie Liss. 1996. Acoustic characteristics of less-masculine-sounding male speech. *Journal of the Acoustical Society of America* 99(6). 3738–3748.

Barrett, Rusty. 1995. Supermodels of the world, unite!: Political economy and the language of performance among African American drag queens. In William Leap (ed.), *Beyond the lavender lexicon*, 207–226. Amsterdam: Gordon and Breach Science Publishers.

Barrett, Rusty. 1997. The "homo-genius" speech community. In Anna Livia & Kira Hall (eds.), *Queerly phrased*, 181–201. Oxford: Oxford University Press.

Besnier, Niko. 2002. Transgenderism, locality and the Miss Galaxy beauty pageant in Tonga. *American Ethnologist* 29(3). 534–566.

Besnier, Niko. 2004. The social production of abjection: Desire and silencing among transgender Tongans. *Social Anthropology* 12(3). 301–323.

Boellstorff, Tom. 2004. Gay language and Indonesia: Registering belonging. *Journal of Linguistic Anthropology* 14(2). 248–268.

Boellstorff, Tom. 2005. *The gay archipelago: Sexuality and the nation in Indonesia.* Princeton, NJ: Princeton University Press.

Boellstorff, Tom & William Leap. 2004. Introduction: Globalization and "new" articulations of same-sex desire. In William Leap & Tom Boellstorff (eds.), *Speaking in queer tongues: Globalization and gay language*, 1–21. Chicago: University of Illinois Press.

Bourdieu, Pierre. 1977. *Outline of a theory of practice.* Cambridge: Cambridge University Press.

Bourdieu, Pierre. 1979. *Distinction.* Cambridge, MA: Harvard University Press.

Bourdieu, Pierre. 1990. *The logic of practice.* Cambridge: Polity Press.

Bourdieu, Pierre. 1991. *Language and symbolic power*, 5th edn. Cambridge, MA: Harvard University Press.

Bourdieu, Pierre & Loïc Wacquant. 1992. *An invitation to reflexive sociology.* Cambridge: Polity Press.

Brubaker, Rogers & Frederick Cooper. 2000. Beyond "identity." *Theory and Society* 29. 1–47.

Bucholtz, Mary. 2009. From stance to style: Gender, interaction and indexicality in Mexican immigrant youth slang. In Alexandra Jaffe (ed.), *Stance: Sociolinguistic perspectives*, 146–170. Oxford: Oxford University Press.

Bucholtz, Mary & Kira Hall. 2004. Theorizing identity in language and sexuality research. *Language in Society* 33(4). 469–515.

Bucholtz, Mary & Kira Hall. 2005. Identity and interaction: A sociocultural linguistic approach. *Discourse Studies* 7(4–5). 585–614.

Butler, Judith. 1990. *Gender trouble: Feminism and the subversion of identity*. London: Routledge.

Butler, Judith. 1993. *Bodies that matter: On the discursive limits of "sex."* London: Routledge.

Cameron, Deborah. 2011. Sociophonetics and sexuality: Discussion. *American Speech* 86(1). 98–103.

Cameron, Deborah & Don Kulick. 2003. *Language and sexuality*. Cambridge: Cambridge University Press.

Cameron, Deborah & Don Kulick. 2005. Identity crisis? *Language and Communication* 25(2). 107–125.

Campbell-Kibler, Kathryn. 2011. Intersecting variables and perceived sexual orientation in men. *American Speech* 86(1). 52–68.

Chesebro, James (ed.). 1981a. *Gayspeak: Gay male and lesbian communication*. New York: Pilgrim Press.

Chesebro, James. 1981b. Introduction. In James Chesebro (ed.), *Gayspeak: Gay male and lesbian communication*, ix–xvi. New York: Pilgrim Press.

Choo, Hae Yeon & Myra Marx Ferree. 2010. Practicing intersectionality in sociological research: A critical analysis of inclusions, interactions and institutions in the study of inequalities. *Sociological Theory* 28(2). 129–149.

Crenshaw, Kimberlé. 1989. Demarginalizing the intersection of race and sex: A black feminist critique of antidiscrimination doctrine, feminist theory and antiracist politics. *The University of Chicago Legal Forum* 140. 139–167.

Crenshaw, Kimberlé. 1991. Mapping the margins: Intersectionality, identity politics and violence against women of color. *Stanford Law Review* 43. 1241–1299.

Crist, Sean. 1997. Duration of onset consonants in gay male stereotyped speech. *University of Pennsylvania Working Papers in Linguistics* 4(3). 53–70.

Crossley, Nick. 2003. From reproduction to transformation: Social movement fields and the radical habitus. *Theory, Culture & Society* 20(6). 43–68.

Davis, Kathy. 2008. Intersectionality as buzzword: A sociology of science perspective on what makes a feminist theory successful. *Feminist Theory* 9(1). 67–85.

Day, Conniee & Ben Morse. 1981. Communication patterns in established lesbian relationships. In James Chesebro (ed.), *Gayspeak: Gay male and lesbian communication*, 80–86. New York: Pilgrim Press.

Eckert, Penelope. 2000. *Linguistic variation as social practice: The linguistic construction of identity in Belten High*. Oxford: Blackwell.

Eckert, Penelope. 2002. Demystifying sexuality and desire. In Kathryn Campbell-Kibler, Robert Podesva, Sarah Roberts, & Andrew Wong (eds.), *Language and sexuality: Contesting meaning in theory and practice*, 99–110. Stanford, CA: CSLI.

Eckert, Penelope. 2008. Variation and the indexical field. *Journal of Sociolinguistics* 12(4). 453–476.

Eckert, Penelope. 2012. Three waves of variation study: The emergence of meaning in the study of sociolinguistic variation. *Annual Review of Anthropology* 41. 87–100.

Eckert, Penelope & Robert Podesva. 2011. Sociophonetics and sexuality: Toward a symbiosis of sociolinguistics and laboratory phonology. *American Speech* 86(1). 6–13.

Fai, Diane. 1988. A study of the (-ing) variable in the Ottawa male community. In *Actes du colloque: Tendances actuelles de la recherche sur la language parlée*, 35–40. Quebec: Centre International de Recherche sur le Bilinguisme/International Center for Research on Bilingualism.

Gaudio, Rudolf. 1994. Sounding gay: Pitch properties in the speech of gay and straight men. *American Speech* 69(1). 30–57.

Gaudio, Rudolf. 1997. Not talking straight in Hausa. In Anna Livia & Kira Hall (eds.), *Queerly phrased*, 416–429. New York: Oxford University Press.

Gaudio, Rudolf. 2009. *Allah made us: Sexual outlaws in an Islamic African city*. Oxford: Blackwell.

Grenfell, Michael. 2014. Methodology. In Michael Grenfell (ed.), *Pierre Bourdieu: Key concepts*, 2nd edn., 213–228. Durham, NC: Acumen.

Hall, Kira. 1995. Lip service on the fantasy lines. In Kira Hall & Mary Bucholtz (eds.), *Gender articulated*, 183–216. New York: Routledge.

Hall, Kira. 1997. "Go suck your husband's sugarcane!: Hijras and the use of sexual insult. In Anna Livia & Kira Hall (eds.), *Queerly phrased*, 430–460. New York: Oxford University Press.

Hall, Kira. 2005. Intertextual sexuality: Parodies of class, identity and desire in liminal Delhi. *Journal of Linguistic Anthropology* 15(1). 125–144.

Hall, Kira. 2009. Boys' talk: Hindi, moustaches, and masculinity in New Delhi. In Pia Pichler & Eva Eppler (eds.), *Gender and spoken interaction*, 139–162. Basingstoke, UK: Palgrave Macmillan.

Hall, Kira & Veronica O'Donovan. 1996. Shifting gender positions among Hindi-speaking hijras. In Victoria Bergvall, Janet Bing, & Alice Freed (eds.), *Rethinking language and gender research: Theory and practice*, 228–266. London: Longman.

Hanks, William F. 2005. Pierre Bourdieu and the practices of language. *Annual Review of Anthropology* 34(1). 67–83.

Hayes, Joseph. 1981. Gayspeak. In James Chesebro (ed.), *Gayspeak: Gay male and lesbian communication*, 45–57. New York: Pilgrim Press.

Johnstone, Barbara & Scott Kiesling. 2008. Indexicality and experience: Exploring the meanings of / aw /-monophthongization in Pittsburgh." *Journal of Sociolinguistics* 12(1). 5–33.

Jones, Lucy. 2011. "The only dykey one": Constructions of (in)authenticity in a lesbian community of practice. *Journal of Homosexuality* 58(6–7). 719–741.

Jones, Lucy. 2012. *Dyke/girl: Language and dentities in a lesbian group*. Basingstoke, UK: Palgrave Macmillan.

Kiesling, Scott. 2004. Dude. *American Speech* 79(3). 281–305.

Kiesling, Scott. 2009. Style as stance: Stance as the explanation for patterns of sociolinguistic variation. In Alexandra Jaffe (ed.), *Stance: Sociolinguistic perspectives*, 171–194. Oxford: Oxford University Press.

Knapp, Gudrun-Axeli. 2005. Race, class, gender: Reclaiming baggage in fast travelling theories. *European Journal of Women's Studies* 12(3). 249–265.

Kulick, Don. 1998. *Travesti: Sex, gender and culture among Brazilian transgendered prostitutes*. Chicago: University of Chicago Press.

Kulick, Don. 2000. Gay and lesbian language. *Annual Review of Anthropology* 29. 243–285.

Kulick, Don. 2005. The importance of what gets left out. *Discourse Studies* 7(4–5). 615–624.

Laplanche, Jean & Jean-Bertrand Pontalis. 1973. *The language of pyscho-analysis*. London: Karnac Books.

Leap, William. 1993. Gay men's English: Cooperative discourse in a language of risk. *New York Folklore* 19. 45–70.

Leap, William. 1996. *Word's out: Gay men's English*. Minneapolis: University of Minnesota Press.

Leap, William & Tom Boellstorff (eds.). 2004. *Speaking in queer tongues: Globalization and gay language*. Urbana-Champaign: University of Illinois Press.

Legman, Gershon. 1941. The language of homosexuality: An American glossary. In George Henry (ed.), *Sex variants: A study of homosexual patterns*, 1149–1179. New York: Hoeber.

Levon, Erez. 2006. Hearing "gay": Prosody, interpretation and the affective judgments of men's speech. *American Speech* 81(1). 56–78.

Levon, Erez. 2010. *Language and the politics of sexuality: Lesbians and gays in Israel*. Basingstoke, UK: Palgrave Macmillan.

Levon, Erez. 2014. Categories, stereotypes and the linguistic perception of sexuality. *Language in Society* 43(5). 539–566.

Livia, Anna & Kira Hall. 1997. "It's a girl!": Bringing performativity back to linguistics. In Anna Livia & Kira Hall (eds.), *Queerly phrased*, 3–20. Oxford: Oxford University Press.

Maton, Karl. 2012. Habitus. In Michael Grenfell (ed.), *Pierre Bourdieu: Key concepts*, 2nd edn., 48–64. Durham, NC: Acumen.

Matsuda, Mari. 1991. Beside my sister, facing the enemy: Legal theory out of coalition. *Stanford Law Review* 43(6). 1183–1192.

McCall, Leslie. 2005. The complexity of intersectionality. *Signs* 30(3). 1771–1800.

Moonwomon, Baird. 1985. Towards a study of lesbian language. In Sue Bremner, Noelle Caskey, & Baird Moonwomon (eds.), *Proceedings of the first Berkeley Women and Language Conference*, 96–107. Berkeley, CA: Berkeley Women and Language Group.

Munson, Benjamin & Molly Babel. 2007. Loose lips and silver tongues, or, projecting sexual orientation through speech. *Language and Linguistics Compass* 1(5). 416–449.

Ochs, Elinor. 1992. Indexing gender. In Alessandro Duranti & Charles Goodwin (eds.), *Rethinking context: Language as an interactive phenomenon*, 335–358. Cambridge: Cambridge University Press.

Pharao, Nicolai, Marie Maegaard, Janus Møller, & Tore Kristiansen. 2014. Indexical meanings of [s+] among Copenhagen youth: Social perception of a phonetic variant in different prosodic contexts. *Language in Society* 43(1). 1–31.

Podesva, Robert. 2007. Phonation type as a stylistic variable: The use of falsetto in constructing a persona. *Journal of Sociolinguistics* 11(4). 478–504.

Podesva, Robert. 2008. Three sources of stylistic meaning. *Texas Linguistic Forum* 51. 134–143.

Queen, Robin. 2007. Sociolinguistic horizons: Language and sexuality. *Language and Linguistics Compass* 1(4). 314–330.

Queen, Robin. 2014. Language and sexual identities. In Susan Ehrlich, Miriam Meyerhoff, & Janet Holmes (eds.), *The handbook of language, gender and sexuality*, 2nd edn., 203–219. Oxford: Blackwell.

Rampton, Ben. 2007. Neo-Hymesian linguistic ethnography in the United Kingdom. *Journal of Sociolinguistics* 11(5). 584–607.

Shoaps, Robin. 2004. Morality in grammar and discourse: Stance-taking and the negotiation of moral personhood in Sakapultek wedding counsels. Santa Barbara: University of California unpublished PhD dissertation.

Silverstein, Michael. 1985. Language and the culture of gender: At the intersection of structure, usage and ideology. In Elizabeth Mertz & Richard Parmentier (eds.), *Semiotic mediation: Sociocultural and psychological perspectives*, 219–259. Orlando, FL: Academic Press.

Smyth, Ron, Greg Jacobs, & Henry Rogers. 2003. Male voices and perceived sexual orientation: An experimental and theoretical approach. *Language in Society* 32(3). 329–350.

Stanley, Julia P. 1970. Homosexual slang. *American Speech* 45(1–2). 45–59.

Taylor, Ben. 1996. Gay men, femininity and /t/ in New Zealand English. *Wellington Working Papers in Linguistics* 8. 70–92.

Valentine, D. 2003. "I went to bed with my own kind once": The erasure of desire in the name of identity. *Language & Communication* 23(2). 123–138.

Weldon, Laurel. 2008. Intersectionality. In Gary Goertz & Amy Mazur (eds.), *Politics, gender and concepts: Theory and methodology*, 193–218. Cambridge: Cambridge University Press.

Wong, Andrew, Sarah Roberts, & Kathryn Campbell-Kibler. 2002. Speaking of sex. In Kathryn Campbell-Kibler, Robert Podesva, Sarah Roberts, & Andrew Wong (eds.), *Language and sexuality: Contesting meaning in theory and practice*, 1–21. Stanford, CA: CSLI Publications.

Woolard, Kathryn. 1985. Language variation and cultural hegemony: Toward an integration of sociolinguistic and social theory. *American Ethnologist* 12(4). 738–748.

Yuval-Davis, Nira. 2011a. Beyond the recognition and re-distribution dichotomy: Intersectionality and stratification. In Helma Lutz, Maria Teresa Herrera Vivar, & Linda Supik (eds.), *Framing intersectionality: Debates on a multi-faceted concept in gender studies*, 155–169. London: Ashgate Publishing.

Yuval-Davis, Nira. 2011b. *The politics of belonging: Intersectional contestations*. London: Sage.

2

How Does Oppression Work?

INSIGHTS FROM HONG KONG LESBIANS' LABELING PRACTICES

Andrew D. Wong

Intersectionality theory has attracted increasing attention from sociolinguists in recent years (see, e.g., Mallinson 2006; Morgan 2007; Lanehart 2009; Levon 2011). For those familiar with the study of language variation and change, the word *intersectionality* immediately brings to mind the interaction of social variables like gender, ethnicity, and social class. As a theory, however, intersectionality is not just about the interaction of social variables. It grew out of black feminists' attempts to expose the limitations of gender as a single analytical category (hooks 1981; Davis 1983). The term *intersectionality*, coined by legal scholar Kimberlé Crenshaw (1989, 1991), was originally used to critique the tendency to treat race and gender as mutually exclusive categories, which was commonplace in academic research, antiracist politics, and the feminist movement. Sociologist Patricia Hill Collins (2000), another major figure in this area, provides a succinct explanation in her book *Black Feminist Thought*:

> Intersectionality refers to particular forms of intersecting oppressions, for example, intersections of race and gender, or of sexuality and nation. Intersectional paradigms remind us that oppression cannot be reduced to one fundamental type, and that oppressions work together in producing injustice. (21)

In other words, intersectionality underscores how different axes of social difference reinforce and intersect with each other to create specific forms of identity and oppression. This theory was initially used to emphasize the multidimensionality of black women's lived experience. Over time, it has also been applied to the discussion and analysis of the experiences of others who are multiply burdened and marginalized because of their race, gender, sexuality, and nationality (McCall 2005; Nash 2008).

Sociolinguists have been particularly successful at demonstrating how intersectionality theory illuminates identity-related linguistic practices. Dodsworth & Mallinson (2006) explore the idea that the multiplicative nature of race, gender, sexuality, and social class produces contextualized experiences, which are then manifested locally in linguistic and other social practices. Using this idea to frame apparently conflicting phonetic data from an individual speaker, they show how the phonetic data actually reflect the speaker's personal tensions as a marginalized member of his community. In a similar vein, Mallinson (2008) examines how diverse life experiences in an Appalachian community shape residents' use of a variety of linguistic resources to construct complex identities and to articulate differing social orientations toward race and region. More recently, heeding the call for greater attention to individuals' lived experiences, Levon (2011) demonstrates how two groups of Israeli lesbian activists attend to the intersection of gender and sexuality differently and how this difference results in the two groups attaching distinct meanings to the same linguistic practice. Taken together, these studies remind us of the necessity to take the beliefs and lived experiences of the people we study seriously in order to understand their linguistic practices.

Nevertheless, intersectionality is not solely a theory of identity formation. As previously discussed, it also calls attention to the ways in which axes of social differentiation interact with each other to produce systematic inequality. Intersectionality theorists believe that multiply marginalized subjects offer a unique vantage point for understanding how power is exercised and resisted (Collins 2000). Those who are multiply marginalized, as critical race theorist Mari Matsuda (1987) argues, "speak with a special voice to which we should listen" (324). Taking this insight as its point of departure, this chapter examines the labeling practices of two groups of Hong Kong lesbians (activists and non-activists) in order to reveal how power operates through language at the intersection of gender and sexuality and to expose the kinds of oppression that lesbians experience in Hong Kong society.

After a brief discussion of the role of power in distributional sociolinguistics, I describe below the methodology of the study and the sociohistorical environment in which the research was conducted in order to contextualize the analysis of labeling practices that follows. While activists' labeling practices shed light on how androcentrism is imposed on women within the sexuality-based social movement in Hong Kong, an examination of non-activists' labeling practices reveals the symbolic means through which same-sex desire is rendered invisible, as well as non-activists' complicity in the process. Not only does this study provide support to Levon's (2011) observation that intersections are underspecified and can only be understood through empirical investigation, but it also shows how labeling practices offer valuable insights in such an endeavor.

Power and Distributional Sociolinguistics

This chapter, like the others in this volume, demonstrates how distributional sociolinguistics can illuminate complex social issues and relationships. Specifically, it is concerned with the ways in which language mediates the workings of power. At its most basic level, power may be construed as the ability to control or influence the actions of others. While many variation studies focus on the structural aspects of the interplay between diachronic change and synchronic variation, the notion of power often enters into the equation in accounts of social motivations for language variation and change. Eckert's (1989, 2000) study of phonological variation in an American high school stands out as a prime example. On the whole, the girls in this community make greater use of phonological variation than the boys. Offering ethnographic evidence to support her claim, Eckert attributes this to the fact that while the boys can gain power and status through direct action and physical prowess, the girls have to rely on language and other symbolic means to develop a "whole person" image designed to gain them influence within their own social groups. Looking at the role of gender in sociolinguistic variation from a different perspective, Kiesling (1998) examines the use of the variable (ING) (e.g., *walking* vs. *walkin'*) in an American college fraternity. While most of the fraternity men use primarily the standard variant (i.e., *-ing*) during weekly meetings, several members use the vernacular variant (i.e., *-in'*) more frequently than the standard variant. Kiesling argues that the men with higher rates of the vernacular variant use this linguistic resource to index confrontational stances and working-class cultural models, which are crucial to the construction of a persona based on physical power.

Power also figures prominently in many interactional sociolinguistic studies of cross-gender and cross-cultural communication. Interactional sociolinguistics, like the traditional study of language variation and change, seeks to describe and explain socially conditioned patterns of variation in language use. While variationists focus primarily on differences in grammar and pronunciation, interactional sociolinguists study variation of a different kind. They are interested in such aspects of interaction as turn-taking conventions, politeness strategies, and paralinguistic cues (e.g., pitch, prosody, intonation, and volume). One prolific line of research has explored the occurrence of overlapping speech in different kinds of social interactions. Taking note of the multifunctionality of this discourse strategy, various studies (e.g., Zimmerman & West 1975; Tannen 1981; James & Clarke 1993) have investigated who uses overlapping speech to dominate social interactions, who uses it as a means to show rapport and involvement, and in what contexts this strategy is employed for these purposes. These studies, like Eckert's and Kiesling's discussed previously, bring into relief the centrality of power in distributional sociolinguistics.

It may seem rather unorthodox to look at variation in labeling practices for insights into how power works. Labeling, as Cameron & Kulick (2003) explain, is not simply a matter of putting words on things that have always been there waiting to be named; it has the power of changing our perception of the social world. The emergence of the categories *homosexual* and *hetero-sexual*, for example, brought into being what we now call sexual orientation or sexual preference, which had not been part of previous understandings of sexual behavior. McConnell-Ginet (2002) also reminds us that the cognitive structure underlying a social category label is not a definition but a set of beliefs and values about the category that the label denotes. Thus, labels like *gay, queer,* and *homosexual* are not merely different ways of calling the same people; they symbolize competing systems of sexual understanding. As such, they serve as an ideal site for investigating the contestation of power and ideology.

Doing Research on Language and Sexuality in Hong Kong

I drew the data for this study from a larger project on language and sexuality in Hong Kong. I conducted fieldwork in 2001 to examine how different ideologies about same-sex desire materialize through labeling practices. It was an exciting time to carry out research on sexual minorities in Hong Kong. Following the decriminalization of homosexuality in 1991, the cultural space for those with same-sex desire began to expand exponentially. Bars, saunas, dance clubs, and other entertainment establishments catering to lesbians and gay men sprang up all over the city. There emerged a proliferation of gay web sites and publications (including pornographic ones), testing the limits of tolerance and the freedom of publication guaranteed by the Hong Kong Basic Law. Organizations providing social and cultural activities to different sexual minority groups (e.g., gay Christians, lesbians, and bisexual women) were founded one after another within a few short years. Collaboration among these organizations led to the formation of a nascent sexuality-based social movement and a series of well-publicized conferences in which activists from Hong Kong, Taiwan, mainland China, and overseas Chinese communities came together to discuss issues concerning Chinese sexual minorities. Most pertinent to this study, these activists appropriated the Chinese word *tongzhi* (often glossed as 'comrade'), which was a popular address term in Communist China, as an umbrella label for all sexual minorities (similar to *LGBT*—lesbian, gay, bisexual, transgender, in English).[1] (I will discuss this label in more detail in the section "Activists' Labeling Practices.") Despite these rapid and promising social changes, the angst following the return of Hong Kong from British to Chinese sovereignty in 1997 failed to subside. Many lesbians and gay men continued to wonder if the freedoms they had come to enjoy would disappear overnight. It was in this social and historical context that I carried out the research reported in this chapter.

For the larger project, I collected data from both male and female leaders of various *tongzhi* organizations (i.e., activists), as well as lesbians and gay men who were not involved in the *tongzhi* movement in any capacity (i.e., non-activists). I used three data sources to shed light on my research question: semistructured interviews, observations of labeling practices in everyday interaction, and informal discussions through which I obtained insights into ideologies about same-sex desire. I divided the semistructured interview into two parts. In the first part, I asked research participants to discuss topics that would generate the use of labels to refer to those of non-normative sexual orientation (e.g., sexuality, kinship, and coming out). To prevent my use of labels from influencing theirs, I refrained from using *gay, lesbian, tongzhi, tung-sing-lyun je* 'homosexual,' and other obvious labels. Instead, I used the Cantonese equivalents of such expressions as 'those of non-normative sexual orientation,' 'those with same-sex desire,' and 'those attracted to the same sex.' In the second part, I explicitly asked research participants to talk about labels for sexual minorities (e.g., how *tongzhi* and *gay* are different from each other, and whether or not they use *tongzhi* as a label for self-identification). Research participants' evaluations of *tongzhi* and other labels complement data from the first part of the interview, which provide the basis for the analysis of their use of labels in discourse. Given the focus of the present chapter on lesbians' labeling practices, I restrict the following discussion to female activists and non-activists.

Non-activists' Labeling Practices

Quite early on during my fieldwork, I was struck by non-activists' lack of explicit reference to same-sex desire in both interviews and casual conversations even when discussing coming out, sexuality-based social movements, and sexual minorities in Hong Kong. Non-activists circumvent the issue of specifying same-sex desire through the use of such deictic expressions as *li-di yan* 'these people,' *go-di yan* 'those people,' and *gam ge yan* 'this kind of person.' What first caught my attention was Louise's use of this strategy during our interview.[2] I was introduced to Louise by a male activist, who became acquainted with her when they both participated in a panel discussion on homosexuality. She seemed rather wary of researchers and journalists, and was the only person who requested that her interview not be tape-recorded. When describing her experience of coming out to her mother, Louise did not talk about sexual orientation directly. Instead, she used the following deictic expressions to avoid specifying same-sex desire:

yi-ga ngo hai **gam**.
'Now I'm like **this**.'
ngo hai yat go **gam ge yan**.
'I am **this kind of person**.'
yi-ga ngo hai di **gam ge yan**, lei jip-m-jip sau a?
'Now I am **this kind of person**. Are you going to accept me?'

The use of this strategy is by no means restricted to the non-activists I interviewed. Rob, who oversaw the outreach activities of a large organization for sexual minorities, stated that many who called the organization's hotline would use *li-di yan* 'these people' and *go-di yan* 'those people' to refer to lesbians and gay men. Rodney Jones, who has conducted extensive research on same-sex cultures in Hong Kong and mainland China, mentioned that gay men in Beijing often use the Mandarin equivalent of 'people like us' when talking about same-sex desire (personal communication). In a sense, 'people like us' is similar to *li-di yan* and *go-di yan*: Whomever these expressions refer to, the group they belong to does not have a name, and their desire is best left unspoken.

Louise was not the only non-activist who used deictic expressions to get around naming same-sex desire. In example (1), Bonnie discusses the main reason she decided to become involved in organizations for sexual minorities: participating in these organizations allows her to meet others like herself, so that she can "better understand what is out there." She uses the deictic expression *li-go san-fan* 'this identity,' as well as the circumlocution *dou-hai tung ji-gei yat-yeung ge yan* 'people like me,' when discussing this subject matter.

(1)   Bonnie
       Interviewer:
       dan-hai lei wui-m-wui   But do you take the initiative to
          jyun-dang heui   go to various
       di wui chaam-ga di wut-dung a? organizations to participate in
                                         their activities?

       Bonnie:
       dou-wui yau   I do.
       je-hai ji-gei dou hai **li-go san fan**   well, I have **this identity**.
       je-hai dou wui heui   I sometimes go to
       dou-hai tung ji-gei yat-yeung   places where there are
          ge yan
       ge dei-fong   **people like me**
       heui liu-gaai ha la.   to better understand what is
                                         out there.

In addition to deictic expressions and circumlocutions, non-activists avoid specifying same-sex desire through the use of ellipsis. Ellipsis is the omission of words that are assumed to be understood by the addressee. For instance, April said that if she wanted to find out if someone is a lesbian, she would say:

keui	hai-m-hai	[ellipsis]	a?
she	is-not-is	[ellipsis]	Question Marker

'Is she [ellipsis]?'

instead of *keui hai-m-hai* **lesbian** *a?* 'Is she a **lesbian**?' Thus, she would rely on the addressee's shared background knowledge to supply the omitted word. As this example shows, although ellipsis generally is anaphoric and follows an explicit antecedent (e.g., *I'm Chinese and John is, too.*), it could also be licensed by shared knowledge in the discourse.

The use of ellipsis is extremely common in non-activists' accounts of how they disclosed their same-sex desire to others. In example (2), Linda responds to my question of whether or not she has told anyone in her family that she is attracted to the same sex. She says that she told one of her cousins about her same-sex attraction, but she did not do so directly. The act of coming out is encapsulated in lines 7 and 8: Linda mentioned to her cousin that she did not like children and was not planning to get married. Other than the two main narrative clauses in lines 3 and 7, Linda's narrative consists mostly of clauses that explain why her cousin had probably known about her same-sex attraction before she came out to him: first, he lives in Australia where there are many lesbians and gay men (lines 2 and 11–12); and second, her cousin could infer from her outlook that she is a lesbian (lines 9–10). Notice Linda's use of ellipsis in lines 5 and 12. Same-sex desire is not mentioned explicitly through the use of labels in her narrative.

(2)　Linda

Linda:

ngo yau go tong-a-go ji.　　　　　One of my cousins knows.

Interviewer:

hai lei uk-kei yan wa bei keui ji a?　　Did your family tell him?

Linda:

1. m-hai	No
2. yan-wai keui hai Ou-Jau jyu	because he lives in Australia
3. gam keui lei taam ngo	he came to visit me
4. gam a	so
5. keui recognize dou ngo hai [ellipsis] lo	he recognized that I was [ellipsis].

6. gam tung ngo haang-gaai	One time, he was taking a walk with me
7. ngo wa ngo mou mat lam-jyu git-fan	I said I wasn't planning to get married
8. ngo yau m-hai hou jung-yi sai-lou-jai	I didn't really like kids
9. je-hai ngo di concept	I mean, my concepts
10. from ngo ge outlook	from my outlook
11. yan-wai keui hai Ou-Jau jyu	because he lives in Australia
12. Ou-Jau dou hou-do [ellipsis]	there are a lot [ellipsis] in Australia.

Non-activists' use of ellipsis in their stories about coming-out experiences is antithetical to the Western notion of coming out and defeats the putative purpose of coming-out stories. Many (e.g., Curtis 1988) have argued that coming-out stories bind together lesbians and gay men of different races, social classes, and educational backgrounds. In the introduction to an anthology of lesbian coming-out stories, Julia Penelope & Susan Wolfe (1995) state:

> For years, the coming out story has been among the first of the stories exchanged among wimmin [sic] . . . *We tell our pasts to intensify the bonds between us and to tear away "the veil of silence" which separates us.* Sharing our stories is a way of coming to know ourselves. . . . These coming out stories are the foundation of our lives as Lesbians, as real to ourselves; as such, our sharing of them defines us as participants in Lesbian culture, as members of a community. (6–11; emphasis added)

At least according to the dominant gay and lesbian ideology in the United States, coming out is supposed to be about self-liberation, the celebration of one's same-sex desire, and, as the quote points out, the tearing away of "the veil of silence." The proclamation of one's same-sex desire is arguably the most important element of coming out. Yet in non-activists' accounts of coming-out experiences, same-sex desire is often left unsaid. Also lacking in these narratives is a strong sense of self-affirmation associated with the Western notion of coming out (Wong 2009). Non-activists simply present their coming-out experiences in a matter-of-fact manner.

Non-activists' use of ellipsis, circumlocutions, and deictic expressions to leave same-sex desire unspecified stems from their general dislike for labels that refer to sexual minorities. Non-activists often equate mentioning same-sex desire explicitly with giving undue emphasis to sexuality. Despite their sexual orientation, many of them believe that they are essentially the same as heterosexual people and do not necessarily share a sense of commonality with others who desire the same sex. For Louise, labels like *lesbian* and *tongzhi* only make it easier for others to categorize and stereotype her. As far as she is concerned, they do not serve any purpose. Similarly, when discussing various labels for sexual minorities in the interview, April questioned the necessity of using *tongzhi* or *tung-sing-lyun je* 'homosexual' to highlight same-sex attraction:

> Sometimes I wonder why I have to call myself *tongzhi* or *tung-sing-lyun je*. Heterosexuals don't walk around telling everyone that they are hetero-sexual. . . . I actually prefer not to label myself as *tongzhi* or *tung-sing-lyun je*. I don't really like these labels because they categorize me. They take out a certain part of my identity and magnify it. . . . I don't like to highlight my sexual orientation. For me, it is sort of like highlighting a particular sex organ. It's rather strange to me.

Amy echoed April's opinion:

> I rarely use these labels. Even *tung-sing-lyun je* or *lesbian*. I don't like to categorize myself in this manner. Perhaps, I am what these labels refer to. But when I hear these terms, I don't feel like they are about me. I don't think it's necessary to use them.

Pauline, who is April's partner, said that to identify herself, she would rather use her own name than labels like *lesbian* and *tongzhi*. If same-sex desire is indeed the topic of discussion, many non-activists prefer to state their sexual attraction instead of using *lesbian* or *tongzhi*. As Bonnie explained, "I actually don't use any labels for myself. I only know that I'm attracted to women."

Non-activists' general dislike for labels for sexual minorities is consistent with their belief that sexuality (especially same-sex desire) is an insignificant part of a person's identity: as a personal and private matter, it has no place in the public domain and should be compartmentalized from other aspects of life such as family and work. This belief has not completely made same-sex desire a taboo subject, but it has certainly led to non-activists' practice of leaving same-sex desire unspecified in many situations.

Given this belief, it should come as no surprise that many non-activists consider coming out an utterly absurd idea. They do not see the need to tell anyone—even close friends—about their sexual orientation because they strongly believe that it is their own business. They are also concerned about the potential of coming out to adversely affect their relationships with others. However, not all parents are in the dark about their children's sexual orienta-tion; rather, they prefer not to bring it out in the open. As Linda explains:

> It's very difficult to hide it from your family. They can tell from your every-day behavior. They can tell from the books you read. They can tell from your friends and the way you talk to them on the phone. It's one thing to know, but it's quite another to talk about it openly. It's fine if they don't want to. I can respect that.

In fact, it is rather common for lesbian and gay Hongkongers to introduce same-sex partners to their families as "best friends" (Chou 2000); however, the true nature of same-sex relationships is rarely discussed. Even though Linda's mother is aware of her sexual orientation, she never talks about it or asks Linda any questions about personal relationships.

Non-activists' silence and their families' reticence on sexuality reinforce each other. In the name of social harmony, both parties operate on a "don't ask, don't tell" principle to keep same-sex desire unspecified. In example (3), Amy describes a recent incident in which her mother expressed approval of her same-sex relationship. Setting up the scene for the main narrated event, which begins in line 14, Amy first explains her mother's previous disapproval (lines 7–10) and a possible reason for her change of heart (lines 11–12).

(3)   Amy

1. gam jan-jan-jing-jing gong	So I really told them
2. sing-ying hai **[ellipsis]**	acknowledging that I am [ellipsis]
3. dou hai li-paai ge ja	only recently.
4. jau hai hou-laak	well, okay
5. gin ngo part-na gin-jo gei-chi la	they had met my partner several times
6. gam yau yat-chi jing-jing jo-dai king-gai	one time, we sat down to have a good chat
7. e, yan-wai kei-sat	um, because actually
8. ngo a-ma jau m-hai hou	my mother didn't really
9. jan-hai m-hai hou jip-sau **[ellipsis]** ge ja	didn't really accept **[ellipsis]**
10. yi-chin m-hai hou jip-sau **[ellipsis]**	in the past, she didn't accept **[ellipsis]**
11. daan-hai gam-chi ho-lang gin-dou	but perhaps this time she noticed
12. gam, li-yat-go part-na bei-gaau stable di	that this partner was more stable
13. gam-yeung le	so
14. keui jau ji-gei wa bei ngo teng	she herself said to me
15. je hai keui gan ngo gong ge	she told me herself
16. e, wa,	um, she said,
17. e, "ngo dou ji-dou lei hai **gam ge yeung** ga lak."	um, "I know that you are **this way.**"

18. e, "ji-yiu lei gok-dak hoi-sam ge   um, "as long as you're happy,
19. ngo m-wui faan-deui lei lo."   I won't be against it."
20. gam yeung lo.   Just like that.

Although Amy's mother took the initiative to talk to Amy and express her approval, her use of the deictic expression *gam ge yeung* 'this way' (as reported by Amy) in line 17, just like Amy's use of ellipsis in lines 2, 9, and 10, keeps same-sex desire unspecified. As this example shows, even if parents accept their children's same-sex sexual orientation, they prefer not to talk about it directly, and their children are often more than happy to go along.

This "don't ask, don't tell" principle may seem to work quite well. In reality, it does not. Given that the true nature of same-sex relationships is often left unsaid, it is often difficult for non-activists to talk to their families about emotional problems. There are also limits to how much parents and siblings are willing to accept. Carla and Deana have been together for seventeen years. Their families just assume that they are "best friends." As Carla explains, however, a same-sex partner can never become part of the family:

We often have dinner with my family, but if it is a big holiday like
Chinese New Year's Eve, my family doesn't like it when I bring her home.
My family thinks that holidays are for the whole family to get together.
It doesn't matter how close we are, my "friend" is still an outsider. She
doesn't have the same last name. They think my "friend" has a family as
well. Why doesn't she go home? Why is she having dinner with us?

Despite parents' and siblings' apparent acceptance of same-sex relationships, lesbians in Hong Kong still face tremendous pressure from all sides to get married. April and Pauline have been living together for several years. Although their families have visited their small one-bedroom apartment and seen that there is only one bed in the entire place, they never inquire about the nature of April and Pauline's relationship. However, they often pester April and Pauline with questions about boyfriends and marriage. The same problem arises at the workplace. To deal with nosy coworkers who want to know everything about her personal life, Deana has resorted to concocting outrageous stories to explain why they have never seen her with a man. She has told some that she is divorced and has given up on relationships. To others, she has said that her boyfriend cannot be seen with her in public because he is married and his wife does not know about their relationship.

As previously discussed, non-activists' labeling practices and their "don't ask, don't tell" principle both stem from the belief that their sexuality is an insignificant part of their identity and should be compartmentalized from other aspects of their lives. While it might be tempting to argue that non-activists must overcome their compartmentalization of sexuality in order to develop a fuller sense of self, cultural relativists would caution against understanding these beliefs and practices through a Western lens. Ultimately, however, we need to adopt a critical perspective to examine whose interests are served and which relations of domination are maintained through these beliefs and practices. Non-activists' labeling practices, like their "don't ask, don't tell" principle, help reproduce heteronormativity by reinforcing the heterosexist ideology that same-sex desire has no place in the public domain. In fact, non-activists themselves are complicit in their own subordination. Through their use of ellipsis, circumlocutions, and deictic expressions to leave same-sex desire unspecified, lesbians and gay men are rendered invisible within Hong Kong society.

Activists' Labeling Practices

Unlike non-activists, gay and lesbian activists in Hong Kong make no attempt to exclude same-sex desire from public discussion, nor do they avoid using labels that specify sexual minorities. The sexuality-based social movement that emerged in Hong Kong in the early 1990s has two main goals. First, it strives to break down the public/private dichotomy. Activists aim to bring same-sex desire into public discussion through the use of nonconfrontational strategies. They consider this a prerequisite for their fight for equal rights. Second, the movement emphasizes that sexuality should not be separated as an independent domain. Activists assert that it is an important part of a person's identity and is essential to one's understanding of the self. However, they believe that it should not overshadow other aspects of a person's life (e.g., work and family); instead, the sexual should be integrated into the social.

Many activists, both male and female, use *tongzhi* as an umbrella term (similar to *LGBT*) when discussing issues about sexual minorities with journalists and researchers (Wong 2008). Chou Wah-Shan (2000), a Hong Kong activist/scholar who has written extensively on same-sex desire in Chinese cultures and is partly responsible for the popularization, provides the following definition:

> *Tongzhi* is the most popular contemporary Chinese word for lesbians, bisexuals, and gay people. . . . *[T]ongzhi* refers not only to *tongxinglian* [homosexuality] but to all forms of sexual practice that have been marginalized by hegemonic heterosexism. That explains why the category *tongzhi* is most welcome to nonhomosexual *tongzhi*, such as bisexual women, sadomasochists (S/Mers), and all other sexual minorities who cannot be subsumed under the category *gay* or *tongxinglian*. (1–3)

As Table 2.1 shows, the label has a long history, and its meaning has changed over the years. *Tongzhi*, which is often glossed as "comrade," was first adopted by Nationalist revolutionaries in Republican China. It was then taken up by Chinese Communists to refer to those fighting for Communist ideals. After 1949, it was used as an address term by the general public. Since the opening

TABLE 2.1

Important milestones in the history of *tongzhi* since 1911

	1911 Republican China	1949 Communist China	1978 The opening up of the market economy	Late 1980s The beginning of the *tongzhi* movement	Mid-1990s–Present
Mainland China	"comrade"	"(Communist) comrade"	"(Communist)"	"(Communist) comrade"	"(Communist) comrade"
	Address term for Nationalist revolutionaries	Address term for the general public	The term *tongzhi* became disfavored.	"sexual minorities"	"sexual minorities"
				Term of reference used by gay rights activists	Term of reference used by gay rights activists and mainstream newspapers
Hong Kong	"comrade"	"(Communist) comrade"	"(Communist)"	"(Communist) comrade"	"(Communist) comrade"
		The use of *tongzhi* "comrade" as an address term was widely known in Hong Kong, but it was rarely used due to its Communist and political connotations.			

up of the market economy of China in 1978, it has become disfavored due to its political connotations (Fang & Heng 1983). In the late 1980s, it was appropriated by gay and lesbian activists in Hong Kong as an all-inclusive label to refer to those of non-normative sexual orientation (i.e., lesbians, gay men, bisexuals, and transgender people). Even in mainstream Hong Kong newspapers, *tongzhi* has for the most part replaced derogatory labels that were commonly used in the past (Wong 2005).

Gay rights activists' appropriation of *tongzhi* serves as a symbolic form of resistance against not only Western gay and lesbian ideologies but also heterosexism in Hong Kong. Unlike *gay, lesbian,* and *queer, tongzhi* is an indigenous label that emphasizes the cultural specificity of same-sex desire in Chinese societies (Chou 2000: 2). Activists exploit the revolutionary connotations of the term and its suggestions of solidarity, intimacy, and striving for liberty. Like Chinese revolutionaries, activists use the term to present a public, collective, and political front. They call on Chinese sexual minorities to join the common endeavor of fighting for equality and to challenge the heterosexist beliefs that same-sex desire should remain unspoken and should be excluded from the public domain (Wong & Zhang 2000).

Both male and female activists use *tongzhi* as a superordinate term when presenting the collective whole to journalists and researchers. This is particularly evident when they talk about the *tongzhi* circle/community *(hyun/se-keui)*, organizations for sexual minorities, and sexual-based social movements in Hong Kong and elsewhere. They also use *tongzhi* as an umbrella term when making generalizations about same-sex cultures or discussing issues pertaining to all sexual minorities—for example, coming out, public acceptance, and discrimination against those of non-normative sexual orientation. In example (4), Veronica, a core member of Queer Sisters (a queer feminist group in Hong Kong) contemplates whether or not it was difficult to be a *tongzhi* in primary or secondary school in the old days.

(4)   Veronica

yau jung-hok lei gong le	If we're talking about secondary school
kei-sat yi yat-go **tongzhi** san-fan le	for someone who is a **tongzhi**
jung-hok wa-je siu-hok ge gaai-dyun	in secondary school or primary school
mou mat laan-dou ge	it wasn't difficult.
ngo gok-dak yau m-wui	I think there wasn't
dak-bit bei yan kei-si la	any discrimination in particular
di yan m-wui seung-hoi lei ga	people wouldn't hurt you.

Veronica's discussion is not limited to lesbians and bisexual women; rather, it applies to others of non-normative sexual orientation as well. Her use of *tong-zhi* appears to be all-inclusive since members of all sexual minorities face the potential threat of discrimination and societal rejection.

When the context requires specifying the gender of the referent, female activists often modify *tongzhi* with either *laam* 'male' or *leui* 'female.' In example (5), Erica, another core member of Queer Sisters, speaks on behalf of the organization and gives several examples of its educational programs and activities. Notice her use of *leui tongzhi* 'female *tongzhis*' instead of *tongzhi* in this case to specify that the programs cater to lesbians and bisexual women.

(5) Erica

pei-yu ngo-dei yau mong-seung din-toi	For example, we have an Internet radio station
gong yat-di ho-yi bong dou **leui tongzhi**	we have programs that can help **female tongzhis**
tung uk-kei yan kau-tung ge jit-muk la	communicate with their families
wa-je lei dim-yeung come out a	or how do you come out?
wa-je lei dim-yeung chyu-lei	or how do you deal with
gung-jok seung ge aat-lik a	pressure at work?
lei dim-yeung ho-yi jou hou ji-gei le?	how do you improve yourself?
gam-yeung	so on and so forth.

Nevertheless, female activists believe that for some male activists, *tongzhi* is just another label for "gay man." One reason for this belief has to do with female activists' experience in the *tongzhi* movement. In theory, women are included under the label *tongzhi*. Whether it is "*Tongzhi* Week," "*Tongzhi* Day," or "*Tongzhi* Conference," women are encouraged to take part in all the events and activities. However, female activists complain that women are only granted the role of silent participant. At best, lesbians' and bisexual women's concerns are addressed only insofar as they are shared by gay men. At worst, women's issues are considered peripheral to the goals of the *tongzhi* movement. This has led female activists to conclude that *tongzhi* merely means "gay men" and that male *tongzhi* activists' vision has been imposed on lesbians and bisexual women. Another reason has to do with how male activists use the label *tongzhi* in discourse. Male activists' androcentric vision manifests itself in their cognitive structure underlying the label. Figure 2.1 shows two taxonomic hierarchies.

Like female activists, male activists use *tongzhi* as an umbrella term to refer to all sexual minorities, but the two hierarchies differ when the referent is

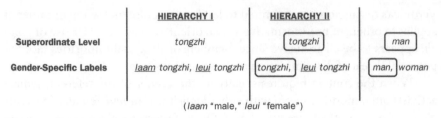

FIGURE 2.1 Two taxonomic hierarchies

male: some male activists modify *tongzhi* with *laam* 'male,' but others use the label without the modifier. In other words, for those who adopt Hierarchy II, *tongzhi* refers to "all sexual minorities" or "gay men." The use of *tongzhi* in this case is similar to the generic use of the English word *man*. Many female activists object to this practice because it effectively equates male *tongzhis'* reality with the reality for all sexual minorities.

The use of *tongzhi* as a male-specific term becomes problematic when the topic of discussion is the *tongzhi* movement in general. In example (6), a male activist, Sam, discusses a particular turning point in the *tongzhi* movement. He claims that the publication of a gay pornographic magazine was an important milestone for the *tongzhi* movement.

(6)   Sam

1. je yi bei-gaau cheut-kei lei gong le   So what was rather
                                                                        surprising was that

2. e, 97 lin cheut-jo bun bun-dei ge   um, in 97, there emerged
                                                                        a local

3. chyun-gin-baan ge ***tongzhi*** jaap-ji   all-nude ***tongzhi*** magazine
    ji-hau le

4. gam jau e   So

5. [Interviewer: (laughter)   (laughter)]

6. hou jung-yiu ga   This is very important

7. m-hai, kei-sat li-bun syu le   No, this magazine in fact

8. hai ***tongzhi*** go lik-si leui-bin   in ***tongzhi*** history

9. Hung-Fung le   Hung-Fung

10. hai hou jung-yiu ge yat-bun syu   is a very important
    lei ge   magazine

11. yan-wai li-bun syu cheut-jo   Because after the
    ji-hau le   publication of this
                        magazine

12. ling-dou yau hou-do yan dou   some people felt that
    gok-dak

13. yau yat go	there was a
14. ho-lang hai cho-gok	perhaps it was an illusion
15. yik dou ho-lang hai jan-hai si-sat	or perhaps it was true
16. jau hai wa	the fact that
17. e, Heung-Gong deui-yu li-go *tongzhi* ge fun-yung dou hou-chi hai daai-jo	the acceptance of ***tongzhis*** in Hong Kong has improved

Remember that in Hierarchy I, *tongzhi* is only used as an umbrella term, and when the context requires the use of a male-specific label, the modifier *laam* 'male' is used. To get a sense of what this sounds like to those who adopt this taxonomic hierarchy, we may substitute *tongzhi* with *LGBT* in the English translation in line 3: "an all-nude *LGBT* magazine" sounds rather odd, especially because only gay men are featured in this magazine. In addition, this male activist looks at *tongzhi* history from a male perspective and presents this perspective as the unmarked one—"male *tongzhi* magazine" is equated with "*tongzhi* magazine" in line 3, "male *tongzhi* history" with "*tongzhi* history" in line 8, and "male *tongzhis*" with *tongzhis* in line 17. In other words, male *tongzhis'* reality is presented as the reality for all sexual minorities.

This example shows that the oppression that lesbians and bisexual women experience in the *tongzhi* movement is not complete isolation or exclusion; rather, it is a form of symbolic violence exercised through male *tongzhi* activists' imposition of their androcentric vision on other sexual minorities. The imposition of one's view of the world on others is perhaps more effective than any other form of power—be it coercion, control of resources, or monopoly in decision-making. As linguistic anthropologist Susan Gal (1995) rightly claims: "the strongest form of power may well be the ability to define social reality, to impose visions of the world. And such visions are inscribed in language, and most important, enacted in interaction" (178).

Conclusion

This study demonstrates how labeling practices can shed light on the ways in which power operates through symbolic means at the intersection of gender and sexuality. Hong Kong lesbians who are not part of the *tongzhi* movement use ellipsis, deictic expressions (e.g., *go-di yan* 'those people'), and circumlocutions (e.g., *tung ji-gei yat-yeung ge yan* 'people like me') to keep same-sex desire unspecified. Through their labeling practices, non-activists participate in their own subjugation by rendering themselves invisible within the wider community and reinforcing the heterosexist ideology that same-sex desire has no place in the public domain. An examination of activists' labeling practices illustrates another manner in which oppression works. Female activists' adoption of the label *tongzhi* puts them in a double bind. For both male and female activists, *tongzhi* serves as a mode of resistance against heterosexism and Western gay and lesbian ideologies. Through their use of the term, however, some male activists impose their androcentric viewpoint on lesbians and practically erase them from the movement. The oppressed effectively become the oppressors. Not solely the property of those at the very top of the social hierarchy, power is dispersed throughout the social fabric and moves in a multitude of directions from a multitude of sites. Instead of asking who has power, we should examine the ebb and flow of power at different locations. In other words, we need to investigate how power flows through social structures and how power relations work at different social intersections.

Any discussion of oppression through symbolic means inevitably leads to the question of whether or not it is any less "real" or "effective" than other kinds of oppression (e.g., physical coercion). In some sense, symbolic domination is more insidious and resistant to change than physical domination. As we have seen in the case of non-activists, the perspective of the dominant group is so thoroughly naturalized that subordinate groups adopt it as their own, begin to observe and analyze the world from that perspective, and become complicit in their own subordination. This form of symbolic power is embedded in their thoughts and actions, and gives a veneer of legitimacy to the order of things. Oppression through symbolic means produces material effects as well. The use of *tongzhi* as an all-inclusive label masks the reality that within the *tongzhi* movement, resource allocation is based on criteria and agendas set by male activists, who personify the movement and give it its public image. Studying oppression through symbolic means should not be taken as a denial of the importance of other forms of oppression. Oppression takes many different forms that are intimately tied to each other, and they work together to result in the sufferings of subordinate groups.

Intersections, as Levon (2011) argues, are theoretical constructs that are underspecified. They can only be understood through empirical investigation of lived experience and social practice. Not only does the present study lend credence to this idea, but it also shows how labeling practices offer a useful perspective in such an endeavor. We cannot establish a priori how power operates at a given social intersection. Those presumably at the same social intersection may experience oppression differently and give us distinct insights into the workings of power. Intersectionality reminds us to take power differentials into account and challenges us to examine how language serves as a tool for oppression—as well as a tool for resistance—at various intersections of social differentiation. This, I believe, is the most important lesson from intersectionality theory. We can learn a tremendous amount from the linguistic practices of multiply marginalized subjects, and what we learn will go a long way toward unraveling the social forces underlying linguistic variation and change.

Notes

1. *Tongzhi* is the *pinyin* (romanization) of the Chinese word in Mandarin. In Cantonese, it is pronounced as *tung4-ji3* (4—low falling tone; 3—midlevel tone). Since all the interviews were conducted in Cantonese, Cantonese (rather than Mandarin) romanization is used in this chapter. The only exceptions are the terms *tongzhi* and *gay. Tongzhi* is used more often than its Cantonese counterpart in academic writing in English (see, e.g., Chou 2000), and *gay* is a loanword from English. The romanization used in this chapter is based on the Yale system (see Matthews & Yip 1994). For easier reading, tones are not indicated.

2. All names are pseudonyms.

References

Cameron, Deborah & Don Kulick. 2003. *Language and sexuality.* New York: Cambridge University Press.

Chou, Wah-Shan. 2000. *Tongzhi: Politics of same-sex eroticism in Chinese societies.* New York: Harrington Park Press.

Collins, Patricia Hill. 2000. *Black feminist thoughts.* New York: Routledge.

Crenshaw, Kimberlé. 1989. Demarginalizing the intersection of race and sex: A black feminist critique of antidiscrimination doctrine, feminist theory, and antiracist politics. *The University of Chicago Legal Forum* 140. 139–167.

Crenshaw, Kimberlé. 1991. Mapping the margins: Intersectionality, identity politics, and violence against women of color. *Stanford Law Review* 43(6). 1241–1299.

Curtis, Wayne (ed.). 1988. *Revelations: A collection of gay male coming out stories.* Boston: Alyson Books.

Davis, Angela. 1983. *Women, race and class.* New York: Random House.

Dodsworth, Robin & Christine Mallinson. 2006. *The utility of intersectionality theory in variationist sociolinguistics.* Paper presented at the 80th annual meeting of the Linguistic Society of America. Albuquerque, NM.

Eckert, Penelope. 1989. The whole woman: Sex and gender differences in variation. *Language Variation and Change* 1(3). 245–268.

Eckert, Penelope. 2000. *Linguistic variation as social practice.* Malden, MA: Blackwell.

Fang, Hanquan & J. H. Heng. 1983. Social change and changing address norms in China. *Language in Society* 12(4). 497–507.

Gal, Susan. 1995. Language, gender, and power: An anthropological review. In Kira Hall & Mary Bucholtz (eds.), *Gender articulated*, 169–182. New York: Routledge.

hooks, bell. 1981. *Ain't I a woman: Black women and feminism.* Cambridge, MA: South End Press.

James, Deborah & Sandra Clarke. 1993. Women, men, and interruptions: A critical review. In Deborah Tannen (ed.), *Gender and conversational interaction*, 231–280. New York: Oxford University Press.

Kiesling, Scott. 1998. Men's identities and sociolinguistic variation: The case of fraternity men. *Journal of Sociolinguistics* 2(1). 69–99.

Lanehart, Sonja. 2009. Diversity and intersectionality. *Texas Linguistics Forum (Proceedings of the 17th Annual Symposium About Language and Society—Austin)* 53. 1–7.

Levon, Erez. 2011. Teasing apart to bring together: Gender and sexuality in variationist research. *American Speech* 86(1). 69–84.

Mallinson, Christine. 2006. *The dynamic construction of race, class, and gender through linguistic practice among women in a black Appalachian community.* Raleigh: North Carolina State University. PhD dissertation.

Mallinson, Christine. 2008. The linguistic negotiation of complex racialized identities by black Appalachian speakers. In Kendall A. King, Natalie Schilling-Estes, Lyn Fogle, Jia Jackie Lou, & Barbara Soukup (eds.), *Sustaining linguistic diversity: Endangered and minority languages and language varieties,* 67–80. Washington, DC: Georgetown University Press.

Matsuda, Mari. 1987. Looking to the bottom: Critical legal studies and reparations. *Harvard Civil Rights-Civil Liberties Law Review* 22. 323–399.

Matthews, Stephen & Virginia Yip. 1994. *Cantonese: A comprehensive grammar.* New York: Routledge.

McCall, Leslie. 2005. The complexity of intersectionality. *Signs* 30(3). 1771–1800.

McConnell-Ginet, Sally. 2002. "Queering" semantics. In Kathryn Campbell-Kibler Robert Podesva, Sarah Roberts, & Andrew Wong (eds.), *Language and sexuality: Contesting meaning in theory and practice,* 137–160. Stanford, CA: CSLI.

Morgan, Marcyliena. 2007. When and where we enter: Social context and desire in women's discourse. *Gender and Language* 1(1). 119–129.

Nash, Jennifer C. 2008. Re-thinking intersectionality. *Feminist Review* 89(1). 1–15.

Penelope, Julia & Susan Wolfe (eds.). 1995. *The original coming out stories.* Freedom, CA: The Crossing Press.

Tannen, Deborah. 1981. New York Jewish conversational style. *International Journal of the Sociology of Language* 30. 133–149.

Wong, Andrew. 2005. The reappropriation of *tongzhi. Language in Society* 34(5). 763–793.

Wong, Andrew. 2008. On the actuation of semantic change: The case of *tongzhi. Language Sciences* 30(4). 423–449.

Wong, Andrew. 2009. Coming-out stories and the "gay imaginary." *Sociolinguistic Studies* 3(1). 1–34.

Wong, Andrew & Qing Zhang. 2000. The linguistic construction of the *tongzhi* community. *Journal of Linguistic Anthropology* 10(2). 248–278.

Zimmerman, Don & Candace West. 1975. Sex roles, interruptions and silences in conversation. In Barrie Thorne & Nancy Henley (eds.), *Language and sex: Difference and dominance,* 105–129. Rowley, MA: Newbury House.

3

Social and Linguistic Representations of South African Same-Sex Relations

THE CASE OF *SKESANA*

Stephanie Rudwick and Thabo Msibi

Introduction

In South Africa, gender relations continue to be deeply embedded in the country's patriarchal social structure, which, at the same time, intersects in complicated ways with racial, ethnic, sexual, and linguistic identity constructions. For example, same-sex relationships, while constitutionally protected, are far from being "widely accepted" in South African society. Often, the arguments presented against same-sex relations are drawn from essentialized and patriarchal notions of manhood and womanhood, with the belief that a linear and given relationship exists among sex, gender, and sexuality. Love relationships, in general, are often characterized by "patriarchal thinking" and actions, and heteronormativity simply remains, in many different facets, rooted in the consciousness of most South Africans. In this chapter we broadly aim to demonstrate that this is also the case in same-sex relationships and that there are diverse social and linguistic representations of this reality.

The chapter is based on semiethnographic research in the *eThekwini* area of South Africa (Durban metropolitan area), focusing on the situation of African men who engage in same-sex relations and who have knowledge of a linguistic variety termed *isiNgqumo*.[1] IsiZulu is the base language of this variety and it can be described as a sociolect or genderlect, spoken primarily by Zulu men in the KwaZulu-Natal region who engage in same-sex relations. In observing the lives of isiNgqumo-speaking men over three years, we found that the traditional Zulu custom of *hlonipha*, which has complex social and linguistic facets, plays a significant role in the social and linguistic behavioral codex of these men. Our study also reveals a connection of the isiNgqumo lexicon and the *hlonipha* language lexicon, which is a linguistic variety employed to demonstrate respect. This chapter further portrays the social and linguistic complexities of the identity trajectories of a particular subgroup of African men who engage in same-sex relations and who self-identify as *skesana*, most of whom have knowledge of isiNgqumo.

Drawing on intersectionality theory (Crenshaw 1989; Collins 2000; McCall 2005; Levon 2011), we discuss multiple formations of gender identities in relation to this particular language use. The isiNgqumo lexicon is characterized largely by what Zulu speakers refer to as "deep" lexicon, an almost "archaic" form of isiZulu, comparable to Shakespearean English. A closer examination also reveals that there are lexical items that are drawn from the *hlonipha* language, in some instances also termed *isiHlonipho sabafazi* ('women's language of respect'). This linguistic variety can be described as a politeness register primarily employed by Zulu females before and after marriage. *Hlonipha* [lit. 'respect'] language usage and social actions are representative for very particular power dynamics in Zulu society. Women who obey the *hlonipha* custom are generally showing referential submissiveness toward males and other persons who are considered superior in the sociocultural hierarchy.

We argue in this chapter that *skesana* men not only socially obey the custom of *hlonipha* but, in some instances, also make usage of an isiNgqumo variety which draws from the *hlonipha* lexicon. This suggests that isiNgqumo is a linguistic means that is deeply gendered and linked to a patriarchal cultural system constructing femininity as an inferior subject position. Within this gendered order, isiNgqumo can create tension-riddled identity categories and allows for complex positioning of African men who engage in same-sex relations, many of whom draw on heteronormative and heteropoleric categories in the construction of their sexual and gender identities. We further argue that men who know isiNgqumo, engage in same-sex relations, and self-identify as *skesana*—who, ironically, themselves experience widespread discrimination in the broader South African public—exhibit social and linguistic behavior that contributes to the perpetuation of the matrix of oppression in the gender landscape of the country. This, however, does not discount the emancipatory and agentive possibilities that the use of isiNgqumo may offer these men in some instances. Rather, it shows the multifaceted nature of sexual identities, and of the linguistic varieties associated with certain sexualities.

Cognizant of the contested panoptic use of Western sexual identity labels in African contexts, we use the rather lengthy concept of "men who engage in same-sex relations" in referring to our participants. Western sexual categories are increasingly being questioned in African contexts given their failure to capture the varied ways in which same-sex engagement is understood and enacted in these locales. Recently for instance, Sigamoney & Epprecht (2013) have shown, through an extensive study of more than 1,000 South African township youth, how concepts like "homosexuality" and other Western categories of identification fail to resonate with the local people as many often do not know the concepts or do not understand their meanings. In fact, Sigamoney & Epprecht found that the sheer majority of township youth and police officers in their study did not use the word *homosexual*, with less than 5% of their participants using it to refer to men and women who manifest same-sex desires. While the same study also revealed that *gay* and *lesbian* were often the preferred terms by study participants, we are also guarded in using these terms as these often take on particular localized meanings which differ drastically from those used in the West (see Msibi 2013a). Additionally, queer theory has highlighted the fluid nature of identification, thereby troubling the assumed static nature of labels such as *gay* and *lesbian* (Jagose 1997). We are, however, also constrained from labeling the participants *queer* due to the sparse use of this concept in contexts like South Africa. The general concept of "men who engage in same-sex relations" assists therefore in not only avoiding an imposition of concepts but also in highlighting the complexities of sexual identification.

We begin our argument by providing a brief background on the particularities of studies on African sexuality. This is followed by a discussion on the conceptual and theoretical positions adopted in this chapter. Then we introduce isiNgqumo as a South African genderlect and draw a connection to the *hlonipha* language variety. By exploring the genealogy of the *skesana* identity as a subject position constructed by African men who engage in same-sex relations, we showcase the ways in which the heteronormative, gendered positioning of this identity may have been informed by historical patterns of same-sex practices in South African mineral mines (mine sexual politics), with same-sex sexual engagements among men primarily defined along traditional, heteronormative gender lines. We also demonstrate how *hlonipha* social and linguistic behavior plays a role in the constructions of these sexual and gender identities.

African Sexuality: A Brief Background

Epprecht's (2004, 2006) historical accounts of dissident sexuality in Southern Africa aptly demonstrate how same-sex acts and relationships occurred in pre-modern South Africa.[2] He also explains, however, that "homosexuality as an identity or lifestyle choice did not exist when the pressures to have sex for reproduction were so over-determined by material, political, spiritual and other cultural considerations" (Epprecht 2004: 224). Today, however, this has changed, and many African gays and lesbians do indeed construct distinct same-sex identities on the basis of a particular lifestyle. By that we do not mean to say that their same-sex sexuality per se is a choice or that all men who engage in same-sex relations exclusively claim a "gay" identity; most participants in this study indicated that they were "born gay," but there is a complex array of lifestyles available for Africans who engage in same-sex relations today, with conceptions of "gayness" ranging from one context to the next.

The gendered nature of sexuality and identity prevalent specifically among African gay men in South Africa has been described as quite heteronormative (McClean & Ngcobo 1995; Reddy & Louw 2002), in a sense that there is always either an "active" or a "passive" participant in sexual intercourse whose role is rather clear-cut and stable. This essentially means that much African same-sex activity accommodates heterosexual gender roles (i.e., same-sex partnerships and marriages where one man is the "man" and the other the "woman"). To this day, many African men who openly claim a gay identity are quite "feminine" and perform primarily a passive act during sex. This is not to say that African masculine men do not claim gay identities or that such men do not play "passive" sexual roles. Rather we argue that for many of the men who visibly claim "gay" identities, this normative positioning holds. This speaks as much to the discrimination that men who claim "gay" identities face as it does to the patriarchal conditions of the context. Men who outwardly claim gay identities are often assumed to want to be women, with derogatory labels such as *sis-bhuti* (sister-brother) used against them, particularly in rural, conservative South African contexts. For many African Nguni language speakers, this "effeminate" identity positioning is termed *skesana*. This specific sexual and gender identity construct and its linguistic representations are the focus of this chapter.

The heteronormativity at play in many "gay" African relationships is the vantage point for us. Without this continuous prevalence of heteronormativity in the post-apartheid state, the linguistic variety of isiNgqumo would probably not thrive in quite the way it does. It is the frequent femininity and effeminate associations with the speakers of the variety in combination with a lexicon that is deeply culturally rooted which allows the language to thrive and develop further on a daily basis.

Theoretical Framework

Within the field of linguistic anthropology, it has been argued that "one of the greatest weaknesses of previous research on identity [. . .] is the assumption that identities are attributes of individuals or groups rather than of situations" (Bucholtz & Hall 2004b: 376). Importantly for this chapter, identities are constructed in social actions and the products of particular circumstances; they can always shift and renew themselves from one situation to another and from one time to another. Hence, the sexual and gender identities that are produced and performed through language by the participants in this study are highly context- and time-dependent and vary from one individual to the next, taking into account the idiosyncrasies of the individuals involved, the situation, and the subject matter of the communicative act. The linguistic experience and identity performance of a "gay"-identifying Zulu-speaking man based in deep rural Nkandla will certainly be different, for instance, from that of a Zulu-speaking man based in the urban and cosmopolitan city of Durban.

In order to demonstrate the preceding more aptly, this chapter draws on Crenshaw's (1989) theory of intersectionality in highlighting the varied ways in which language, gender, sexuality, race, and nation intersect to produce particular ways of identification and linguistic practices. Recognizing limitations of deracializing women's experiences, Crenshaw used intersectionality as a tool to understand the discursive locations of black women's experiences. For Crenshaw, and other black feminist scholars who built on her theories, the feminist movement assumed a similarity of experience among women, forgetting the insidious ways in which race shapes women's experiences. Intersectionality was therefore a theoretical response by black feminist scholars who recognized the importance of identifying interconnections that exist between different forms of identity (e.g., race, class, gender, and sexuality) in maintaining systems of oppression (Collins 2000). The term *intersectionality* is drawn upon to trouble the notion of a linear or singular identity, in seeking to showcase the many aspects of selfhood (Davis 2008).

Intersectionality further recognizes that there is no one way of being a woman, gay, black, and so on. Identity is centered on the subject and the subject's performance of identity across time, place, and space. More recently, intersectionality has been adopted by post-structural and post-colonial sexuality theorists to explore the multiple ways of sexual identification and to deconstruct the limiting and, at times, necessary sexual identity labels (see the edited collection from Taylor, Hines, & Casey 2010). Like Nash (2008), we are aware of the limitations of intersectionality as a theoretical position, in particular its ubiquitous use as a theoretical tool highlighting the lives of those in the margins, without sufficiently engaging with the intersectional systems that produce dominant identities. In this chapter, we use intersectionality to understand the ways in which various forms of identification among *skesanas* intersect to produce particular forms of sexual and linguistic performances. Such identifications include that of a Zulu man who linguistically behaves more like a Zulu "woman" and who takes on roles that would, from a traditional African perspective, be reserved for females. Just as the *skesana* identity is informed by multiple forms of identification, we concede that constructions of other more dominant forms of sexual identification are produced through similar and competing intersectional systems.

A study that examines language in relation to sexuality and identity also benefits from Bucholtz & Hall's (2004a, 2004b, 2005) "tactics of intersubjectivity." These tactics can index sameness and/or difference among speakers, they can appear consecutively or simultaneously in interaction, and they can also occur in contradictory ways. There is adequation vis-à-vis distinction, authentication vis-à-vis denaturalization, and authorization vis-à-vis illegitimation. Through these tactics, speakers of a particular linguistic variety construct identity positions for themselves and others. Because different participants may understand the same linguistic act as motivated by different tactics, the tactical outcome is negotiated during the interaction, rather than established prior to the conversation. Bucholtz & Hall's conceptualization of sexual and gender identities in relation to language are useful for explaining how speakers employ linguistic resources in order to express sexual and gender roles in same-sex relationships.

This chapter also employs the concept of heteronormativity to expose the ways in which heterosexuality is normalized in daily discourses via "othering" forms of sexual identification outside the normative positioning (Kumashiro 2002). Othering, in this context, is a process where individuals who fall out of the boundaries of mainstream society in terms of their sexual and gender orientation are negatively perceived and, at times, even ostracized. Heteronormativity is enacted through various ways, including language, texts, and actions. For instance, Murray (2012) has shown, using a close textual analysis of two fictional texts with lesbian identities, how even fictional texts can reflect a heteronormative male gaze, thereby silencing lesbian identities. Reid (2006) and Msibi (2013b) have also shown how in some South African contexts those who engage in same-sex relations may conform to heteronormative constructions of sexuality, with those who take "bottom" sexual roles (i.e., being penetrated) often perceiving themselves as women in the relationships, while those who play the "top" position (i.e., doing the penetration) often consider themselves "men" in the relationships. In this current study, we demonstrate the pervasive heteronormative enactment of sexuality through the gendered ways in which isiNgqumo is employed by the *skesanas* interviewed.

Language usage does not necessarily have to be gendered but the term *genderlect* has been coined to define a linguistic variety that indexes the gender or sexual identity of a speaker, or expresses different language usage among men and women. Although by now widely criticized, the term emerged from previous studies in the Anglo-Saxon context that have also used the terms *women's* and *men's* language by compiling lists of lexical and grammatical features (Lakoff 1975) or discussed male-female miscommunication patterns (Tannen 1990). Since the 1990s, sociolinguistic scholars have distanced themselves from such essentialized notions of gender categories and work with Holmes & Meyerhoff's (2005) avoidance of the idea "that there is a natural basis for separating the social world into two and only two sexes and genders" (8). We nevertheless employ the term *genderlect* following Motschenbacher's (2010) theorization of genderlects as referring to the way that language "plays a significant role in the performative construction of gender" (49). Accordingly, the term is not used as a simple binary concept but framed in postmodernist thought where stereotypes of gendered communication can be critically interrogated. From this perspective, the concept of genderlect can also consider "the variable ways people do gender linguistically" (Motschenbacher 2007: 263) and the role "genderlectal stylization plays in the discursive formation of gendered identities" (Motschenbacher 2007: 270).

Fieldwork

This chapter is informed by semiethnographic data and individual interviews over a period of three years. During this time, the authors and their research assistants spent time in the *eThekwini* region townships to meet isiNgqumo-speakers and to "hang out" with them. We also spent substantial time in one particular Durban bar which at the time was frequented by many young Zulu men who engage in same-sex relationships. A multitude of casual conversations occurred during these periods in the field and often led us to meet again elsewhere. This study is informed by the many candid accounts of isiNgqumo-speakers in these informal circumstances. Only some of these were voice recorded, others written down in terms of field notes. The recorded interviews mostly took place within the participant's home and in public places of their choice. Although these interviews were not supposed to be open-ended, on occasion they turned into conversations that lasted many hours. While interviews were generally semistructured, many turned into lengthy narratives. Although we voice-recorded a total number of twenty-six participants for this study, and there were three particular individuals whose interesting stories triggered more engagement with us and caused us to meet them repeatedly. This allowed us to get a detailed view of their lives and how isiNgqumo and *hlonipha* intersect. For this chapter, we privilege the narratives of these three participants. We present a brief synopsis of these individuals and their lifestyles in the case studies that follow. However, prior to the presentation of these case studies, it is important to present a brief discussion on the two linguistic varieties under discussion in this chapter.

ISINGQUMO

Only a few years have passed since isiNgqumo first attracted attention among South African sociolinguists and gender scholars (Rudwick & Ntuli 2008; Rudwick 2010; Msibi 2013a). Thus far, no comprehensive lexicon of isiNgqumo has been published, although we have met several isiNgqumo-speaking individuals who intend to compose such a volume. We provide a short list of lexical items in the appendix to demonstrate that the isiNgqumo lexicon transcends a mere sexual register by the incorporation of many nonsexual lexical items. Grammatically, isiNgqumo is based on the Nguni language family. The variety can be considered a genderlect as by speaking it "people do gender linguistically" (Motschenbacher 2007: 263), but also because it is virtually exclusively employed by "gay" men. The interviewees unanimously claimed that lesbians make no use of the variety.[3] Only two participants conceded that some heterosexual women who have close contacts and friendships with African gay males may have some passive knowledge of isiNgqumo and they referred to these women jokingly as "fag hags."

IsiNgqumo's distinctive feature is not its grammar but its lexicon. According to Rudwick & Ntuli (2008), *isiNgqumo* words belong to the lexical categories of nouns, adjectives and verbs and these are by no means limited to sex discourse. The authors suggest that there are no distinct prepositions, adverbs or pronouns in the lexicon of *isiNgqumo*, which we can confirm from the data we collected. As has been noted in the context of "gay speech varieties" before (Baker 2002; Cage 2003; Rudwick & Ntuli 2008), overlexification is taking place where semantic frames of the lexical items mostly revolve around sex discourse.

In regard to the etymology of isiNgqumo, researchers have not been of one voice. McLean and Ngcobo (1995) claimed that *isiNgqumo* words are primarily based on "deep" isiZulu and suggested that this fact "could be related to the intensely patriarchal nature of Zulu society and the greater need for secrecy" (184). Many participants in this study also indicated that isiNgqumo emerged as a "secret" language. Others, however, flagged more its role as a language of belonging and as an identity building device. While some scholars have distinguished clearly between certain gay languages as *either* a "secret language" *or* a "language of belonging" (Boellstorff 2004: 182), isiNgqumo does not seem to have such a singular role in South African black gay society (Rudwick & Ntuli 2008). Although isiNgqumo usage seems more prevalent in lower socioeconomic gay circles and semiurban, township settings, it is not spoken only by *skesanas* as one particular group of men who engage in same-sex relationships. We argue here that its complex role in the lives of many black gay men in South Africa who engage in heterogeneous lifestyles creates its multifaceted functions as a genderlect, an antilanguage, a secret code, a language of belonging, and a linguistic means to perform distinct gender and sexual identities.

HLONIPHA PRACTICE, LANGUAGE USAGE, AND THE CONNECTION WITH ISINGQUMO

The social and linguistic custom of respect (*hlonipha*) is a cultural pillar of South African Nguni and Sotho society and can be understood as a complex behavioral codex that requires deferential conduct. In traditional Zulu society, it is primarily married Zulu women who uphold *hlonipha* in its strictest sense (Zungu 1985), but the custom per se is not restricted to women.[4] Zulu men also use *hlonipha*, for instance in respect of elders, superiors and ancestors.

Hlonipha can manifest itself in multifaceted relations of superordination and subordination and is essentially based on mechanisms that control language use, posture, gesture, movements, dress code, and other dynamics of a material nature or status.

However, in its most common linguistic form and contextualized in rural Zulu settings, the *hlonipha* language can also be regarded as a genderlect, because traditionally, speaking *hlonipha* is primarily expected from Zulu wives and wives-to-be and expresses a very particular form of femininity (Rudwick 2013). In this context, the variety has been termed *isiHlonipho sabafazi* (Finlayson 2002) and it is indexical of the perceived socially inferior status of women in Zulu society (Herbert 1990). The linguistic aspect of the custom primarily includes the avoidance of certain terms but comprises also, in its traditional form, an entire core lexicon of specific *hlonipha* words. The social aspect of *hlonipha* involves the avoidance of any kind of behavior which is considered disrespectful. Even to this day in Zulu traditional society, this includes, for instance, the refraining from wearing trousers by women, showing disagreement to an older or superior person, or speaking in what would be considered an inappropriate manner. Several scholars (Hanong Thetela 2002; Rudwick & Shange 2006; Rudwick 2013) have shown how *hlonipha* language embodies ambiguities and problems in regard to gender equality that are deeply rooted in African patriarchy. Women who speak *hlonipha* language to their husbands and male relatives project a traditional kind of Zulu femininity which can be characterized as submissive. Although these projections and representations may render speakers of *hlonipha* quite vulnerable, the code is endorsed in rural Zulu society due to its cultural rootedness.

In this chapter, we argue that *hlonipha* also plays a crucial part in the power dynamics of some same-sex African relationships in South Africa. In the list that follows, we exemplify some terms from the *hlonipha* vocabulary that are employed and sometimes also recontextualized in isiNgqumo (partly from Msibi 2013a):

- *umchakisana*—'boy'
- *imalasi*—'dog'
- *umfazi*—'a respectable (married) woman/wife,' 'a respected feminine partner in a same-sex relationship'
- *ukuphumela*—'to like someone'
- *ukutukela*—'to cry'

The fact that there is some overlap between the *hlonipha* language and isiNgqumo suggests that avoidance and respect may also play an important role in African same-sex relationships.[5] The intersection of lexical items between the two varieties may, however, also be explained by the fact that both linguistic codes are, to a large extent, based on an archaic form of isiZulu. More generally, isiZulu speakers refer to this way of speaking as "deep" isiZulu.

Leap (2004) provides an example of *hlonipha* language usage among men in a gay newspaper called *Exit*, where a Zulu (male) writer is proposing marriage to an *indoda* ('man') which would include the payment of *ilobolo* ('bride-wealth'), in order to make him/her *unkosikazi* ('a respectable woman/ feminine man'). He also writes that as a result of this marriage she or he would *ngiyoku hlonipha* ('show respect toward her/his partner'). As Leap (2004) rightly argues, "by proposing to practice *hlonipha* on the indooda's [*sic*] behalf, the writer suggests a powerful strategy to asserting the legitimacy of their relationship within Zulu tradition" (152). As can be deduced from the preceding list, the lexical item *umfazi* is a term capturing respect for one's (feminine) partner in a same-sex relationship, and several participants in our study confirmed that they consider *umfazi* an isiNgqumo word. The usage of *umfazi* implies a certain gendered order which creates tension-riddled identity categories, essentially because an *umfazi* is primarily respected because she or he knows how to practice *hlonipha* which, in most instances, means that she is submissive to her man. This evidently allows for complex positioning of African men who engage in same-sex relations and also suggests that they, ironically, draw on heteronormative and heteropoleric categories.

Both *hlonipha* and *ilobolo* could be regarded as cultural pillars in Zulu society, and it is not uncommon that Zulu men who engage in same-sex relations would like to endorse either practice. Although same-sex desire and Zulu culture poses a point of contention for many common Zulu people, some African men who engage in same-sex relations have found creative ways to reconcile their "gay" lifestyle with Zulu cultural norms. For instance, in 2013 Thoba Sithole and Cameron Modisane, both young African males, made international and national headlines when they decided to host South Africa's first traditional African wedding, which appealed both to Zulu and Tswana cultures. This same-sex wedding ceremony triggered a storm of criticism from Zulu traditionalists, including the Zulu royal house, for what was perceived as a mockery of Zulu culture. For Thoba and Cameron however, being "gay" simply did not go hand in hand with a rejection of their African cultures, but rather it necessitated an integration of their "gay" identities within these cultures. Unfortunately, however, this integration has done little to challenge gender constructions in these cultures that are based on unequal power relations and have social and linguistic consequences.

Three Case Studies

Many of the isiNgqumo-speakers we met during the fieldwork self-identified as *skesana*. The following three case studies also illustrate the variable lifestyles of the *skesanas* we interviewed. The few snippets of conversation, which are marked in italics, emerged during the fieldwork in informal conversations and interviews and they are chosen because they poignantly capture what many other *skesana* participants have expressed in different words.

Lebo is a twenty-one-year-old township resident who lives with his mother and two sisters in a small brick house.[6] He identifies as *skesana*, refers to himself as a "girl," and claims that even his mother has accepted his chosen gender identity the way it is because she only ever speaks about *her girls* when talking to someone about her children.[7] Lebo does not know his father, but he has a close relationship with his mother who works as a domestic worker in Durban. Lebo himself earns some money from a part-time waiter job in a small pizzeria and claims that more than a part-time job is not feasible for him because he is fully responsible for the household while his one sister is study-ing and the other is *simply lazy*. He repeatedly asserts that he loves running the household and describes cooking, cleaning, and *making the place look nice* as his passions. On the weekends, Lebo commonly meets his friends who are also mostly *skesanas* and with whom he likes going to clubs in town. It is in this cir-cle of his friends that he speaks extensive isiNgqumo which, according to his own description, he *loves* and uses eloquently. *We* [he and his *skesana* friends] *love to gossip, you know*, he proclaims and describes how they would each pick a *straight* man when they go out, talk in isiNgqumo about him during the night, and as best case scenario lure him into bed toward the end of the night. While Lebo has dated two men over a not insignificant period of time and would have liked to think of himself as *umfazi* in these relationships—the hlo-nipha term for a married woman—he never had a stable long-term relation-ship. Although his mother knows most of his *skesana* friends, and claims that she thinks of him as female, he is not sure how she would react if he brought a boyfriend home. Lebo claims to be entirely happy about his body with no intentions for a gender reassignment, but he emphasizes that he is *definitely the woman* in the relationship with a man. When asked about *hlonipha*, Lebo asserts that without him showing *hlonipha* toward his partners, he would not be able to "score": *They* [the kind of men he dates] *like to be served, you know, so we do everything to please him*, he says while giggling. Lebo would employ the term *ubaba* for his male partners, a *hlonipha* term for a respected man.

Sky is a thirty-one-year-old well-dressed self-proclaimed *skesana* whom we met in a Durban café. Right at the beginning of the meeting, he emphati-cally proclaimed that—though his body may suggest otherwise—*I am a full-blown woman*. He lives in Umlazi, the largest township in the Durban metropolitan area where we visited him subsequently and where he runs a very small, doubtfully lucrative business making and selling clothes. He says that "style" is very important to him, that his style is feminine and that he does not like dating someone who does not have "style." Speaking isiNgqumo is *a way of life* for Sky; he boasts being one of the best isiNgqumo speakers in KwaZulu-Natal and would like to compose a dictionary of the linguistic vari-ety someday. Sky is currently dating a forty-six-year-old teacher who, as he phrases it, is "a bit of a big daddy," meaning that he is well established and sup-ports Sky financially and emotionally. When Sky is at his lover's place, he says he *tries to be a good woman* to him, washes, cooks, and cleans, and shows him the respect he *deserves as a man*. Sky would like to undergo a gender reassign-ment but stated that since his father is still alive it is an "impossibility," at least for now. Apparently, as he explains, it is *an issue of* hlonipha, showing respect to his father by not changing his sex.

Blessing is a twenty-three-year-old teacher at a primary school around Durban. He recently moved to Durban after having lived most of his life in a small town on the South Coast of the KwaZulu-Natal province. He cur-rently lives with his partner, who is quite masculine, and who is also a teacher. During one of the interview sessions, we arrived as he was receiving an instruction from his partner: *Ngicela ungenzele iwashing. Ngyakthuma, ngcela ungenzele iwashingi* ('Please can you wash my clothes . . . I'm asking that you please wash my clothes').[8] Without any sort of irritation, Blessing started col-lecting his partner's clothes for washing. For him, this was the role he was meant to perform as a "female" partner. He was the "bottom" in the relation-ship, *umama wekhaya* ('the woman of the house,' as he puts it). This, he claims, requires a demonstration of *inhlonipho* ('respect') toward the *man of the house*. Blessing feels very constrained by his profession. He is expected to behave like a man, dress up like other men, and relate to children in his school like other men would. However, he finds this challenging as it limits possibilities for self-expression: *Well if you are gay, you have to show it. You have to wear tight clothes, you have to be neat and you have to be colorful. You can't just be untidy like all the straight men. . . .* For Blessing, being masculine means a lack of interest in one's physical appearance, something he believes "straight" men care little about. He is a fluent isiNgqumo speaker, and often uses the language when *ezinye izimeshi zivakashile* (other gay friends visit).[9] Blessing is also a spiritual man who occasionally goes to church.

We presented the three cases in this section in order to demonstrate that while there are differences in the lifestyles and identities of *skesanas* who live in the Durban metropolitan area, the overwhelming majority of self-identified *skesanas* in this area have knowledge of isiNgqumo and consider *hlonipha* a salient aspect in their relationships with other men and their life more broadly.

Constructing a *Skesana* Identity

It was previously suggested that, in particular, African "gay" men who identify as *skesanas* make usage of *isiNgqumo* (Rudwick & Ntuli 2008; Ntuli 2009) and that it is they who identify most strongly with the linguistic variety. The etymol-ogy of the term *skesana*, and the social construct associated with it, arguably have their roots in the early and mid-nineteenth-century mine environment.

South African mines were based on the migrant labor market, and mineworkers were away from their wives and families for many months throughout the year in what was a predominantly male-dominated environment. Ntuli (2009) also traces the etymology of the term *skesana* to the mine environment. He writes that "if a gay boy or man [at the mines] called himself a *skesana* it meant that he was the wife or the submissive lover in the relationship and he should be with the other *skesanas* in their section of the sheebeen" (68).[10] In their seminal piece, Moodie, Ndatshe, & Sibuyi (1988) describe same-sex acts in the South African mines as heteronormative in a sense that the "boy-wives" of otherwise "straight" mineworkers took on the social and sexual role women would in a heterosexual relationship, with others even expected to dress in women's attires to please their "husbands" (Murray, 2000; Epprecht, 2013).[11] Gunkel (2010) similarly, suggests that miners who engaged in same-sex relationships could maintain their heterosexual identity by considering *skesanas* and *izinkotshane* ("boy-wives") as women rather than men. Although in the post-apartheid state "gay" life offers alternatives to "traditional" and dominant femininities and masculinities, South Africans in same-sex relationships often do not challenge these hegemonic structures (Potgieter 2006).

In an influential work on African sexuality, a *skesana* has been defined as a young man who "likes to be fucked" (McLean & Ngcobo 1995: 164), in other words, a man who desires the kind of sex with a man where he engages in the "passive" role only. The African men who call themselves *skesanas* are, by and large, feminine and effeminate and tend to be quite visibly "gay" in South Africa. *Skesanas* have further been described as desiring "masculine men who could be considered "accidental homosexuals," because they have sex with men whom they believe to be intersex or someone who pretends to be "female" (McLean & Ngcobo 1995: 166).[12] Some *skesanas* see themselves as women (Reddy & Louw 2002; Ntuli 2009; Rudwick 2010; Msibi 2013a), and others as "gay" men (McLean & Ngcobo 1995). This was the case for our participants, including Lebo, Sky, and Blessing.

While it is generally not uncommon for South African black men who desire same-sex engagements to be intimate with men whom they consider to be "straight," the case of the *skesanas* (and other similar identifications such as "ladies, discussed later) has its roots in a thoroughly heteronormative *weltanschauung* (worldview). McLean & Ngcobo (1995) aptly quote one of their informants saying "My male lover is not gay, he is just heterosexual. I am always the woman in a relationship" (166). Several of our interviews echoed similar statements. When *skesanas* make use of the adjective "straight" in reference to their partners, this not only encapsulates sexual behavior but also appearances that are stereotypically masculine and behavioral notions such as toughness (Reddy & Louw 2002). To have sex with such men represents a significant conquest for some *skesanas*. Importantly, African men who engage in same-sex relations and identify as *skesana* rarely date each other or are sexually intimate with each other, and in the rare cases where this does occur, the act is not considered "sex," even if it results in an orgasm (McLean & Ngcobo 1995).

Our fieldwork suggests that *skesana*-identified men often form close friendships to the extent that they may love each other on a platonic level, but because many of them think of themselves as women, they would not be with another *skesana* as this would be tantamount to a lesbian relationship.[13] Due to their heteronormative perspective, many *skesanas* also report finding lesbians "strange" because they are with a person who has the same gender identity. What is crucial is that all the interviewees who explicitly identified as *skesana* viewed their femininity as *naturally given* and thought it to be "unnatural" that two *men-men* would have sex or an intimate relationship with each other. *Skesanas*, due to their affiliation with traditional Zulu femininity, show submissiveness to their male partners, just as women do in many African heterosexual relationships. It has been argued that *skesanas*, as the "female" partners, "may be subject to the demands of their partners" just as women are in many heterosexual relationships (Reddy & Louw 2002: 91). It is this unequal power relation which often also leads *skesanas* to adopt *hlonipha* toward their partners, which in many cases includes serving their partner on the domestic level.

The identity as a *skesana* is by no means fixed, rather, as has been noted in several works, such identities may take on particular, localized, and idiosyncratic meanings. For instance, Reid (2006, 2013) has shown how "gay" identities can emerge and be practiced in other South African contexts. Reid introduces readers to "ladies," who are *skesana* equivalents in Ermelo, a small town in another province in South Africa. These are effeminate men who maintain female social and sexual roles, and ideally get sexually involved with "gents" ("straight" men known for or suspected of being available as sexual partners to homosexual men) and *injongas*. The ladies often use so-called jolly-talk, a gay linguistic variety equivalent to isiNgqumo, to communicate. Like the *skesanas*, *ladies* see their sexual identifications as closely intertwined with their gender identities; they perceive themselves as women and expect to be treated like women in their relationships with other men.

There may also be some parallels in the construction of *skesana* identities and the Israeli *oxtša* (Levon 2012), who are described as "young, *effeminate gay men* [. . .], who are *physically slight*, wear makeup and the latest designer clothing, and are *obligatorily passive during sex*" [emphasis added] (189). Importantly, however, in Levon's (2012) study it is argued that most gay men in Israel are *not* using *oxtšit* as a means to express an alternative, *oxtša* identity but, rather, that they just make use of unsystematic use of *oxtšit* words in conversation without self-identifying as an *oxtša*. This is in stark contrast to our study. The participants in our study openly identify as *skesana* and isiNgqumo is an important aspect of the gay subgroup of *skesanas* examined here. This is not to say that all isiNgqumo-speakers are *skesanas* or that all *skesanas* speak isiNgqumo, but it is safe to argue that South African gay men who identify as *skesana* know and speak, to some degree, the linguistic variety. While the speaking of isiNgqumo is not the sole marker of a *skesana* identity, it is a salient one. The vocabulary of isiNgqumo may also be far more extensive than other "gay" varieties examined in the literature. In fact, one of our interviewees claimed that isiNgqumo has *well over 1,000 words*; others said that it is a *full-blown* language, with others demanding for it to acquire the status of the twelfth official language in South Africa (see also Rudwick & Ntuli 2008).[14]

Conclusion

From our study, it is clear that isiNgqumo linguistic practices among the *skesana* men we interviewed are highly gendered, with *hlonipha* playing quite a major role in the ways in which the men both perceive themselves and also how they relate to their partners. The agency presented by the *skesana* identities, in terms of debunking both gender and sexual categories, is at a cursory glance quite profound. This is a context where gender and sexuality are heavily policed, and where a very strict gender order exists: men are expected to exhibit masculine traits. Deviation from this expectation often carries some form of punishment. However, deeper scrutiny of their gender and sexual identification performances suggests a troubling irony: these men construct their identifications along very fixed gender binary lines (male/female), informed by heteronormativity. While the men exhibit agency by constructing their identifications beyond the normative expectations, their reconstructed identifications do little to shift the heteronormative and patriarchal social system. Heteronormativity is simply re-created within their same-sex relationships by employing diverse social and linguistic means. This not only highlights the dominance of patriarchy in a transformed, "equal" post-apartheid South Africa, it also demonstrates the extent to which fixed binary systems inform gender practices.

While this chapter certainly does not present an exhaustive account of possible intersections between isiNgqumo and the *hlonipha* language variety, we hope that this initial exposition will trigger further and more in-depth research. Our chapter has shed light on the ways in which heteronormativity finds expression in how some same-sex desiring individuals perform their sexualities, as well as the role of language in such expressions. We also hope that further research in this vein will work to expose in more detail the patriarchal nature of *hlonipha* and isiNgqumo linguistic practices.

List of isiNgqumo Words

1. abajuketi = students
2. affair = the township gay words for relationship

3. amafezela = straight men
4. amaqaphelo = eyes
5. ayine = fuck
6. gweni = darling
7. imalasi = dog
8. imbakhla = Indian person
9. imbhamo = food
10. imbube = those who switch between playing penetrative and receptive roles in homosexual sex
11. imfazo = war
12. imju = father
13. injonga = those who play the active, penetrative (butch or top) role in homosexual sex
14. iqnege = handsome man/one's boyfriend
15. isichibi = beer
16. isidudula = car
17. isitabane = hermaphrodite
18. izimbovu = women
19. izimvakazi = clothes
20. kehlo = a marriage ceremony between men in migrant labor hostels
21. mantloana = housie-housie
22. maskingalane = guard
23. umfundisi = elder
24. morabaraba = a board game similar to draughts, played with bottle-tops
25. mteto = the set of rules governing relationships between men in migrant labor hostels
26. obhabsi basethi = the sandwiches are here
27. obhovu = girl
28. panga = a home-made township axe
29. pantsulas = a macho township guy
30. portfolio = ones assigned role as either a skesana or injonga
31. regina Mundi = Sowetho's principle cathedral famous for anti-apartheid gatherings in the 1980s
32. shaya ndlwabu = to masturbate
33. skesana = those who switch between playing penetrative and receptive roles in homosexual sex
34. ubukhwashu = black person
35. udayi = white person
36. ukubhedlela = to sleep
37. ukubhuluza = to give birth
38. ukucoshela = to listen
39. ukufaza = to bitch
40. ukufoza = to smoke
41. ukujuketisa = to teach
42. ukukala = to look
43. ukuqeqa = drink

44. ukushaya emqhumeni = to go to work
45. ukushaya/ukuguza = to go/walk
46. ukutekula = to cry
47. ukuwindi = to desire (someone)
48. umambhu = mother
49. umambhu = old woman
50. umjuketisi = teacher
51. umngeni = water
52. umqhumo = work
53. umqingo = phone
54. umvelo = beautiful (nature originally)
55. umchasikana = boy
56. iqenge = boyfriend
57. ukuphumela = to like someone
58. ukuzinza = to stay
59. isitende = a home
60. ukuluthula = to kiss
61. ushwili = a boy too young for a person to be in a relationship with
62. umbhamo = food
63. ukugaya = to drink alcohol
64. umjukethisi/abajukethisi = teacher/teachers
65. isichibi/inkeshezi = drink about to be finished
66. isidudula = fat person
67. inju = father
68. Nozitshwaxa = God
69. Isigeqo = a drink
70. Openi-Money (comes from penny)
71. Imbube = certain type of traditional music
72. uvele/ubonakele = pretty individual
73. mvakazi = clothes
74. ukutukela = to cry
75. isifico = medicine
76. bhadlaza = to buy
77. umahothelana = hot spirits/drinks

Notes

1. We largely refrain from using Western identity categories such as *gay, lesbian*, etc., given the contested nature of these labels in African settings. We use instead the broad concept of men who engage in same-sex relations given the provision this offers for the wide encapsulation of varied same-sex performances and identifications.

2. Of course, other scholars have written about same-sex behaviors in native African societies. For example, the renowned anthropologist Evans-Pritchard (1970) described marriages between two men and the phenomena of "boy-wives" among the Azande in present-day Zaire.

3. This is not surprising, as many lesbians residing in townships make usage of a linguistic variety, traditionally employed by urban males, termed *Tsotsitaal* which is considered an urban mixed-code employing English extensively (for more detail, see Rudwick, Nkomo & Shange 2006).

4. For close detail on the "traditional" practice of *hlonipha* among Zulu women, see Raum (1973).

5. Many more lexical items than the five displayed here belong to what is considered the *hlonipha* lexicon and are part of what is considered "deep isiZulu."

6. The participants have been given pseudonyms in order to assure their confidentiality.

7. During our second meeting with Lebo, we met in a Durban restaurant. While not dressing overly feminine, the waiter in the restaurant greeted us with "Hello girls" which evidently pleased Lebo and put a big smile on his face.

8. *Ngyakuthuma* does not have an English equivalent. However, *ukuthuma* (lit. 'sending someone somewhere') is often done by someone in authority, giving instruction to a subordinate position to do something. For instance, a parent can direct (*thuma*) their children to do some chore. It is often an instruction given by a "dominant" person to a "subordinate" for some task to be done.

9. This is a colloquial term for overly effeminate gay men. This has similar meaning to *skesana*.

10. *Shebeen* is the colloquial term for unlicensed bars in South African townships.

11. 'Boy-wives,' known as *izinkotshane*, were often younger male miners who were lured through financial gifts and other luxuries to "marry" older men. The older men would in turn receive sexual favors, mostly through *ukuhlobonga* (thigh sex), with the younger men not allowed to reciprocate. Additionally, it was expected that the young men would perform "wifely" duties such as "adopting feminine attire, wearing false breasts fashioned from coconuts, putting on scent, keeping their faces well-shaven, and even sipping wine or other sweet liquors (as opposed to the 'husbands' manly swilling of beer)" (Epprecht 2013: 61). Although *izinkotshane* and *skesanas* differed in that the former often identified themselves as heterosexual while the latter saw themselves as women, both identities provided sexual services in the mines and both took on "female" roles which subscribed to heteronormativity in the relationships they engaged in.

12. These men are called *injongas* and most *skesanas* do not consider them "gay."

13. Reid's (2006) work confirms this finding through his discussion of the *ladies* (skesana equivalents) in the context of Mpumalanga province, in Ermelo. Reid notes that the idea that two *ladies* could be together in a relationship was met with "thigh-slapping hilarity" by his participants, as this would constitute "lesbianism." One of the participants noted, in response to the question as to whether she or he could be in a relationship with her/his friend who was also a lady, that "I love him very much, but I am not a lesbian!" (Reid 2006: 139).

14. South Africa has eleven official languages, namely, Zulu, Xhosa, Sotho, Northern Sotho, Tswana, Swati, Ndebele, Venda, English, Afrikaans, and Tsonga.

References

Baker, Paul. 2002. *Polari—The lost language of gay men*. London & New York: Routledge.

Boellstorff, Tim. 2004. "Authentic, of course": Gay language in Indonesia and cultures of belonging. In William L. Leap & Tim Boellstorff (eds.), *Speaking in queer tongues*, 181–201. Chicago: University of Illinois.

Bucholtz, Mary & Kira Hall. 2004a. Theorizing identity in language and sexuality research. *Language in Society* 33. 469–515.

Bucholtz, Mary & Kira Hall. 2004b. Language and identity. In Alessandro Duranti (ed.), *A companion to linguistic anthropology*, 369–394. Malden & Oxford: Blackwell Publishing.

Bucholtz, Mary & Kira Hall. 2005. Identity and interaction: A sociolinguistic approach. *Discourse Studies* 7 (4–5). 585–614.

Cage, Ken. 2003. *Gayle—the language of kinks & queens: A history and dictionary of gay language in South Africa*. Johannesburg: Jacana Press

Collins, Patricia H. 2000. Gender, black feminism, and black political economy. *The Annals of the American Academy of Political and Social Science* 568(1). 41–53.

Crenshaw, Kimberlé. 1989. Demarginalizing the intersection of race and sex: A black feminist critique of antidiscrimination doctrine, feminist theory and antiracist politics. *The University of Chicago Legal Forum* 140. 139–167.

Davis, Kathy. 2008. Intersectionality as buzzword: A sociology of science perspective on what makes a feminist theory successful. *Feminist Theory* 9(1). 67–85.

Donham, Donald L. 1898. Freeing South Africa: The "modernization" of male-male sexuality in Soweto. *Cultural Anthropology* 13(1). 3–21.

Epprecht, Marc. 2004. *Hungochani. The history of dissident sexuality in Southern Africa*. Montreal, Quebec, Canada: McGill-Queen's University Press.

Epprecht, Marc. 2006. "Bisexuality" and the politics of normal in African ethnography. *Anthropologica* 48(2). 187–201.

Epprecht, Marc. 2013. *Hungochani: A history of dissident sexuality is southern Africa*, 2nd edn. Montreal, Quebec, Canada: McGill-Queen's University Press.

Evans-Pritchard, Edward E. 1970. Sexual inversion among the Azande. *American Anthropologist* 72(6). 1428–1434.

Finlayson, Rosalie. 2002. Women's language of respect: "Isihlonipho sabafazi." In Rajend Mesthrie (ed.), *Language in South Africa*, 279–296. Cambridge: Cambridge University Press.

Gunkel, Henriette. 2010. *The cultural politics of female Sexuality in South Africa*. New York: Routledge.

Hanong Thetela, Puleng. 2002. Sex discourses and gender constructions in Southern Sotho: A case study of police interviews of rape/sexual assault victims. *South African Linguistics and Applied Language Studies* 20(3). 177–189.

Herbert, Robert K. 1990. Hlonipha and the ambiguous woman. *Anthropos* 85. 455–73.

Holmes, Janet & Miriam Meyerhoff, 2005. Different voices, different views: An introduction to current research on language and gender. In Janet Holmes & Miriam Meyerhoff (eds.), *The handbook of language and gender*, 1–18. Oxford: Blackwell.

Jagose, Annamarie. 1997. *Queer theory: An introduction*. New York: New York University Press.

Kumashiro, Kevin, K. 2002. *Troubling education: "Queer" activism and anti-oppressive pedagogy*. New York: Routledge

Lakoff, Robin. 1975. *Language and woman's place*. New York: Harper & Row.

Leap, William L. 2004. Language, belonging and (homo)sexual citizenship in Cape Town, South Africa. In William L. Leap & Tim Boellstorff (eds.), *Speaking in queer tongues, globalization and gay language*, 134–162. Chicago: University of Illinois Press.

Levon, Erez. 2011. Teasing apart to bring together: Gender and sexuality in variationist research. *American Speech* 86(1). 69–84.

Levon, Erez. 2012. The voice of others: Identity, alterity and gender normativity among gay men in Israel. *Language in Society* 41. 178–211.

McCall, Leslie. 2005. The complexity of intersectionality. *Signs* 30(3). 1771–1800.

McLean, Hugh & Linda Ngcobo. 1995. "Abangibhamayo bathi ngimnandi (Those who fuck me say I'm tasty)." In Marc Gevisser & Eduard Cameron (eds.), *Defiant desire. Gay lesbian lives in South Africa*, 158–185. New York & London: Routledge.

Moodie, T. Dunbar, Vivienne Ndatshe, & British Sibuyi. 1988. Migrancy and male sexuality in the South African gold mines. *Journal of South African Studies* 14(2). 228–256.

Motschenbacher, Heiko. 2007. Can the term "genderlect" be saved? A postmodernist re-definition. *Gender and Language* 1(2). 255–278.

Motschenbacher, Heiko. 2010. *Language, gender and sexual identity: Poststructuralist perspectives*. Amsterdam & Philadelphia: John Benjamins.

Msibi, Thabo. 2013a. Homophobic language and linguistic resistance in KwaZulu-Natal, South Africa. In Lillian L. Atanga, Sibonile E. Ellece, Lia Litosseliti, & Jane Sunderland (eds.), *Gender and language in Sub-Saharan Africa*, 253–274. Amsterdam & Philadelphia: John Benjamins.

Msibi, Thabo. 2013b. Denied love: Same-sex desire, agency and social oppression among African men who engage in same-sex relations. *Agenda* 27(2). 105–116.

Murray, Jessica. 2012. The layered gaze: Reading lesbian desire in selected South African fiction. *Current Writing: Text and Reception in Southern Africa* 24(1). 88–97.

Murray, Stephen O. 2000. *Homosexualities*. Chicago: University of Chicago Press.

Nash, J. C. 2008. Re-thinking intersectionality. *Feminist Review* 89. 1–15.

Ntuli, Mduduzi. 2009. IsiNgqumo: Exploring origins, grows and sociolinguistics of an Nguni urban-township homosexual sub-culture. Durban: University of KwaZulu-Natal, unpublished MA thesis.

Potgieter, Cheryl. 2006. Masculine bodies, feminine symbols: Challenging gendered identities or compulsory femininity. *Agenda* 67. 116–127.

Reddy, Vasu & Ronald Louw. 2002. Black and gay: Perceptions and interventions around HIV in Durban. *Agenda* 53. 89–95.

Reid, Graeme. 2006. How to become a "real gay": Identity and terminology in Ermelo, Mpumalanga. *Agenda* 20(67). 137–145.

Reid, Graeme. 2013. *How to be a real gay: Gay identities in small-town South Africa*. Pietermaritzburg, South Africa: UKZN Press.

Rudwick, Stephanie. 2010. Gay and Zulu—we speak isiNgqumo. Ethnolinguistic identity constructions. *Transformation* 74. 112–134.

Rudwick, Stephanie. 2011. Defying a myth: A gay sub-culture in contemporary South Africa. *Nordic Journal of African Studies* 20(2). 90–111.

Rudwick, Stephanie. 2013. Gendered linguistic choices among isiZulu-speaking women in contemporary South Africa. In Lilian L. Atanga, Sibonile E. Ellece, Lia Litosseliti, & Jane Sunderland (eds.), *Gender and language in Sub-Saharan Africa*, 233–251, Amsterdam & Philadelphia: John Benjamins.

Rudwick, Stephanie & Magcino Shange. 2006. Sociolinguistic oppression or expression of "Zuluness"? "IsiHlonipho" among isiZulu-speaking females. *Southern African Linguistics and Applied Language Studies* 24(4). 473–482.

Rudwick, Stephanie, Khathala Nkomo, & Magcino Shange. 2006. "Ulimi lwenku-luleko": Township "women's language of empowerment" and homosexual linguistic identities. *Agenda: Empowering women for gender equity* 67(2/3). 57–65.

Rudwick, Stephanie & Mdudzi Ntuli. 2008. IsiNgqumo: Introducing a gay black South African linguistic variety. *Linguistics and Applied Language Studies* 26(4). 445–456

Sigamoney, Veronica & Marc Epprecht. 2013. Meanings of homosexuality, same-sex sexuality, and African-ness in two South African townships: An evidence-based approach for rethinking same-sex prejudice. *African Studies Review* 56(2). 83–107.

Tannen, Deborah. 1990. *You just don't understand: Women and men in conversation.* London: Virago.

Taylor, Yvette, Sally Hines, & Mark E. Casey (eds.). 2010. *Theorizing intersectionality and sexuality.* Basingstoke, UK: Palgrave Macmillan Ltd.

Weston, Kath. 1993. Lesbian/gay studies in the house of anthropology. *Annual Review of Anthropology* 22. 339–367.

Zungu, Phillis J. 1985. *A study of hlonipha terms amongst Zulu.* Durban, South Africa: Department of Zulu, University of Natal.

4

Sorry Guys!

THE DISCURSIVE CONSTRUCTION OF QUEER SPATIALITY
IN JAPANESE WOMEN-ONLY CLUB FLYERS

Claire Maree

Mobility and Movement—Alternative Spaces and Promotional Flyers

In the 1990s, a "boom" of interest in gay culture and entertainment exploded within popular Japanese culture. A range of new clubs and bars began to spring up in Shinjuku ni-chōme (an area of central Tokyo known as a gay entertainment area since the 1950s) and beyond. One of the women-only clubs that emerged during that time has become the longest-running women-only club event operating in the Tokyo area: Monalisa/Gold Finger[1] (1991–). The women-only space of Monalisa/Gold Finger offered an alternative to clubs catering for gay male and/or mixed gay and straight clientele. It can be understood as queer space, or, as Halberstam (2005) notes, "space enabled by the production of queer counterpublics" (6).

Scholarship on counterpublics focuses on the public "circulation of non-dominant communicative strategies" (Loehwing & Motter 2012: 35). Warner (2002) suggests that counterpublics rely on the circulation of texts which call into being audiences in a way "that is constitutive of membership and its affects" (122). Newsletters and mini-komi (short for mini komyuinikēshon ['mini communication']) produced by feminist and/or lesbian editorial collectives in Japan are examples of such counterpublic texts. As Vera Mackie (1992) notes in her overview of Japanese feminist media in the 1980s and 1990s, "newsletters provide an alternative sense of community for many of the producers and readers" (25). The Monalisa/Goldfinger flyers invoke a sense of belonging to an alternative queer spatiality which privileges women only. As such, they can also be understood as examples of counterpublic texts.

The flyers are also multimodal texts that traverse LGBT[2] networks and market the advertised club space as *desirable* to women only. These are sexed texts (Baker 2008) which "(re)produce and/or contest particular ideas and beliefs about gender and sexuality" (Milani 2013a: 208). Milani (2013a) argues that queer linguistics must engage in multimodal analysis in order to seriously engage with the "complexity of *sexed* meanings in public texts" (211). A multimodal analysis of the image, text, layout and design used to brand and sell women-only space in club flyers will uncover the "semiotic complexity and richness" (Iedema 2003: 39) of the medium, and how this complexity is utilized to invoke potential club-goers as *belonging* to women-only space. This chapter argues that the use of image, graphics, and text constitute stances that style the event and position women-only space as a desirable alternative to normative spatiality. Stance-taking refers to positionality (Jaffe 2009) and includes the evaluation, positioning, and alignment with others (du Bois 2007) performed in language encounters. The highly sexualized imagery used to promote the space as *women only*, not *lesbian only*, troubles heteronormative representations of female desire. The flyers also provide an outline of how imaginings of women-only space in 1990s Tokyo has shifted to respond to trends and fashions within mainstream and alternative culture.

Queer(y)ing Space

Work in queer studies has queer(y)ed normative notions of space and time, and explored alternative ways of inhabiting modern societal and cultural surroundings and/or institutions. While there is a growing body of Japanese discourse studies informed by queer studies (Abe 2010; Maree 2007, 2013), there has been little linguistic analysis of queer spatiality in Japanese discourse. Indeed, to date much of the work on "queer space" has been situated in the global and national machinations of Euro-American sociocultural politics (Edelman 2004; Halberstam 2005; Freeman 2010).

There is a strong history of women's activism and community building in modern and contemporary Japan. From the suffragist movement of the early 1900s, women have organized to create supportive and inclusive spaces and places. Separatist women-only spaces in the form of social events, community centers, and publishing collectives, however, are typically traced back to the women's liberation movements. These emerged from women's need to create places separate from mysogynistic operations of student political movements in the 1970s. Crenshaw's foundational work on intersectionality has stressed that intragroup differences are often conflated and ignored by all-encompassing notions of gender and/or sexual identity (Crenshaw 1991). This is noted in Japan, too. As self-identified lesbian women began to engage with issues of heterosexism within the women's liberation movement, they also began to build their own spaces. This pattern of identifying ignorance and/or trivializing of issues arising from the intersections of gender with other axes of discrimination such as sexuality, or nationality, or physical ability has resulted in dissention among groups (Iino 2006, 2008; Izumo et al. 2007). Break-away groups have created alternative material spaces and media communications such as newsletters and *mini-komi*. Women's groups have also used information leaflets and flyers to increase the visibility of their publications and to encourage participation in the events they organize.

Historically, social spaces staffed by women who identified as *onabe* (stone-butch—a colloquial term for cross-dressing women), known as *onabe* bars, have operated in various locations across the Tokyo metropolis since at least the 1950s (*Bessatsu Takarajima 64* 1987; McLelland 2004; Maree 2014). These spaces, however, catered mainly to heterosexual male customers. In the 1970s and early 1980s, monthly parties and events for women emerged from the collective organizational activities of women's groups. Most events were transient and operated monthly, sometimes from a variety of premises. For example, the earliest recorded lesbian group in Japan formed by Suzuki Michiko in 1971, *Wakakusa no kai* (Young Grass Club), ran home parties for its members.[3] It was not until Bar Sunny, a type of small bar establishment known as a snack (*suna-kku*), opened in 1984, and two lesbian (*rezubian*) bars, Ribonne (*Ribonnu*) and Mars Bar (*Māzu Bā*), opened in 1985 in Shinjuku ni-chōme that a women-only space shifted from private parties to more commercially based spaces. Whereas in the 1970s and early 1980s, media and social spaces were run by collectives, many of whom who shared resources with feminist groups or on premises provided by sympathetic gay men, these newer spaces were of a more commercial and less transient nature.

As Ingram, Bouthillette & Retter (1997) said, "In the fragments of queer-friendly public spaces available today, a basis for survival, contact, communality and sometimes community has begun" (3). Material spaces provided opportunites for women to meet, discuss, and organize. Media spaces provided by editorial collectives in the form of newsletters and *mini-komi* also enabled connections and communities (Mackie 1992). Promotional and information flyers have acted as a "portal" (Lalonde 2014: 19) or critical linkage to the material and media spaces they advertise.

WOMEN-ONLY CLUB SPACE MOVING AROUND
THE METROPOLIS: A BRIEF HISTORY OF MONALISA/GOLDFINGER

A trailblazer in queer community event organizing and an entrepreneur, Chigalliano (Don★King Chigalliano; a.k.a Chigar) started Monalisa/Gold Finger in 1991 as a "girls only night" at Deep, a rented club space in the Akasaka area of central Tokyo.[4] Inspired by clubs in the United Kingdom, Chigalliano aimed to organize and provide a space for Tokyo women that would be edgy and exciting. The need for a bigger venue to accommodate more women was the impetus for moving the club from Deep to Gold (in the Shibaura area of Tokyo), one of the hippest club venues in Tokyo at the time. Monalisa and Monalisa Pink were subsequently held monthly in venues scattered around the central Tokyo district. The event reopened as Gold Finger in 1997. With a new name, and moving from venue to venue, it continues to operate in the metropolis. Chigalliano has also opened a bar named Motel in Shinjuku ni-chōme, operating as Gold Finger circa 2013. Monalisa/ Gold Finger has been covered widely in national and international media, and Chigalliano proudly promotes it as the longest-running women-only event of its kind. Although Monalisa/Gold Finger has traversed locations and clubs around the central Tokyo metropolis, it has maintained consistency as a monthly, women-only event. One consistent feature is the use of promotional flyers.

PROMOTIONAL FLYERS AND CLUB FLYERS

Promotional flyers have circulated in Japan since the seventeenth century. Advertising handbills known as *hikifuda* or *ebira* became popular with merchants in the Edo, or Tokugawa period (1603–1868) with the spread of woodblock printing (Salter 2006). Woodblock artists, some of whom became acclaimed artists of the period, designed the exquisite flyers. Distributed in the major cities of Osaka and Edo (now known as Tokyo) *hikifuda* and *ebira* were valuable media forms used to promote merchant's wares. The use of handbills and flyers remains a part of Tokyo's contemporary cityscape.

Promotional flyers are passed to commuters on the streets, stacked at the entrances of cafes and clubs, wedged between the pages of newspapers and theatre programs, and distributed in bundles at festivals and events. A kind of viral marketing which relies on circulation via established networks and flows of people in public space (Young 2011), flyers and handbills are also items of public discourse (Scollon 1997) which circulate the landscape of a given geospatial location. Club flyers, as Jon Savage writes in the introduction to a collection of flyers from the British rave scene, "are an integral part of the urban landscape" (Beddard & Savage 1995: 6). A highly visual medium, flyers communicate not just information about the event but information about the positioning of the event within its contemporary culture. As Mukherjee & Chowdhury (2012) note in their analysis of flyers to promote study abroad programs, flyers may "indirectly communicate an embedded first impression" (580) about spaces and places. This is true of club and dance event flyers, too, which, as Amanda Lalonde (2014) writes in her work on Buddy Esquire's hip-hop flyers, are "a kind of portal—the first glimpse of the scene, the first indistinct hint of the music" (19). Promotional flyers act to style the promoted event by situating it within contemporary culture.

Don't Miss It!! Going Your Way!!: Monalisa/Gold Finger Flyers

Flyers have been part of the Monalisa/Gold Finger promotional arsenal since the event's inception. The earliest flyers were made by cutting and pasting text and images to paper, and reproduced via printing. With the spread of accessible digital technologies, the production method shifted to a digital base, and desktop publishing has significantly influenced the style of flyers in general (Beddard & Savage 1995). Professional graphic artists who are leaders in their fields design Monalisa/Gold Finger flyers. Placed in club venues, cafes around Tokyo, and handed to women at events, with the rise of the Internet and web technology, Monalisa/Gold Finger flyers are now also available online.

As Savage notes, the "baseline of any flyer is information" (Beddard & Savage 1995: 6). Typically, each Monalisa/Gold Finger flyer will contain information about the date, admission cost, DJ and VJ, special guests and shows for the event, notes about the theme and dress code (if applicable), a map of the venue, sponsorship details, dates for the following event, a note about admission requirements pertaining to age and/or gender/sex, and perhaps a special deal available to clients on presentation of the flyer.[5] The particular theme of the event largely governs the overall design, including color, font, illustrations, and/or photographs. The map marks the flyer as belonging to a specific locality and club scene. As club music styles, fashions, and music tastes change, the conceptualization of women-only space as demonstrated through the language and images used in the flyers also subtly alters. To facilitate an analysis of the flyers, it is necessary to have a general understanding of the Japanese writing system.

JAPANESE WRITING SYSTEM

Writing in Japanese necessarily involves at least three scripts; *Kanji* (Sino-Japanese characters), *hiragana* (cursive syllabary), and *katakana* (boxed syllabary), as well as Roman letters and Arabic numerals. Conventionally, Sino-Japanese characters are used for lexical items, *hiragana* for function words, and *katakana* for onomatopoeia and loanwords from non-*Kanji*–based languages. *Katakana* is also used for onomatopoeia, slang and taboo words, interjections, and phonaesthesia (Tranter 2008).

While conventions are adhered to in more formal styles of public discourse, writers in cyberspace, editors of popular magazines, and advertising copywriters creatively negotiate writing conventions for stylistic effect (Tranter 2008; Gottlieb 2009, 2010, 2011; Bartal 2013). Roman script is used in advertising, and English, French, and other European languages also decorate commercial media. As Gottlieb (2009) notes, there has always been elements of "language play" (74) in Japanese writing. Unconventional combinations of punctuation borrowed from European languages (such as "!!" and "?!") are popular in advertising and digital media. A variety of alternative scripts and symbols are also used in personal communications using both paper and digital technologies (Kataoka 2003; Nishimura 2003, 2008; Miller 2004, 2011; Miyake 2007).

Stereotypes about scripts, and the association of scripts with specific styles have a constitutive effect. For example, Sino-Japanese characters are associated with erudition, *hiragana* with softness, *katakana* with modernity and popular culture, and Roman scripts with commerciality (Smith & Schmidt 1996; Tranter 2008). It is expected, therefore, that the creative use of different scripts will be a feature of the flyers and be representative of the Monalisa/Gold Finger club identity as a women-only space.

JOIN!! ALL Womyn: Branding and Promoting Women-Only Space

Monalisa, Monalisa Pink, Gold Finger, Girl Friend by Gold Finger: The event names all derive from cult-status figures that draw on cultural associations of mystery, beauty, sexiness, and strength. These concepts inform the branding of this women-only space. Interviews and magazine reports on the club indicate that the branding is successful. In a report published in the magazine *Weekly Ascii*, the club is described as 'fashionable' (*oshare*) and the club-goers as a "wide diversity" of women including 'boyish girls,' *kogyaru* ('little girls'), a "heavily pregnant woman," and "a group communicating in sign language" (Munakata 1997: 21).[6] Branding involves creating "associations and expectations" around products and service including "a specially designed representation developed to represent implicit values, ideas, and characteristics of the product or the users of the product," which aims to separate it from other products and services in the market (Rausch 2008: 137).

Monalisa/Gold Finger is branded as a women-only club which differs not only from more conventional mixed straight and/or gay club events but also from *onabe* bars, women-only monthly parties run by community collectives, and lesbian bars operating in the Tokyo metropolis in the 1990s. In the sections that follow I focus on three elements foundational to marketing the space as desirable to a diverse group of women: the Monalisa/Gold Finger logos; salient images which populate the flyers; and descriptions of the space which appear as "fine print" text on the flyers.

STRONG AND SIMPLE: MONALISA/GOLD FINGER LOGOS

The July 1994 flyer (Figure 4.1) is the earliest flyer in the corpus under consideration, and contains an example of the early Monalisa logo (Figure 4.2). The early logo is a simple design of white text on black background with a central white rectangle. The event name MONALISA appears as the top line of text, and the

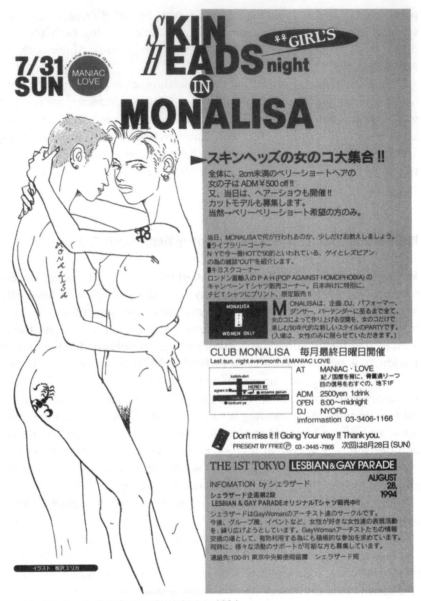

FIGURE 4.1 Skin Heads Girl's Night MONALISA July 1994

bottom line of text boldly brands the event as WOMEN-ONLY. Capitalized Roman script is used for both lines of text, and Monalisa appears as one word. The use of capitalization, and the white typeface presents a strong image.

Monalisa Pink flyers from the corpus also make use of this articulation of Monalisa logo. However, as the event matures, the logo is overhauled. The October 1995 flyer for monalisa pink (Figure 4.3) shows the newer style. The

FIGURE 4.2 Early monalisa logo

design remains simple and bold. The logo makes use of differently sized fonts and a combination of upper- and lower-case lettering for the block of text over two lines: monalisa, PINK. Although not incorporated into the logo itself, the circular cut out of pert breasts drawn in stylized cartoon design (Figure 4.4) is used in combination with the logo on the flyers from this time. The breasts are a highly sexualized yet bold image of strong womanliness which nevertheless retains a pop, tongue-in-cheek quality. In Monalisa Pink flyers from 1997, a circular cut-out of the kissing witches (depicted in Figure 4.4) is used in place of the cartoon-like breast cut-out.

In 1997, Monalisa Pink transforms into the club event known as GOLD FINGER. The logo for the event is heavily modeled on its namesake, *Gold Finger* (1964) from the cult 007 James Bond series (Figures 4.5 and 4.6). The most common reproduction of the logo features two silhouetted women top right and bottom left aiming to shoot. The "i" of FINGER takes the shape of a tube of lipstick, which is an item associated with glamorous femininity, and perhaps in the context of James Bond imagery connotes a possibility of danger and intrigue. In the period of transition from the event known as Monalisa to the event known as Gold Finger, "monalisa" is inscribed down the length of the lipstick.[7] Roman script is used exclusively in the logos.

Roman script is common to the commercial sphere where a wide variety of scripts compete for attention with the visual linguistic landscape.[8] English often appears in advertising (Barnes & Yamamoto 2008; Tranter 2008) and Romanized transliterations of Japanese brand names is not uncommon. The Monalisa/Gold Finger logos can, therefore, be understood as strong symbols which incorporate conventions from commercial language use in Japan. Furthermore, as Sebba (2009) notes in his work on the sociolinguistics of writing, script choices are also tied to identitites. Nonconventional orthographic choices can work to demarcate group identity and subcultural affiliations (Sebba 2009). As we shall see, Roman script, English vocabulary, capitalization, and alternative spellings using *katakana* to replace conventional Sino-Japanese

FIGURE 4.3 monalisa PINK Jan–March 1995

Note: The "JUN" here appears to be a typographical error. It should read "JAN."

characters are combined to demarcate the women-only focus of the events and to style them as a contemporary, desirable alternative space. The logos and script choices therein brand the club event in a subculturally rich way.

SALIENT IMAGES: BOLD, SEXUAL, KITSCH

Bold, sexual, pop and kitsch illustrations as well as photographic images are a major focal point of the Monalisa/Gold Finger flyers. Some of the images are

FIGURE 4.4 monalisa PINK October 1995

replicated in flyer designs over several months, giving an impression of continuity and contributing to the overall styling of the space. The earlier flyers made use of illustrations and stills taken from movie tie-ins. The later flyers make use of illustrations and other graphics, but they also make greater use of photography. Photographs are either from unknown stock sources or from in-club shots of the Bond Girls taken by the resident photographer. Monalisa/Gold Finger has long had a policy of limiting photography to ensure a safe

FIGURE 4.5 Bikini Night GOLDFINGER July 2000 (front)

FIGURE 4.6 Bikini Night GOLDFINGER July 2000 (back)

environment for its clients, and consequently, there is little use of crowd shots or visuals of club-goers. Similar bans on photography were in place for sections of the Tokyo Lesbian and Gay Parade in the 1990s. This is linked to the precarious nature of women's sexuality and the experiences of harassment and discrimination queer women (and men) face in the wider Japanese society.

FIGURE 4.7 Gold Finger logo sticker circa 2014

Note: Available to download from the Gold Finger website: http://www.goldfingerparty.com/links/.

The July 1994 Monalisa flyer (Figure 4.1) is a typical example of the earlier design. The illustration by prolific *manga* artist Sakurazawa Erika[9] occupies one side of the flyer, and textual information occupies the other. The phrase *Skin Heads Girl's Night in Monalisa* is designed over four lines at the top and is perhaps initially the most eye-catching or salient (Kress & Van Leeuwen 1996) element of the flyer. The *S* and *H* are in italics, and the word *girl's* is prefaced by the symbol ♀♀ in what appears to be a speech balloon. Visually, "♀♀ girl's" modifies "skin heads." If we look closer, the women portrayed in the *manga*-like illustration are also marked: one woman with the ♀♀ symbol on her left upper arm and the other woman with the word *monalisa* written across her upper arm and a scorpion on her buttock. The depiction of full breasts and pubic hair adds to the erotic defiance of the image. The depiction of pubic hair and genitalia in illustrations and audiovisual materials was heavily regulated until the 1990s (for a full discussion, see Allison 1998). The image, here too, demands attention and gives a clear message of the theme of the night, and the passionate promise of excitement the event flyer is making. It overrides the headline as the most salient part of the flyer composition overall.

This flyer clearly brands the event with its theme "Skin Heads Girl's Night in Monalisa" in English text through the headline, and with the visual image that occupies the left side of the flyer. Indicated with a triangular pointer to the right of the image, and positioned below the screamer headline is a Japanese representation of the theme *sukinhezzu no onna no ko daishūgō*!! The use of double exclamation marks, which are punctuation marks taken from English and adopted into contemporary Japanese writing, gives the phrase a sense of urgency and importance. This text could be glossed in either of two ways: first to mean "huge gathering of skinhead girls!!"; second to be a call for "skin head girls to gather!!" In the phrase *onna no ko* (lit. 'girl'), the final *ko* (lit. 'child') is rendered in *katakana* コ (*ko*) instead of the Sino-Japanese character 子 (*ko*).[10] This alternative spelling may be likened to the use of -*z* instead of *s* in "girlz." The nonconventional choice of script fits smoothly with the *katakana* used for the loanword *sukin hezzu* and double exclamations marks. Exclamation marks are also borrowed from the Roman script and are not used in formal

written Japanese. The use of excessive punctuation is more frequent in adver-
tisements (Seeley 2000), and double and sometimes triple exclamation marks
are a feature of contemporary digital writing styles. Through the use of nonconventional script and excessive punctuation, the linguistic elements of the
text bind to the highly sexualized image to create a cohesive representation
of the event theme. Being a skin-head girl in 1994 Tokyo is a departure from
conventional heteronormative femininity. Both script and image reinforce the
alternative stylistics of contemporary fashions trends.

The July 2000 flyer for GOLD FINGER (Figures 4.5 and 4.6) is representative of the later style of flyers in the corpus. Printed on both sides, the
front is split into two frames.[11] The left side is an advertisement for the spon-
sor beverage (details are also included on the back of the flyer). The product
name is printed onto an illustration of an hourglass-shaped bikini clad torso.
The figure is framed top and bottom; the product tag line on top, its location
branding "made in France" with connotations of high quality, excellence, and
extravagance at the bottom. The composition of the right side mimics the beverage advertisement. A photograph of a woman clad in a Gold Finger bikini
with flowers decorating the low-rise bikini pants fills most of the right side.
The woman's body is oriented toward the ad itself. The theme "Bikini Night"
and the date "7/28 (FRI)" overlay the torso. The style and placement of the cursive font also mimic the product name in the advertisement. The color tone of
brown and yellow with the product names in white is common to both sides.
The top banner of color for the club event, however, is in an eye-catching red.
The tag line "THE MOST EXCITING WOMEN-ONLY PARTY" (in capitalized Roman script) is brown except for the phrase *women-only* in yellow. The
Gold Finger logo appears bottom center. The realness of the photograph pulls
the eye to the image on the right. This is not imagined bronzed flesh, but *real*
glamor and sensuality. This, then, is the most salient part of the flyer overall.

The reverse side of the flyer also pulls our attention to the image on the
bottom left. There is a reproduction of a highly stylized 1950s bikini-clad
beauty. Her index finger is near her lips and her other hand is placed to her
ear. She appears as an alluring figure, framed in stars and enticing us to join
her. The theme "Bikini Night" appears to her right, and immediately below
it in Japanese a request to 'please come in a bikini' [*bikini de kite ne*]. The
positioning of this phrase next to the photographic image, and the use of the
informal request form *kite* ('come') followed by the interactive particle *ne*, suggests that the bikini-clad fifties model is addressing the reader; requesting her
to wear a bikini on the night. The interactive particle *ne* invites the involvement of the interactive partner (Katagiri 2007; Lee 2007; Okamoto 1995), with
the assumption that the partner will understand the utterance and the feelings
with which it is uttered (Lee 2007). The use of interactive particles which are
features of conversational interactions is a kind of "synthetic personalization"
(Fairclough 1989, 1994, 2001)—a process whereby producers of mass-media

texts use language to address each reader as if they were being spoken to as an individual. In her work on the construction of gender in teenage magazines, Talbot (1992, 1995) has shown how magazine editors use language to construct a friendship between the producers of the magazine and the readers. Drawing on this work, Nakamura (2004) demonstrates how interactive particles (also known as sentence-final particles) are one linguistic form used to construct interactions which contribute to forming a sense of a shared community in Japanese youth magazines. The Monalisa/Gold Finger flyers also address readers as members of a shared community of club-going women desiring to partake in the activities mapped out by the organizers.

THE "FINE PRINT": SPACE CREATED BY GIRLS TO BE ENJOYED BY GIRLS

In addition to branding the event as women only through the use of logos that index strong female figures, the use of commercially salient script choices and bold, sexual, kitsch images which contest contemporary notions of female sexuality, the flyers also contain sections of text that demarcate the space as accessible to women only. Typically, these are in a relatively small, black font on the front of the flyer. Font is an essential component of graphic design. It shapes the visual language of the flyer and influences the overall impression (Bartal 2013). The plain style of the descriptors marks them as informational components of the flyer overall, or as "the fine print" that offers a full disclosure of the event. The language, script choices, and punctuation used in the fine print constitute the club's official stance towards potential clients.

The flyer from July 1994 (Figure 4.1) contains a one-sentence description followed by a note in parentheses, as in example (1). The text appears to the right of the logo, and below details of the "library corner'" selling Japanese language editions of *Out* magazine, and the "kiosk corner" stocking Pop Against Homophobia t-shirts. A large "M," in a font size the height of two lines, visually marks the one sentence paragraph as separate from the logo. The text emphasizes the event as women-only in planning and production as well as clientele, and is followed by a short declaration of the entrance regulations in parentheses.

(1) July 1994 flyer
MONALISA wa, kikaku, DJ, pafōmā, dansā, bātendā ni itaru made subete, onna no ko ni yotte tsukuriageru kūkan o, onna no ko dake de tanoshimu '90 nendai-teki na atarashii sutairu no PARTY desu. (Nyūjo wa, josei nomi ni kagirasete itadakimasu.)

'MONALISA is a new 90s style PARTY; a space created by girls entirely from planning, DJ, performers, dancers to bartenders, to be enjoyed by girls only. (Entrance is restricted to women-only.)'

The description on the 1994 flyer promotes Monalisa as an innovative space (*kūkan*) in a contemporary 1990s style ('90 *nendai-teki*) created by and for girls (*onna no ko*) only. The listing of staff further emphasizes that the entire (*subete*) team is comprised of girls-only (*onna no ko*). Consistent with the nonconventional script used in the theme, *onna no ko* (girl) is written as 女のコ (*girlz*). Interestingly, this sentence ends with the distal form of the copula *desu*. Japanese verbs may take either the direct or distal style. The distal style indexes both a public persona and distance from the addressee (Cook 1996; Maynard 2004; Dunn 2010). It is used in formal speech and certain forms of essay writing, but not in public discourse such as newspaper articles. The final sentence in parentheses in (1) further underscores the women-only nature of the event through the use of the noun *josei* (woman). It shifts to a more formal register through the use of the humble honorific verb + causative + *itadaku* form. This form is found in service encounters. The distal -*masu* form of the verb is also used here. The literal translation would be "humbly receive permission to limit entry to women only."[12]

Example 1 shows the mixture of nonconventional orthography and conventional politeness strategies that are found in the flyers. Conventionally, writers are warned not to mix the distal and direct styles in written Japanese; however, style mixing is common in Japanese writing (Maynard 2004). In (1), the distal style is maintained, but the juxtaposition of alternative orthography and formal speech constitutes stance-taking by the writer. The alternative orthography used here positions both the staff and potential club-goers as nonconventional *girlz*, at the same time as it addresses readers in the distal style used in service encounters. The descriptive text, therefore, creates a hip, club-like vibe while maintaining a professional stance.

Another creative strategy used in the fine print of the flyers can be noted in the use of English, which is common to the commercial language of advertising (Barnes & Yamamoto 2008; Kuppens 2009). For example, a list of the types of women the club welcomes appears as a string of English in flyers throughout the 1990s:

(2)   Band of English framing the image from October 1995

'monalisa PINK is for GAY WOMEN, LIPSTICK LESBIAN, BI SEXUAL, GAY GAL, DYKE, BUTCH, FEM, BITCH ... etc. ALL GIRL WELCOME! GOING YOUR WAY!'

Gay women, lipstick lesbians, bisexual women, gay gal, dykes, butch women, fem women, and bitches are each invoked as potential club-goers through the use of this script. The final phrase "going your way" is the tag line for the events, and enforces the organizers' stance that all women who enter the club space should enjoy their own individual style.

Far from being stereotypical "fine print" in the October 1995 flyer (Figure 4.4), this band of Roman script reproduced in (2) visually frames the top and right side of the illustration of two witches kissing. The theme for the night written in English appears on the bottom, and on the left is a description of the club entrance regulations in Japanese (*monalisa PINK wa, josei dake de tanoshimu '90 nendai-teki na atarashii sutairu no pātī desu* ['monalisa PINK is a new style nineties party enjoyed by women-only']).[13] A description of the Halloween theme in Japanese follows the descriptor.

In three flyers in the corpus from 1998, the alternative spelling *womyn* is used. While this may be a quirk in the transliteration of terms, this non-conventional English spelling is also used in phrases such as *JOIN!! ALL WOMYN* which appears in bright pink on a white background on the January–March 1995 flyer (Figure 4.3). The spelling *womyn* may invoke images of lesbian feminist calls to renounce the androcentric bias of English by replacing he/man grammar/vocabulary (Martyna 1980; Ehrlich 2007) with women-identified viewpoints. Indeed, the Japanese feminist and lesbian feminist communities were readily engaging with lesbian feminist texts written in English from the 1970s. Linguists too have translated selected seminal feminist linguistic texts into Japanese.[14] In the flyers, however, the lesbian feminist term *womyn* is often juxtaposed with terms such as *lipstick lesbians*, *gay gals*, and *bitches* which seem historically removed from 1970s lesbian feminist rhetoric. Indeed, the Oxford English Dictionary lists the first usage of *womyn* from 1970s magazine *Lesbian Connection*. The earliest usage of "lipstick lesbian," which is defined as "a lesbian of glamorous or manifestly feminine appearance and behavior," is listed as Maupin's *Babycakes* (1984) (OED Online 2014).

A quick survey of print material, however, indicates that the feminist spelling of *womyn* is used extensively in the lesbian, bisexual, and queer women's communities in the 1990s. *Kinswomyn* was the name of a popular shot bar which opened in Shinjuku ni-chōme in 1994.[15] The first commercial lesbian and bisexual women's magazine *Furīne* (Phryne; 1995) is also branded as for "WOMYN LOVING" women on the cover (in Roman script). Its sister publication *Anīsu* (Anise; 1996–1997, 2001–2003) is branded as being "for womyn" (also on the cover in Roman script).

The collocation of *womyn* with *lipstick lesbian* also reflects the linguistic trends of the 1990s women's community. リップスティック・レズビアン (*rippusutikku rezubian*), the transliteration of the English *lipstick lesbian* into *katakana*, is included in the community terms listed in the first edition of *Furīne* (Phryne 1995). The definition given (in Japanese) is "a lesbian who is perfectly made up. Isn't too unusual these days, is it?" (Phryne 1995: 174). Although *lipstick lesbian* is not listed in the first edition of *Anīsu* (1996), it does appear again in the Autumn 1996 edition with a slightly shorter explanation: "a lesbian with make-up on." The term *womyn* does not appear in listings of this sort, suggesting that it is sufficiently recognizable not to require a definition.

The positioning of *womyn* alongside terms such as *lipstick lesbian* and *fem*, therefore, must be read within this historical and cultural context. When considering the importation and adaptation of subcultural terminology from languages other than Japanese into Japanese women's communities, "the local lesbian construct of community" (Welker 2010: 373) emerges as the fundamental point of reference. Similarly, as Kuppens (2009) argues, English used as a foreign language in advertising functions as a "linguistic cue" (118) to intended intertextual references to transnational media and other media genres. The flyers, therefore, fuse terms originating in English-speaking lesbian/bisexual queer women's communities and subcultures to meanings that have emerged through local textual and place-making practices. By employing a diversity of terms that are used within the Japanese-language women's community and rendering them in Roman script, the flyers project a complex stance which is both trend-setting and commercial, while striving to emphasize a sense of diversity nestled within the umbrella term *women only*.

In 1997, Monalisa holds its "big final" and the new event Gold Finger is launched in December 1997. Both logos are incorporated into the flyer for the "Grand Opening Party." The flyer contains no Japanese script whatsoever. The tag line "EVERYTHING SHE TOUCHES TURNS TO EXCITEMENT" (in capitalized Roman script) further heightens the event's intertextual connectivity (Kuppens 2009) with the James Bond 007 cinema phenomenon from which the event takes its name. Around this time, the Bond Girls also take center stage as a hand-picked group of performers and dancers who entertain clubbers with staged shows. They are described as 'cute and sexy' (*kyūto de sekushī*) (March 1999), ready to welcome and please. The Bond Girl "tip service" where clubbers can purchase Gold Finger money to place into the girls' costumes also becomes a promoted part of the event.

Whereas the politely humble "Entrance is restricted to women-only" was used in the 1994 flyer (Figure 4.1), the English phrases *SORRY BOYS* (July 1998) (see (3) and Figure 4.8) and *Sorry Guys* (January 1999) (see (4) and Figure 4.9) enter the flyer discourse in the late 1990s. In the example from the July 1998 flyer, the description of the women-only stance in Japanese is considerably shorter than that in example (1). Furthermore, the entrance regulation is expressed in a colloquial phrase transposed from English. The use of colloquial English "Sorry Boys" creates a more casual stance, which is markedly different from the descriptive sentence from the 1994 flyer that ends with the distal form of the copula *desu*. The use of "boys" complements the use of *gāruzu-onrī* ('girls-only') in the descriptor.

(3)　July 1998 flyer
　　　GOLD FINGER wa gāruzu onrī de tanoshimu naitokurabu ibento desu. Sorry Boys.

　　　'GOLD FINGER is a night-club event enjoyed by girls-only. Sorry Boys.'

FIGURE 4.8 GOLDFINGER July 1998

(4) January 1999 flyer
GOLD FINGER '99. . . . Suriringu na dansu chūn ni, bondo gāruzu ni
yoru guramarasu na shōtaimu. Otona no josei no tame no wan-naito
fantajī. Sorry Guys.

'Thrilling dance tunes and glamorous showtime by the Bond Girls.
A one-night fantasy for adult women. Sorry Guys.'

What could be interpreted as a recasting of the category of *women* is noted
via the use of the phrase *otona no josei* (adult women) in the January 1999
flyer (Figure 4.9). As the phrase *MUST BE OVER 21* is used to state the age
restrictions of the club circa 1997, this does not appear to be related to legal
requirements.[16] Rather, the use of *otona* (adult) to modify "women," which
connotes sophistication through association with adulthood, suggests a new
degree of maturation. In Monalisa/Gold Finger flyers, the terms *adult woman*
(*otona no josei*) and/or *woman* written in capitalized English often appear
with constructions such as *gāruzu naito* ('girl's night'). Whereas the alternative
spelling 女の コ (*onna no ko* = girlz) features in the earlier Monalisa flyers, in

FIGURE 4.9 GOLDFINGER January 1999

the late 1990s the Sino-Japanese character for *woman* is replaced with alternative *katakana* spellings. For example, オンナのコ (*onna no ko* = girlz) and オンナ (*onna* = woman) occur frequently. *Katakana* spellings of non-loanword terms create a disjuncture that visually marks a departure from conventional meaning. Rendering *woman* and *girl* in alternative orthography, therefore, creates semantic distance between traditional or conventional notions of femininity and womanhood.

Shifts in the semantics of Tokyo nightlife can also be traced through the self-reference terms used in the flyers: 'party' in English (circa 1994) or *katakana* (circa 1995); 'club' or 'night club event' in *katakana* (circa 1996; 1998–1999); and *one night fantasy* or *fantasy night* in *katakana* (circa 1999).[17] The term *party* has connotations of a private social gathering comprised of invited guests only. This interpretation is consistent with the formal style used in the descriptor from the 1994 flyer. In contrast, *night club event* suggests a special event held at a commercial premise. The dictionary definition of *naitokurabu* ('nightclub') refers to members-only establishments, which provide alcoholic beverages and entertainment. Positioning Monalisa/Goldfinger as an 'event' (*ibento*, when transliterated into Japanese) is also consistent with terminology uses to refer to themed nights and parties in the LGBT scene. This stance positions the space as a self-contained reoccurring spectacle that is complete with each separate articulation.

Entertainment districts in Tokyo are awash with a wide variety of clubs ranging from those that sell commercial music and entertainment, such as jazz clubs, to host and hostess clubs which sell intimacy and are part of the affect economy (Allison 1994; Takeyama 2010). There are a plethora of terms used to refer to a wide range of venues which sell a variety of services. In the 1990s, de-accented pronunciation of the word *club* emerged from within youth culture to distinguish venues styled as house-music or hip-hop clubs from regular sports clubs and other forms of nightclubs. Note, however, that Goldfinger refers to itself as a "one-night fantasy," not as a "club" as late as 1999.

THE VISUAL AND TEXTUAL LANGUAGE OF THE MONALISA/GOLDFINGER FLYERS

The analysis of a decade of the Monalisa/Goldfinger promotional flyers has illustrated how linguistic and visual representation of women's sexualities challenges the heteronormative notions of female desire and bodies. The iconic naming is highlighted in simple yet strong logos which brand the event as a bold alternative to contemporary club spaces. Highly sexualized images penned by renowned *manga* artists and professional illustrators index female-to-female sexuality and feature prominently in the flyers. Potential clients are visually and linguistically enticed to enter into the fun. Respect for the individual privacy of the club-goers is signaled via the use of in-club shots that do not feature identifiable crowd shots. The visual language of the flyers, therefore, skillfully negotiates a sociocultural context that discourages public engagement with lived experiences of female-to-female desire yet does not negate that desire. In the early flyers, the entrance requirements are articulated using conventionally formal descriptive text that makes use of alternative orthography to reinforce the unconventionality of the space. As the club event matures, the text shifts to a more colloquial style and accompanying text directly addresses potential clients beckoning them to join in the fun. Intersecting notions of womanhood are indexed through terms such as *womyn, gay gal,* and *lipstick lesbian* in English, and *onna-no-ko* ('girlz'), *gāruzu* ('girls'), *otona no josei* ('adult women'). The transient and mobile space is constantly (re)produced as hip and desirable to appeal to a diverse community of club-going women.

Queer(y)ing the Meaning of "Women Only"

Engaging with a corpus of flyers from a ten-year period has identified the changing nature of commercial women-only space. The logos, descriptions, and disclaimers, which limit entry to Monalisa/Goldfinger to women, provide a visual repetition of the parameters of the space. Highly sexualized images are a key part of the visual impact of the flyers. The images index same-sex female desire and mark the club as an enjoyable space for *women* to enjoy themselves *as* women being entertained *by* women. This women-only space is an example of queer spatiality, that is, one of the "place-making practices within postmodernism in which queer people engage" (Halberstam 2005: 6). In Halberstam's (2005) reading of queer space, postmodernism is considered to be both "a crisis and an opportunity—a crisis in the stability of form and meaning, and an opportunity to rethink the practice of cultural production, its hierarchies and power dynamics, its tendency to resist or capitulate" (6). There is tension between the stability of meaning and the potential to rethink space and its meaning. Queer space, in other words, constitutes both a pull toward stability and a push toward change. For Monalisa/Gold Finger, the very category of *women* invoked by the term *women-only* pulls toward the stasis of cis-gender identities, at the same time as it pushes against heteronormative gender and sexuality. In the sociocultural context of 1990s Tokyo, women-only space emerges as a space that attempts to reimagine existing definitions of what constitutes a space that is woman-identified. This tension is further impacted by the commercial demands to reproduce a fashionable nightclub experience in tune with contemporary fashions and trends. This styling of *women-only space* can only be understood in its specific historical context.

In an interview with writer Izumo Marou, Chigar (Chigalliano) explains that she first decided to make a club event where women could dance and enjoy club music at a time when the only lesbian/bisexual women's events were held once a month in rented dance studios and/or gay men's bars. Chigar stresses that the event is a "women-only event" not a "lesbian night" (Chigar & Izumo 1997):

> There is this image of the lesbian. There's a lesbian porn industry, and men are turned on by that, so if you say lesbian, they take it to mean a person

having lesbian sex. (. . .) If you say it is a lesbian night then people say "hey!" and pull away. Because there is this arbitrary delusion. But, there are loads of hetero girls who come because monalisa is fun. So saying sticking to this (event) being (positioned as) a women-only event not a lesbian event, then that gives them an excuse to come. So as the organizer of monalisa one must never say that this space is a lesbian only night. It is somewhere you can enjoy yourself regardless of sexuality. (111)

The marking of the space as *women only* and not as *lesbian only* is a response to two different phenomena. First, it offers an alternative to the image of the "lesbian" in popular Japanese culture, which positions the "lesbian" as pornographic fodder for (heterosexual) male fantasy.[18] The category women only is actively maintained to open the space up beyond the male-centered pornographic view by invoking a diversity of "women." Second, it offers an alternative to the interpretation that *women only* equals lesbian. Whereas in the 1970s and early 1980s, media and social spaces were run by collectives, many of which shared resources with feminist groups or on premises provided by sympathetic gay men, the 1990s gay boom involved a range of new commercial enterprises. Monalisa/Goldfinger emerged at this time as an alternative, not only to the heteronormative club scene but also to the gay male club scene, monthly lesbian parties, and small-scale lesbian bars.

As this chapter has shown, the promotional flyers (re)produce Monalisa/Goldfinger as a desirable alternative through manipulation of image, design, layout, and text. Bold logos, use of English and nonconventional combinations of scripts, and conversational stance combine with eye-catching images of sexualized female forms to create a sense of the pleasure that will be experienced within the women-only space. The flyers identify potential club-goers as young, hip women who are not men, boys, or guys. This stance responds to the complex history of women-only space in Tokyo which often saw the conflation of cross-dressing with same-sex desire in the commercial bar scene. However, through the exclusion of men and a vigilant practice of welcoming all women, the phrase *women only* becomes entangled in a delicate negotiation of postmodern space wherein *woman* is both privileged and contested. A developing awareness of transgender issues that emerged alongside the 1990s gay boom has necessitated engagement with gender and sexuality in alternative ways.[19] Contemporary articulations of the Monalisa/Gold Finger suite of club events and bar spaces include the Boyish Friends events, which welcome female-to-male transfolk, *onabe*, and boi-identified clients.

As already noted previously, Milani (2013a) has argued that queer linguistics must engage in multimodal analysis in order to seriously engage with the "complexity of *sexed* meanings in public texts" (211). Furthermore, he has also claimed that work on linguistic landscapes must engage with gender and sexuality if it is to develop "innovative approaches to language-political issues and aims to continue contributing to the understanding of the ways in which language is imbricated in the (re)production of power in public settings" (Milani 2013b: 22). The Monalisa/Gold Finger flyers are part of the linguistic landscape of contemporary Tokyo. The flyers are examples of a highly mobile medium that traverses a wide diversity of places and spaces. As part of the Tokyo counterpublics, these texts respond to, contest, and (re)produce localized expectations of gender and sexuality and act as a portal to alternative queer spatiality.

Acknowledgments

This research was supported by Japanese Society for the Promotion of Science (JSPS) Grant-in-Aid for Scientific Research (B) (No. 20310155), and with funding from the University of Melbourne, Faculty of Arts Research Grant. I am grateful for this support.

Notes

1. There is a rich history of terminology in Japanese for a range of sexual and gender identities, and the communities that have emerged around self-identifications. For an overview, see (Maree 2014). In this chapter, I will use the acronym LGBT (lesbian/gay/bisexual/transgender) as an overarching term.

2. The club event has had several name changes and in this chapter I will refer to it using a combination of the two main names Monalisa/Gold Finger.

3. *Wakakusa no kai* also produced a newsletter *Wakakusa tsūshin* (Young Grass News, and a self-financed magazine *Ibu & Ibu* (Eve & Eve; 1982–1983). A splinter group unsatisfied with the butch/femme classificatory practices of the parties, formed a publishing collective which published the lesbian mini-komi, *Subarashii onnatachi* (Wonderful women), in 1976. For a discussion on community building in the lesbian community, see Iino 2006, 2008; Sawabe 2008; Welker 2010.

4. In the ten-year period analyzed in this chapter, Chigar spearheaded a number of innovative queer enterprises, for example, the importing of Pop Against Homophobia t-shirts and other paraphernalia, and the production of the Pink Pop Shop (1995) and a Japanese translated mini-edition of *Out* magazine 1995–1996. She also secured commercial sponsorship (from major beverage companies) for the events she organized and collaborated with fashion labels, for example, producing Gold Finger t-shirts in collaboration with Hysteric Glamour in 2000. Many of the Monalisa/Gold Finger parties have film themes in the period 1991–2001, ranging from community-produced videos (such as *Wounded* (1997); *Safer Sex* [lesbian edition, 1998]) to tie-ups with major new releases: *Cowgirls Blues* (1994); *Fresh Kill* (1995); *I Shot Andy Warhol* (1996); *Spice Girl the Movie* (1998); *The Monkey Mask* (2001).

5. For example, a 500 yen discount on the entry price on presentation of the flyer before stipulated time (e.g., 10 p.m.) or if presenting as per the dress code.

6. *Kogyaru* (lit. 'little girls') refers to a subcultural fashion made popular by teenage women 1980s–1990s. For a discussion on *kogaru* and language, see Miller 2004. For a discussion of the *kogyaru* phenomenon, see Kinsella 2005.

7. The flyers from December 1997 and March 1998 feature this design. Segments underlined appear in Roman script.

8. For detailed research on Japanese linguistic landscapes, see Backhaus (2005, 2006, 2007).

9. Sakurazawa Erica debuted in the 1980s and is well known for her girls manga. Her work appears in magazines, books, and cinema adaptations and she regularly appears in print, television, and Internet-based media.

10. *Onna no ko* ('girl') is conventionally written 女の子 using the Sino-Japanese character for 女 (*onna*) + possessive article in hiragana の (*no*) + Sino-Japanese character for child 子 (*ko*). 'Boy' is conventionally written 男の子 (man + possessive particle + child).

11. For convenience I have labeled the side printed in color as the front, and the one in black and white the back.

12. For a recent discussion of this form, see Cook (2013).

13. The distal style can be noted with the use of the copula from *desu*.

14. For example, Robin Lakoff (1975); Dale Spender (1980); Deborah Cameron (1985); Francine Frank, Harriet Wattman, & Frank Ashen (1983).

15. Kinswomyn was revolutionary for not having a cover charge. It closed doors after twenty years in 2014.

16. The legal age of adulthood is twenty in Japan.

17. This is also used in the descriptor for the tie-up with *Spice the Movie* in 1998, and *Queen Kong* in 2001.

18. For discussions in English, see Chalmers (2002) and Maree (2014).

19. Awareness of transgender rights can also be traced to the enactment of The Law Concerning the Special Treatment of the Gender of Individuals with Gender Identity Disorder is commonly referred to as the GID Act. Enacted 2003 (effective 2004) and partially amended in 2008, the act allows individuals who fit the stipulations to legally alter their registered sex. It is important to note that the stipulations allow only those individuals who have undergone surgery and have the genital appearance of the other sex to alter their sex on official documents if they are over twenty years of age, are not currently married, and do not have children under the age of twenty.

References

Abe, Hideko. 2010. *Queer Japanese: Gender and sexual identities through linguistic practices.* New York: Palgrave Macmillan.

Allison, Anne. 1994. *Nightwork: Sexuality, pleasure, and corporate masculinity in a Tokyo hostess club.* Chicago & London: University of Chicago Press.

Allison, Anne. 1998. Cutting the fringes: Pubic hair at the margins of Japanese censorship laws. In Alf Hiltebeitel & Barbara D. Miller (eds.), *Hair: Its power and meaning in Asian culture*, 195–218. Albany: State University of New York Press.

Backhaus, Peter. 2005. Signs of multilingualism in Tokyo: A diachronic look at the linguistic landscape. *International Journal of the Sociology of Language* 175–176. 103–121.

Backhaus, Peter. 2006. Multilingualism in Tokyo: A look into the linguistic landscape. *International Journal of Multilingualism* 3(1). 52–66.

Backhaus, Peter. 2007. ALPHABET Ante Portas: How English text invades Japanese public space. *Visible Language* 41(1). 70–87.

Baker, Paul. 2008. *Sexed texts: Language, gender and sexuality*. London: Equinox.

Barnes, Bradley & Maki Yamamoto. 2008. Exploring international cosmetics advertising in Japan. *Journal of Marketing Management* 24(3–4). 299–316.

Bartal, Orl. 2013. Text as image in Japanese advertising typography design. *Design Issues* 29(1). 51–66.

Beddard, Phil & Jon Savage. 1995. *Highflyers: Clubravepartyart*. London: Booth-Clibborn Editions.

Bessatsu Takarajima 64. 1987. *Onna o aisuru onnatachi no monogatari* (Stories of women who love women). Tokyo: JICC Shuppankyoku.

Cameron, Deborah. 1985. *Feminism and linguistic theory*. London: Macmillan.

Chalmers, Sharon. 2002. *Emerging lesbian voices from Japan*. Richmond, UK: Curzon.

Chigar, Don K. & Marou Izumo. 1997. Kuiā uēbu kurieishon ('Creating queer waves'). *Gendai Shisō* 27(5). 110–116.

Cook, Haruko M. 1996. Japanese language socialization: Indexing the modes of self. *Discourse Processes* 22. 171–197.

Cook, Haruko. M. 2013. A scientist or salesman? Identity construction through referent honorifics on a Japanese shopping channel program. *Multilingua* 32(2). 177–202.

Crenshaw, Kimberlé Williams. 1991. Mapping the margins: Intersectionality, identity politics, and violence against women of color. *Stanford Law Review* 43(6). 1241–1299.

Du Bois, John W. 2007. The stance triangle. In Robert Englebretson (ed.), *Stancetaking in discourse: Subjectivity, evaluation, interaction*, 137–182. Amsterdam: John Benjamins.

Dunn, Cynthia Dickel. 2010. Information structure and discourse stance in a monologic "public speaking" register of Japanese. *Journal of Pragmatics* 42(7). 1890–1911.

Edelman, Lee. 2004. *No future: Queer theory and the death drive*. Durham, NC: Duke University Press.

Ehrlich, Susan (ed.). 2007. *Language and gender volume II—Foundational debates 2: Is language sexist?* New York: Routledge.

Fairclough, Norman. 1989. *Language and power*. Essex, UK: Longman.

Fairclough, Norman. 1994. The authority of the consumer. In Russell Keat, Nigel Whiteley, & Nicholas Abercrombie (eds.), *Conversationalization of public discourse and the authority of the consumer*, 235–249. London & New York: Routledge.

Fairclough, Norman. 2001. *Language and power*, 2nd edn. Essex, UK: Longman.

Frank, Francice, Harriet Wattman, & Frank Ashen. 1983. *Language and the sexes*. Albany: State University of New York Press.

Freeman, Elizabeth. 2010. *Time binds: Queer temporalities, queer histories*. Durham, NC: Duke University Press.

Gottlieb, Nanette. 2009. Language on the internet in Japan. In Gerard Goggin & Mark McLelland (eds.), *Internationalizing internet studies*. New York: Routledge.

Gottlieb, Nanette. 2010. Playing with language in E-Japan: Old wine in new bottles *Journal of Japanese Studies* 30(3). 393–407.

Gottlieb, Nanette. 2011. Technology and the writing system in Japan. In Patrick Heinrich & Christian Galan (eds.), *Language life in Japan: Transformations and prospects*, 140–153. Abingdon, Oxon, UK: Routledge.

Halberstam, Judith. 2005. *In a queer time and place: Transgender bodies, subcultural lives*. New York: New York University Press.

Iedema, Rick. 2003. Multimodality, resemiotization: Extending the analysis of discourse as multi-semiotic practice. *Visual Communication* 2(1). 29–57.

Iino, Yuriko. 2006. The politics of "disregarding": Addressing Zainichi issues within the lesbian community in Japan. *Journal of Lesbian Studies* 10(3–4). 69–85.

Iino, Yuriko. 2008. *Rezubian de aru "watashitachi" no sutorī* ('"Our" story as lesbians'). Tokyo: Seikatsu-shoin.

Ingram, Gordon B., Anne-Marie Bouthillette, & Yolanda Retter. 1997. Lost in space: Queer theory and community activism at the fin-de-millenaire. In Gordon B. Ingram, Anne-Marie Bouthillette, & Yolanda Retter (eds.), *Queers in space: Claiming the urban landscape*, 3–15. San Francisco: Bay Press Incorporated.

Izumo, Marou, Yoshiko Tsuzura, Minako Hara, & Kumiko Ochiya (trans. by James Welker). 2007. Japan's lesbian movement: Looking back on where we came from. In Mark McLelland, James Welker, & Katsuhiko Suganuma (eds.), *Queer voices from Japan: First-person narratives from Japan's sexual minorities*, 195–223. Lanham, MD: Lexington Books.

Jaffe, Alexandra. 2009. Introduction: The sociolinguistics of stance. In Alexandra Jaffe (ed.), *Stance: Sociolinguistic perspectives*, 3–28. Oxford: Oxford University Press.

Katagiri, Yasuhiro. 2007. Dialogue functions of Japanese sentence-final particles "yo" and "ne." *Journal of Pragmatics* 39. 1313–1323.

Kataoka, Kuniyoshi. 2003. Form and function of emotive pictorial signs in casual letter writing. *Written Language & Literacy* 6(1). 1–29.

Kinsella, Sharon. 2005. Black faces, witches, and racism against girls. In Laura Miller & Jan Bardsley (eds.), *Bad girls of Japan*, 143–157. Basingstoke & New York: Palgrave Macmillan.

Kress, Gunther & Theo Van Leeuwen. 1996. *Reading images: The grammar of visual design*. London & New York: Routledge.

Kuppens, An H. 2009. English in advertising: Generic intertextuality in a globalizing media environment. *Applied Linguistics* 31(1). 115–135.

Lalonde, Amanda. 2014. Buddy Esquire and the early hip hop flyer. *Popular Music* 33(1). 19–38.

Lakoff, Robin. 1975. *Language and woman's place*. New York: Harper & Row.

Lee, Duck-Young. 2007. Involvement and the Japanese interactive particles ne and yo. *Journal of Pragmatics* 39. 363–388.

Loehwing, Melanie & Jeff Motter. 2012. Cultures of circulation: Utilizing co-cultures and counterpublics in intercultural new media research. *China Media Research* 8(4). 29–38.

Mackie, Vera. 1992. Feminism and the media in Japan. *Japanese Studies* 12(2). 23–31.

Maree, Claire. 2007. *Hatsuwasha no gengo sotoratejī toshite no negoshiēshon kōi* ('Negotiation as a linguistic strategy of speakers'). Tokyo: Hituzi Shobo.

Maree, Claire. 2013. *"Onē-kotoba" ron* ('On "onē-kotoba"'). Tokyo: Seidosha.

Maree, Claire. 2014. Queer women's culture and history in Japan. In Mark McLelland & Vera Mackie (eds.), *The Routledge handbook of sexuality studies in East Asia*, 230–243. London & New York: Routledge.

Maynard, Senko K. 2004. Poetics of style mixture: Emotivity, identity, and creativity in Japanese writings. *Poetics* 32(5). 387–409.

Martyna, Wendy. 1980. Beyond the "he/man" approach: The case for nonsexist language. *Signs: Journal of Women in Culture and Society* 5(3). 482–493.

McLelland, Mark. 2004. From sailor-suits to sadists: "Lesbos love" as reflected in Japan's postwar "perverse press." *U.S.–Japan Women's Journal* 27. 3–26.

Milani, Tommaso. 2013a. Expanding the queer linguistic scene: Multimodality, space and sexuality at a South African university. *Journal of Language and Sexuality* 2(2). 206–234.

Milani, Tommaso. 2013b. Whither linguistic landscapes? The sexed facets of ordinary signs. *Tilburg Papers in Culture Studies* 53. 1–34.

Miller, Laura. 2004. Those naughty teenage girls: Japanese kogals, slang, and media assessments. *Journal of Linguistic Anthropology* 14(2). 225–247.

Miller, Laura. 2011. Subversive script and novel graphs in Japanese girls' culture. *Language & Communication* 31(1). 16–26.

Miyake, Kazuko. 2007. How young Japanese express their emotions visually in mobile phone messages: A sociolinguistic analysis. *Japanese Studies* 27. 53–72.

Mukherjee, Dhrubodhi & Dalia Chowdhury. 2012. What do the flyers say? Embedded "Orientalist" constructions in social work study abroad programs in the United States. *International Social Work* 57(6). 576–89.

Munakata, Mayumi. 1997, June 30. Flyer report 2: MONALISA at Delight. *Shūkan Asukī*.

Nakamura, Momoko. 2004. "Let's dress a little girlishly" or "conquer short pants": Constructing gendered communities in fashion magazines for young people. In Shigeko Okamoto & Janet S. Shibamoto Smith (eds.), *Japanese language, gender, and ideology: Cultural models and real people*, 131–147. Oxford & New York: Oxford University Press.

Nishimura, Yukiko. 2003. Linguistic innovations and interactional features of casual online communication in Japanese. *Journal of Computer-Mediated Communication* 9. doi: 10.1111/j.1083-6101.2003.tb00356.x.

Nishimura, Yukiko. 2008. *Aspects of Japanese computer-mediated communication.* Sheffield, South Yorkshire, UK: Sheffield Hallam University PhD dissertation.

Okamoto, Shigeko. 1995. Pragmaticization of meaning in some sentence-final particles in Japanese. In Masayoshi Shibatani & Sandra Thompson (eds.), *Essays in semantics and pragmatics: In honor of Charles J. Filmore*, 219–246. Amsterdam & Philadelphia: John Benjamins.

OED Online. 2014. Oxford: Oxford University Press. (December 10, 2014.)

Rausch, Anthony S. P. 2008. Place branding in rural Japan: Cultural commodities as local brands. *Branding & Public Diplomacy* 4(2). 136–146.

Salter, Rebecca. 2006. *Japanese popular prints: From votive slips to playing cards.* Honolulu: University of Hawaii Press.

Sawabe, Hitomi. 2008. The symbolic tree of lesbianism in Japan: An overview of lesbian activist history and literary works. In Barbara Summerhawk & Kimberly Hughes (eds.), *Sparkling rain: And other fiction from Japan of women who love women*, 6–32. Chicago: New Victoria Publishers.

Scollon, Ron. 1997. Handbills, tissues, and condoms: A site of engagement for the construction of identity in public discourse. *Journal of Sociolinguistics* 1(1). 39–61.

Sebba, Mark. 2009. Sociolinguistic approaches to writing systems research. *Writing Systems Research* 1(1). 35–49.

Seeley, Christopher. 2000. *A history of writing in Japan.* Honolulu: University of Hawaii Press.

Shibamoto Smith, Janet S. & David L. Schmidt. 1996. Variability in written Japanese: Towards a sociolinguistics of script choice. *Visible Language* 30(1). 47–71.

Spender, Dale. 1980. *Man made language*. London: Routledge & Kegan Paul.

Takeyama, Akiko. 2010. Intimacy for sale: Masculinity, entrepreneurship, and commodity self in Japan's neoliberal situation. *Japanese Studies* 20(2). 231–246.

Talbot, Mary. 1992. The construction of gender in a teenage magazine. In Norman Fairclough (ed.), *Critical language awareness*, 74–99. Harlow, Essex, UK: Longman.

Talbot, Mary. 1995. A synthetic sisterhood: False friends in a teenage magazine. In Kira Hall & Mary Bucholtz (eds.), *Gender articulated: Language and the socially constructed self*, 143–165. London & New York: Routledge.

Tranter, Nicolas. 2008. Nonconventional script choice in Japan. *International Journal of the Sociology of Language* 192. 133–151.

Warner, Michael. 2002. *Publics and counterpublics*. New York: Zone Books.

Welker, James. 2010. Telling her story: Narrating a Japanese lesbian community. *Journal of Lesbian Studies* 14(4). 359–380.

Young, Laurie. 2011. *The marketer's handbook: Reassessing marketing techniques for modern business*. Chichester, UK & Hoboken, NJ: Wiley.

5

/s/ Variation and Perceptions of Male Sexuality in Denmark

Marie Maegaard and Nicolai Pharao

Introduction

Previous research has shown that in Copenhagen /s/ variation (in both onset and coda) in male speakers is perceived to be strongly linked to sexuality (Pharao et al. 2014). However, this link is only found in standard Copenhagen speech, and not in so-called street language. Street language is a style of speech that differs from standard Copenhagen speech with respect to lexicon, grammar, prosody, and pronunciation. One of the phonetic features that differs from standard Copenhagen speech is the fronted /s/. Street language is usually associated with young speakers in urban heterogeneous environments (Madsen et al. 2013). Furthermore, it is usually associated with a tough, streetwise, and straight masculinity, which is why it is especially interesting that fronted /s/ is also found in this type of speech.

To investigate the relations between variation in /s/, different registers, and social meaning, we carried out an experiment among young Copenhageners. The experiment was a matched guise study where the /s/ quality had been manipulated so that we were able to investigate how even very subtle differences in /s/ quality influenced the stereotypical perceptions of listeners. In this chapter, we use the results of this /s/-study as a basis for further analysis of perceived links between register, sexuality, and other aspects of the perceived identity of the speaker. We use the study of this particular case of linguistic variation to show how different characteristics go together to form recognizable clusters in listeners' perceptions. This is very well illustrated in the results from the /s/-study. Furthermore, by using the theoretical framework of intersectionality, we gain insights into the multifaceted identities that speakers and listeners can construct in interaction by using certain variants while seeing how limited the potential for constructing such identities is, since the stereotypes involved are very strong.

In this chapter, we discuss categories and intersections between them, in relation to the perceptions of both white majority Danes and minority Danes of immigrant backgrounds.

Categories, Stereotypes, and Identifications

Categorization is a fundamental cognitive and sociopsychological process, whereby a complex world is made less complex and more easily perceived (e.g., Allport 1954; Tajfel 1969; Hogg & Abrams 1988; Schneider 2004). As pointed out by Schneider (2004), categorization is closely linked to stereotyping. There is no general agreement on the exact meaning of the term *stereotyping*, and in some accounts it is viewed as an individual phenomenon (e.g., Jones 1997), whereas in others it is seen as a shared social phenomenon (e.g., Mackie 1973; Hogg & Abrams 1988). Schneider provides a definition that is deliberately very simple (and vague) because it is an attempt to minimize the use of constraining assumptions: "stereotypes are qualities perceived to be associated with particular groups or categories of people" (Schneider 2004: 24; Pharao 2013: 48). This definition does not explicitly define stereotypes as individual or collective phenomena, but it is a definition that can be seen as both. In a perception study like the present one, we are interested in the commonly held associations connected to different ways of speaking. This is why in the discussions in this chapter we follow Hogg & Abrams (1988) in that "an important feature of stereotypes is that they are *shared*; that is, large sections of society will agree on what the stereotypes of particular groups are" (65–66). Another aspect of stereotypes that is often mentioned in the literature is that they are wrong or at least inaccurate (cf. Allport 1954; Brigham 1971). Whether or not a stereotype is wrong is something that cannot easily be determined, if at all. On the other hand, it is almost tautological to state that characteristics that are perceived to be associated with entire categories of people will be inaccurate.

Stereotyping is one side of categorization; another is identification. When categorizing the social world, we also categorize ourselves. Self-categorization and self-stereotyping (Hogg & Abrams 1988) are mental processes, but they are linked to the construction of self as taking place in interaction with other social beings. In social identity theory, the focus is not on *identity* but on *social identifications* (Hogg & Abrams 1988). This is in line with recent work in language and sexuality research where the term *identity* is avoided and instead researchers focus on concepts like *desire* and *identification* (Cameron & Kulick 2003). When categorizing the social world we also identify, or disidentify, with other actors, and this places categorization at the heart of social interaction.

Categorization can be studied within many frames, and in this chapter we will use data from an experimental study.

Intersectionality as a Frame

As is clear already from several chapters in this volume, using intersectionality theory as a framework for doing variationist sociolinguistics is not a simple enterprise. Moreover, intersectionality is in itself not easy to define (cf. Levon & Mendes, Chapter 1, this volume). In Crenshaw's (1989) interpretation of the term, it means: "the multidimensionality of marginalized subjects' lived experiences" (139). However, in her discussion of the different views of intersectionality, Yuval-Davis (2011) argues that intersectional analysis should not be limited to marginalized members of society but should encompass all members of society. This position distances her from the origins of intersectionality in black feminism, where a focus on the marginalized is essential. However, this does not mean that Yuval-Davis is not concerned with the empowerment of the marginalized—quite the contrary—but it means that she finds it important to include social agents from the entire social spectrum as objects in an intersectional analysis of social differences and inequality in society. As mentioned in the introduction, in this chapter we will focus not only on perceptions of speakers of ethnic minority background but also on perceptions of speakers of white majority background.

Another important aspect of the intersectional approach that we rely on in this chapter is the mutual constitution of categories. Mutual constitution is important in two senses. As is clear from the social psychological literature referred to earlier, categories are mutually constitutive. The category *white* unavoidably presumes the existence of a *nonwhite* category, and the same goes for all other categories. Delimiting a category automatically leads to delimiting what is *not* part of the category. This means that the construction of a category is always simultaneously the construction of at least one other category. This is one way of looking at mutual constitution, and this is how it is usually understood in social psychology. In much intersectionality work, however, the concept of mutual constitution is used in another sense. For instance, an object for intersectional research could be to examine how class constitutes and is constituted by gender. This connects to what we have later termed an *intracategorical focus*; to examine, for instance, what it means to be in the category *woman* (does it also mean "white" and "middle-class"?). In that sense, the ascription of a person to one category often automatically includes the ascription of that person to other associated categories. This is what psychologists working on stereotypes are also interested in, but where they see stereotypes as largely a psychological concept, critical theorists working within the frame of intersectionality would typically examine discourse revealing these connections. In our view, these connections exist in mental processes of categorization, in sociopsychological phenomena like stereotyping, and in discourse. In the reported study, focus is on stereotypes.

The study presented in this chapter is both intracategorical and intercategorical in its approach (McCall 2005). Our primary focus is on the way in which different clusters of categories are being evoked by listeners depending on the linguistic variation they hear. We are interested in the specific categories that are being evoked (*white, immigrant, homosexual, clever, gangster, posh,* etc.), in the relation between them (which categories go together?), and finally in the varying meanings of specific categories and the boundaries between them (the typical example from the literature being whether "black women" are included in the category *women*). This last point is very much a perspective that needs to be discussed when looking at the results.

A final aspect of intersectionality theory needs to be mentioned here. Intersectional approaches are sometimes criticized for being based on an interpretation of the social world as static (e.g., Puar 2007). Because it is concerned with categories and positions, intersectionality easily becomes focused on structure, and consequently intersectional analyses can lead to patterns seemingly showing stability and constancy, rather than change and process. In an effort to capture the instability and dynamics of belonging, Puar (2007) proposes the concept of *assemblage*, which she borrows from Deleuze & Guattari (1987). While Puar's critique is an important contribution to the ongoing debate on what intersectionality is or should be, in this chapter our aim is to show how individuals are perceived stereotypically, and categories and structure are essential concepts in this endeavor. The analyses presented here will be based on listeners' perceptions of speakers' belonging to different categories. Because the point of departure for this study is to investigate whether very subtle differences in /s/-pronunciation lead to the ascription of speakers to quite different categories, the design of the study offers fixed categories for listeners to consider (see section "Indexicalities of Fronted /s/ in Denmark"). In other words, the fluidity and instability of belonging is undoubtedly a condition for any study focusing on identification in the context of late modernity, and any result will have to be interpreted within that frame, but it is not an aspect that has been incorporated into the actual design of the study. On the other hand, it is important to keep in mind that categories and structure coming out of a study like this are set in a particular historical time and context and that interpretations of what it means to be "Danish," "gangster," "gay," and so on are not fixed but constantly open to negotiation and renegotiation.

Indexicalities of Fronted /s/ in Denmark

Fronted /s/ in Danish is often presented as linked to social meanings like "feminine" and "girlish" when used by female speakers, and social meanings like "feminine" and "gay" when used by male speakers. This is especially the case in public discourse, and in nonlinguists' accounts of the use of fronted /s/. In a reader's comment on a popular scientific website, Videnskab.dk, it is stated:

(1)   Det handler om at være lille/spinkel, kælen og feminin . . . tankevæk-kende at denne talefejl går hånd i hånd med unge pigers barberede kønsdele . . .

'It's all about being small/fragile, affectionate and feminine. . . Thought provoking that this speech impediment goes hand in hand with young girls' shaved genitals. . .'

The reader in example (1) is commenting on an article about "lisping" which many readers seem to interpret as fronted /s/. The comment is obviously about female speakers' use of this variant. In male speakers, the associations seem a bit different, even though femininity is still an often mentioned characteristic associated with the speakers:

(2)   Altså jeg stemmer kun på de flotteste, siger Gustav og stemmer s'erne en ekstra gang

'You know, I only vote for the most handsome ones, Gustav says, voicing his s'es a little extra'

Example (2) is from the Danish tabloid newspaper *Ekstrabladet* (February 23, 2012), describing the reality TV star Gustav, and his apparent lack of knowledge and interest in politics. In the Danish public sphere, Gustav is portrayed as the stereotypical gay diva, and he is frequently ridiculed for his apparent ignorance and self-satisfaction. It is quite evident that both gayness and femininity are related to fronted /s/ in people's associations, but more characteristics seem to go hand in hand with these associations. In example (3), an online article from the National Danish Broadcasting Company describes gay stereotypes:

(3)   De taler med stemte s'er, de har løse håndled, går med make-up og har jobs inden for den kreative branche. Sådan lyder nogle af for-dommene om bøsser, som medierne er med til at bekræfte.

'They speak with voiced s'es, they have loose wrists, wear make-up and hold jobs in the creative industry. This is how some of the preju-dice about gays sound, and the media are helping to confirm it.'
(dr.dk November 11, 2013)

Judging from this, it seems that there are also indexical links between fronted /s/, gayness, and specific job types placing these speakers in the "creative class" (Florida 2002), and thereby ascribing a high degree of cultural capital to them (Bourdieu 1984). Therefore, it could be expected that perceptions of speakers' gayness would be related to perceptions of class belonging (Barrett & Pollack 2005).

This is one part of the indexicality of the use of fronted /s/. On the other hand, recent studies in Copenhagen show that fronted /s/ is also used by young male speakers who are not stereotypically seen as gay (Maegaard 2007; Stæhr 2010). Quite the contrary, they are usually associated with a type of street-wise, tough, heterosexual masculinity. These speakers use features from the so-called street language (Madsen et al. 2010). They also use fronted /s/ which has not been described by linguists as part of the "street" register, but which might be a "street" feature. The fronted /s/ has been identified in studies of the actual speech of Copenhagen youth (Maegaard 2007; Stæhr 2010), and additionally it has been found in popular culture where fronted /s/ is used in parodies of persona types like "tough immigrant boy." This is seen for instance in the 2005 film *Terkel i knibe* by Anders Matthesen, where the character Zaki uses fronted /s/. This evidence indicates that for certain types of male speakers, the use of fronted /s/ does not index gayness or femininity but contributes to constructions of another kind of masculinity where heterosexuality and toughness play a prominent role. However, an association between these boys and use of fronted /s/ is less established in public discourse and awareness.

Pharao et al. (2014) examined the indexicality of the different registers, so-called street and modern Copenhagen, with alveolar versus fronted /s/. In this chapter, we will not be focusing on the indexicalities of /s/ in the two registers but on stereotypical perceptions of speakers as gay or straight, and of minority or majority background. We use the data from the /s/ experiment, because they are well suited for examining correlations between different social attributes based on linguistic variation and thus for looking at quantitative results within an intersectional frame.

EXPERIMENTAL DESIGN

We asked 234 high school students in two schools in Copenhagen to rate eight different sound clips (mean duration 7.6 seconds) produced by four different fifteen-year-old male speakers. High school students were chosen as respondents due to their age. "Street language" is used predominantly by young speakers, and so listeners of this age would presumably have more experience with this type of speech from their daily lives. Two of the speakers spoke "modern" Copenhagen, while the other two spoke "street" Copenhagen.

A number of sociolinguistic studies (Quist 2000, 2008; Maegaard 2007; Madsen 2008; Møller 2009; Ag 2010; Hansen & Pharao 2010; Madsen, Møller, & Jørgensen 2010; Stæhr 2010; Møller & Jørgensen 2011) have described the linguistic features associated with "street." Our stimulus samples include only one characteristic feature of "street," namely, a prosodic pattern that has previously been identified as sufficient for listeners to categorize speech as "street" (see Hansen & Pharao 2010; Pharao et al. 2014 for descriptions of this pattern). Several sociolinguistic studies (e.g., Maegaard 2005; Kristiansen 2009; Møller 2009) have also described the "modern" register, and in this particular study it only differs from the "street" register with respect to the presence absence of the prosodic pattern.

Each speaker was represented by two clips, one containing only alveolar variants of /s/, the other containing only dental variants of /s/. The clips were identical, except for the two different manifestations of /s/, which were spliced into the original (see Pharao et al. 2014 for more details on the method). Example (4) presents a transcript of a speech sample, with occurrences of /s/ marked in bold and underlined.

(4)   så kommer der sådan en vej der går opad og kører ud i den dér sø den hedder Stakitvej øh og når så der er også sådan en øhm sort prik det er en scooterbutik

'then there is a road that goes up there and into the lake that's called Fence road eh and then when there's also kind of ehrm a black spot that's a scooter shop'

Listeners rated each clip on eight personality scales. The selection of scales was based on a prestudy of evaluations of the same speech samples (cf. Pharao et al. 2014). The scales included *confused, intelligent, homosexual, feminine, immigrant, gangster, Nordsjælland* (Northern Zealand, affluent suburbs of Copenhagen), *Vestegnen* (the western area, poorer suburbs of Copenhagen). We use 5-point Likert scales, and listeners responded to questions of the following type: "Does this person seem to you to be [e.g. intelligent]?" Scales ranged from 1 = "no, not at all" to 5 = "yes, very much."

Results

As reported by Pharao et al. (2014), the average ratings on some of these scales were quite similar for the different combinations of register (i.e., "modern" or "street") and /s/-quality (i.e., alveolar or dental). Notably, "modern" clips with dental /s/ were rated highly on both the "homosexual" and the "feminine" scale, whereas all "street" clips were rated highly on both the "immigrant" and "gangster" scales (see Figure 5.1a through 5.1d). The names of the scales are given on the y axes and are shown in the order they appeared on the questionnaire. The mean rating on each of the eight scales is shown with "s" marking the mean rating for the guise containing alveolar /s/ and "s+" marking the mean rating for the guise containing fronted /s/. The longer the line between the two variants, the larger the difference in evaluation.

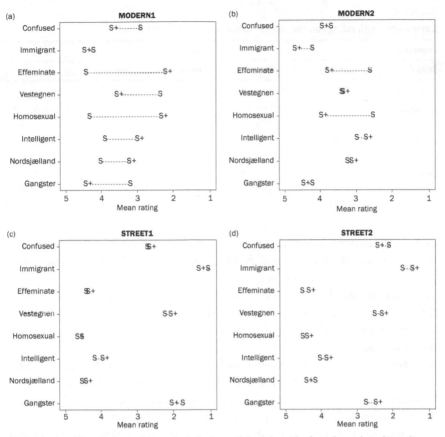

FIGURE 5.1A–D Mean ratings of the guises. Ratings of the [s] and [s+] versions plotted together (reproduced from Pharao et al. 2014: 16)

The plots in Figure 5.1a through 5.1d show a number of similarities and differences in the ratings of the different voices. The major points for us in this chapter are the following: (1) variation in /s/ quality has a large effect on the ratings of the "modern" voices, especially on the scales *feminine* and *homosexual,* and (2) variation in /s/ quality has no or very limited effect on the ratings of the "street" voices.

To provide a quantitative analysis of the possible intersection of the evaluated personality traits, we decided to test whether the correlations between the ratings on the different scales were statistically significant and if so whether they were positive and how large the correlation was. Tests were conducted using Pearson's product moment analysis run in R 3.0.3. We are concerned here with the intersection of sexual orientation and other background factors as well as the intersection of ethnicity and other social factors. Furthermore we are interested in the relationship between the two, since the traits "immigrant" and "homosexual" were the scales on which the two registers differ the most

TABLE 5.1

Correlations with ratings on the scales "homosexual" and "immigrant"

Homosexual			Immigrant		
Scale	Pearson's r	p	Scale	Pearson's r	p
Feminine	0.83	< 0.0001 ***	Gangster	0.67	< 0.0001 ***
Nordsjælland	0.37	< 0.0001 ***	Vestegn	0.39	< 0.0001 ***
Intelligent	0.27	< 0.0001 ***	Confused	0.36	< 0.0001 ***
Gangster	−0.44	< 0.0001 ***	Homosexual	−0.42	< 0.0001 ***
Immigrant	−0.42	< 0.0001 ***	Nordsjælland	−0.41	< 0.0001 ***
Vestegn	−0.32	< 0.0001 ***	Intelligent	−0.39	< 0.0001 ***
Confused	−0.19	< 0.0001 ***	Feminine	−0.38	< 0.0001 ***

in the ratings overall. We have therefore analyzed the data using simple correlation, rather than any type of factor analysis, where the object is to reduce predictors in the dataset on the basis of responses. While such a test could also yield insight into the connections between the different scales used, correlations simply examine the relation between the scales, and in this way links the analyses to the overall theory of intersectionality. Thus, Table 5.1 shows the statistics for the correlation of the two scales "homosexuality" and "immigrant" with the remaining seven scales. Positive correlations are listed first, ordered by effect size, then negative correlations, also ordered by effect size. As can be seen, all of the scales were significantly correlated. Not all of the correlations are equally strong. It is worth noting that "homosexual" and "immigrant" each have one scale with which they have a strong positive correlation, namely, "feminine" and "gangster," respectively. Both also have positive correlations with one of the two scales based on place names, and which we interpret as associated with social class. However, these correlations are not as strong, suggesting that the intersection of sexuality and gender is stronger than the intersection of sexuality and class and that the intersection of ethnicity and class is not as strong as that of ethnicity and toughness.

As can be seen from Table 5.1, there is a clear divide between the eight scales: *homosexual* has a positive correlation with *feminine, Nordsjælland*, and *intelligent*, but negative correlations with *gangster, immigrant, Vestegn*, and *confused*. Unsurprisingly, the opposite pattern is true for the scale *immigrant*. Here, *gangster, Vestegnen*, and *confused* show positive correlations, whereas *homosexual, Nordsjælland, intelligent*, and *feminine* show negative correlations. These correlations obtain when we look at the entire dataset. We have also looked at the correlations in subsets of the data, to examine to what extent they obtain when we only look at reactions to specific combinations of linguistic features. When we focus on the subset of responses to guises with modern prosody and [s+], the correlations between *homosexual* and *confused* and between *homosexual* and *intelligent* are no longer statistically significant.

Looking at responses to the modern guises with standard [s], the correlations between *homosexual* and *confused* and *immigrant* are no longer significant. The other factors remain significantly correlated and with the same valence as previously (although sometimes with diminished degrees of correlation). The trait *confused* then does not appear to be associated with modern prosody in any way. We discuss the loss of significant correlations for *intelligent* and *immigrant* as a function of /s/-quality below.

Turning to correlations in responses to the guises with street prosody, we look first at changes in the correlations between *immigrant* and the other seven factors in the subset of data concerning street guises with [s+]. Both *confused* and *Nordsjælland* turn out not to be significantly correlated with *immigrant*, whereas the remaining correlations are still significant (again with somewhat diminished degrees of correlation). When we look at responses to the street guises with standard [s], we once more find that *confused* is no longer correlated with *immigrant*, and the same is true for *intelligent*. More surprisingly, the (negative) correlations with *homosexual* and *feminine* also turn out not to be statistically significant. As before, we may conclude that *confused* is not strongly associated with street prosody either, and that /s/-quality is not so clearly associated with gender and sexual orientation as we might have expected from previous analyses, at least not when moderated by street prosody. In the following we will go through these results by first discussing the correlations with the scale *homosexual*, and then discussing the correlations with the scale *immigrant*.

CORRELATIONS WITH *HOMOSEXUAL*

The strongest correlation in the set is between *homosexual* and *feminine*, supporting the interpretation that /s/-fronting is stereotypically associated with a particular kind of gayness, namely, the effeminate gay man. This intersection of (homo)sexuality and gender is well known (e.g., LaMar & Kite 1998; Levon 2014). Furthermore, we find positive correlations with place and intelligence for the scale *homosexual*.

The correlation with the place *Nordsjælland* may be linked to the stereotype reported in the quote in example (3), where class belonging is implied. Northern Zealand is where the posh suburbs of Copenhagen are, and also where celebrities and wealthy people supposedly live. This assumed connection between gayness, creativeness, and prosperity is perhaps not well established as statistical evidence, but it is found in discourse at different levels. It is, for instance, communicated by some of the major international companies, both globally and in Denmark. Organizations such as Microsoft, IKEA, and Mærsk all claim that gay employees are a creative resource, and that gay clients and customers constitute a well-funded market, since it is claimed that gay men earn 20% more than straight men, and that they are first movers when

it comes to consumption (Tholl 2010). These organizations organize conferences with the theme of how to improve profit by employing gay staff or target-
ing your marketing activities toward gay consumers (Microsoft 2010). Thus,
the correlation between gayness and class is not surprising, and it is found in
potentially quite influential agents in society, such as international companies.
The term *pink money* is also linked to this view of the gay community as constituting a valuable market.

Valocchi (1999) argues that this focus on consumption developed in the
1990s, and that it reinforced a class bias that was already visible up through
the twentieth century. The shift from gay identity as a political category to a
lifestyle category further consolidated the invisibility of working-class gays in
the gay community. Valocchi's argument rests on both ideology and economy,
and while he stresses the importance of the economic aspect, other scholars, such as Barrett & Pollack (2005), argue that ideological aspects have had
major influence in consolidating this class bias. In any case, the relationship
between sexuality and class is well established as an ideological relationship
where working-class gays are practically invisible. We will get back to this
issue in our discussion of the correlations with the *immigrant* scale, where
we see a similar link between class and sexuality. Ideologically, then, there is
plenty of evidence that a link between gayness and (higher) social class exists
(Valocchi 1999; Barrett 2000; Barrett & Pollack 2005). This way, the perceived
link between gayness, femininity, and upper class is perhaps to be expected
from the respondents in our study as well.

The last positively correlated trait, intelligence, is more surprising. Recall,
however, that this correlation did not obtain for the modern guises with [s+].
In popular discourse, as in examples (1)–(3), the use of [s+] is typically associated with stupidity, ignorance, and simple-mindedness. The fact that the scale
intelligence does not correlate with the scale homosexuality in the modern
[s+] guises does not directly indicate an association with low intelligence
(since we would have then expected a significant but negative correlation).
However, the result does suggest that the presence of fronted /s/ can attenuate
the association between class and competence, and in that sense it is unexpected to find correlations between [s+] and (high) intelligence (in one of
the "modern" speakers). On the other hand, this perceived relation may be
based on the social meanings described earlier. If a person is viewed as higher
class, the person is probably also perceived to have a higher level of education. It is known from many perception studies that traits such as intelligent,
well-educated, articulate, and upper class go together to form a dimension
typically termed *superiority* (Zahn & Hopper 1985). In that sense, it should be
expected that intelligence and upper class are connected.

Just as interesting are the (significant) negative correlations for *homosexual*: while not particularly strong for *confused*, the remaining scales show that
homosexuality is not associated with immigrants, with the western suburbs of

Vestegnen, or with males projecting a gangster-like persona. We will get back to this in our later discussion of homonationalism.

CORRELATIONS WITH *IMMIGRANT*

None of the positive correlations for *immigrant* are as strong as that between *homosexual* and *feminine*, but there is clearly a strong correlation between *immigrant* and being perceived as a "gangster." Also, the correlations with perceptions of place and "cognitive competence" are stronger for *gangster* than *homosexual*: the association of immigrant background with Vestegnen and being confused are (somewhat) stronger than those between *homosexuality* and *Nordsjælland* and *intelligent*. The negative correlations for *immigrant* are all quite strong and as strong or stronger than the negative correlations for the homosexuality scale. Furthermore, intelligence is more strongly negatively correlated with the *immigrant* scale ($r = -0.39$) than it was positively correlated with the *homosexual* scale ($r = 0.27$). That is, while there is a tendency for speakers who have been rated as gay-sounding to be rated more intelligent, there is an even stronger tendency for speakers who have been rated as sounding like immigrants to be rated as less intelligent, in particular when they have [s+] as seen from the lack of a statistically significant correlation between *immigrant* and *intelligent* for the street guises with standard (s). This suggests that the gay stereotype and the immigrant stereotype are not just mirror images in the perceptions of Danish adolescents but rather different stereotypes in which different categories are important. In this sense, it is not only a question of *either/or*, but rather of *more or less*, since the speakers are perceived as having certain characteristics to different degrees. It also suggests that the *immigrant stereotype* is in a sense a stronger stereotype than the *gay stereotype* since the correlations are stronger. This can be interpreted as implying that there is more agreement in the categorization of the perceived immigrant speakers than in the categorization of the perceived gay speakers. Some social psychologists argue that probability is a good measure for comparing strengths of association (Schneider 2004). In our case we interpret the correlations as measures that tell us how strongly correlated one characteristic is to another in listeners' perceptions, and thus how strong the stereotype in question is.

Several of the scales that are (positively or negatively) correlated with *immigrant* can be interpreted as related to class. This is the case with both *gangster* and *Vestegnen*, and it is the case with *Nordsjælland* and *intelligent* as argued previously. Being a gangster is about being independent, streetwise, tough, a gang member, and a criminal. Being gangster-like (or gangsta-like) is also related to rap and hip-hop culture, and thus again related to understandings of ethnicity and perhaps class.

The ascription of the speakers to the western suburbs of Copenhagen, Vestegnen, is a class categorization just as was the case with Nordsjælland.

Vestegnen is where the poorer suburbs are, and where more families of so-called non-western minority background live (Danmarks Statistik 2013). Consequently, when respondents ascribe the speakers to these areas, the categorizations can be seen as either a categorization of class or ethnicity, or—more likely—as both. As Madsen (2013) has argued, "street language" has been analyzed by Danish sociolinguists as primarily linked to ethnicity, while it can in fact be seen to be just as strongly linked to class. As Madsen (2013) states: "linguistic signs that used to be seen as related to migration—identified as ethnic minority rather than majority on an insider/outsider dimension of comparison—are now related to status on a high/low dimension as well" (135). This corresponds perfectly to our results that show that speakers of "street language" are perceived as both lower class and of minority background.

HOMONATIONALISM?

Finally, we will focus on the categorizations of sexuality and gender. As can be seen from Table 5.1, *immigrant* either correlates negatively with *feminine* and *homosexual* (or not at all, as was the case with street guises with standard [s]). This means that speakers judged as immigrants are perceived to be neither gay nor feminine. This corresponds to the social meanings that we know from other studies of "street language" (Stæhr 2010; Madsen 2013), where speakers of "street language" are associated with a specific type of heterosexual, tough, streetwise masculinity. This is again linked to the previous discussions of gayness, femininity, and upper class, where this is more or less the reverse picture.

The perceived relationship between non-Danish minority background and non-homosexuality can be interpreted within the frame of *homonationalism*, which is Puar's notion of homonormative nationalism (Puar 2007). Seen in this perspective, sexuality should be understood through the nation, since both hetero- and queer sexualities are produced by heteronormative and homonormative practices of disciplining that are fostered by nations. In this way, the nation also produces nonheterosexual sexualities which it disciplines and normalizes (Puar 2007). This in turn strengthens the nation in at least three ways: (1) it establishes a homonormativity that strengthens heterosexual institutions, (2) it creates a homosexual consumer segment that polices non-normative sexualities, and (3) it enables a transnational discourse of western modernity and superiority, while producing discourses of racialized and pathological non-western nationalities (Puar 2007). While this queer perspective on the categorizations in our study is different from some of the other arguments we have presented in this chapter, in fact it resembles some of the earlier arguments we have cited. Valocchi's focus on the development of a white gay middle-class consumer segment during the 1990s is an argument that can be seen in this perspective too. Puar interprets this development within the frame of homonormativity (Duggan 2003), and this stresses certain parts of the pattern. According to Duggan (2003), homonormativity can be defined as:

> a politics that does not contest dominant heteronormative assumptions and institutions, but upholds and sustains them, while promising the possibility of a demobilized gay constituency and a privatized, depoliticized gay culture anchored in domesticity and consumption. (179)

In this way, Duggan's perspective offers a critique of the normalizing project of the LGBT (lesbian/gay/bisexual/transgender) community, where certain gay identities are embraced and normalized, whereas other sexual identities are excluded and othered. This argument is brought even further by Puar, who argues that by including gay sexualities in a normative white nationalist discourse, discourses of exclusion of the nonwhite are simultaneously established. This means that by "normalizing" gay relationships through institutions like marriage (Warner 1999), distance and difference are simultaneously created between gayness and the racial "other." This is further elaborated and exemplified below.

Discourses of this type of exclusion in Denmark emerge in many ways. Danish media often run headlines stating, for example, that 'Immigrants attack gays' (*Indvandrere overfalder bøsser*, Information 2001), 'Immigrants are most often behind homoharassment' (*Indvandrere står oftest bag homochikane*, Politiken 2009), 'Homosexuals: immigrants are most often behind hate crimes' (*Homoseksuelle: indvandrere står oftest bag hadforbrydelser*, Jyllandsposten 2013). Headlines like these reproduce discourses of the violent, primitive, sexually restricted, and thus less civilized non-Dane (see, for instance, Nebeling 2011). Danish critical theorists like Nebeling and Bissenbakker argue that this is the dominant discourses of sexuality of non-Danes in contemporary Denmark. The strong correlations we find in our data concerning perceived ethnicity and sexuality confirm this picture, even though the perspective, the methodology, and the analytic measures we use are untypical for a queer-theoretic study.

Discussion

Intersectionality theory emerged as a reaction to what was seen as insufficient accounts of membership and belonging in many feminist studies during the 1970s and 1980s. One of the problems was the very biased and one-sided view of what it means to belong to particular categories. As hooks (1981) remarks when commenting on the bias: "This suggest[s] that the term 'women' is synonymous with 'white women' and the term 'blacks' synonymous with 'black men'" (8). In a way, what the results of the study we report on in this chapter show is that to many young listeners in Denmark, it is actually the case that (stereotypically) all "gays" are "white" and all "immigrants" are "hetero." Furthermore, we have seen how these categories are linked to other categories, creating a fuller picture of the stereotypes. It was evident from the data that stereotypical perceptions of gay men include categorizations of class and ethnicity. Speakers perceived as "gay" are rated as both "feminine" and "upper class" and at the same time *not* gangster-like and *not* of immigrant background. Similarly, we found that speakers perceived as having immigrant background were at the same time perceived as gangster-like and *not* "feminine" and *not* "gay." This shows how different categories intersect in listeners' perceptions in very structured ways, and that categorizations of cultural background and ethnicity combine with categorizations of sexuality in a highly predictable fashion. It is clear from the previous analyses that perceptions of ethnicity and sexuality are to a large degree interconnected. Here, intersectionality becomes highly relevant as a theory providing a perspective that highlights the simultaneous categorization processes that take place when listeners react to the speech samples.

The study is based on variation of /s/-quality, and we have shown (in Pharao et al 2014) that in one register, "modern Copenhagen," this variation changes the perception of the speaker quite dramatically, whereas in the other register, "street language," it has no or little effect. One way of interpreting this is to conclude that the fronted /s/ is actually part of "street language," and that this is why it does not make any difference whether a speaker includes it or not in his speech, when the speech already has several other features characteristic of the "street language." Another interpretation would be that speakers perceived as "immigrants" are simultaneously, and very strongly, perceived as (a specific type of) heterosexual males, and that this categorization makes it very difficult to interpret the fronted /s/ as indexing (feminine) gender or (gay) sexuality. The correlation analyses have shown in a very clear way that different categorizations cluster together to form recognizable identities, and that this clustering is perhaps so influential that even signs that would typically point in another direction, toward other types of identities, are ignored in certain contexts.

References

Ag, Astrid. 2010. *Sprogbrug og identitetsarbejde hos senmoderne storbypiger*. Copenhagen Studies in Bilingualism, Vol. 53. Copenhagen: University of Copenhagen.

Allport, Gordon W. 1954. *The nature of prejudice*. Reading, MA: Addison-Wesley.

Barrett, Donald C. 2000. Masculinity among working class gay men. In Peter Nardi (ed.), *Gay masculinities*, 176–205. Thousand Oaks, CA: Sage.

Barrett, Donald C. & Lance M. Pollack. 2005. Whose gay community? Social class, sexual self-expression, and gay community involvement. *The Sociological Quarterly* 46. 437–456.

Bourdieu, Pierre. 1984. *Distinction: A social critique of the judgement of taste*. London: Routledge.

Brigham, John C. 1971. Ethnic stereotypes. *Psychological Bulletin* 41. 15–38.

Cameron, Deborah & Don Kulick. 2003. *Language and sexuality*. Cambridge: Cambridge University Press.

Crenshaw, Kimberlé. 1989. Demarginalizing the intersection of race and sex: A black feminist critique of antidiscrimination doctrine, feminist theory and antiracist politics. *The University of Chicago Legal Forum*. 139–167.

Danmarks Statistik. 2013. *Indvandrere i Danmark*. Copenhagen: Danmarks Statistik.

Deleuze, Gilles & Félix Guattari. 1987. *A thousand plateaus: Capitalism and schizophrenia*. Minneapolis: University of Minnesota Press.

Duggan, Lisa. 2003. *The twilight of equality? Neoliberalism, cultural politics, and the attack on democracy*. Boston: Beacon Press.

Florida, Richard. 2002. *The rise of the creative class: And how it's transforming work, leisure, community and everyday life*. New York: Perseus Book Group.

Hansen, Gert Foget & Nicolai Pharao. 2010. Prosody in the Copenhagen multiethnolect. In Pia Quist & Bente Ailin Svendsen (eds.), *Multilingual urban Scandinavia. New linguistic practices*, 79–95. Bristol, UK: Multilingual Matters.

Hogg, Michael & Dominic Abrams. 1988. *A social psychology of intergroup relations and group processes*. London: Routledge.

hooks, bell. 1981. *Ain't I a woman?: Black women and feminism*. Boston: South End Press.

Tholl, Sophie. 2010, September 9. Bøsser giver resultat på bundlinjen ('Gays pay off on bottom line'). *Information*, retrieved from http://www.information.dk/245302.

Jones, James M. 1997. *Prejudice and racism*, 2nd edn. New York: McGraw-Hill.

Kristiansen, Tore. 2009. The macro-level social meanings of late modern Danish Accents. *Acta Linguistica Hafniensia* 41. 167–192.

LaMar, Lisa & Mary Kite. 1998. Sex differences in attitudes toward gay men and lesbians: A multidimensional perspective. *Journal of Sex Research* 35(2). 189–196.

Levon, Erez. 2011. Teasing apart to bring together: Gender and sexuality in variationist research. *American Speech* 86(1). 69–84.

Levon, Erez. 2014. Categories, stereotypes and the linguistic perception of sexuality. *Language in Society* 43(5). 539–566.

Mackie, Marlene. 1973. Arriving at "truth" by definition: The case of stereotype inaccuracy. *Social Problems* 20. 431–447.

Madsen, Lian Malai. 2008. *Fighters and outsiders: Linguistic practices, social identities, and social relationships among urban youth in a martial arts club*. Copenhagen: University of Copenhagen PhD thesis.

Madsen, Lian Malai. 2013. "High" and "low" in urban Danish speech styles. *Language in Society* 42. 115–138.

Madsen, Lian Malai, Martha Sif Karrebæk, & Janus Spindler Møller. 2013. The Amager project: A study of language and social life among minority children and youth. *Working Papers in Urban Language and Literacies* 102. 1–25.

Madsen, Lian Malai, Janus Spindler Møller, & Jens Normann Jørgensen (eds.). 2010. *Ideological constructions and enregisterment of linguistic youth styles*. Copenhagen Studies in Bilingualism, Vol. 55. Copenhagen: University of Copenhagen.

Maegaard, Marie. 2005. Language attitudes, norm and gender. A presentation of the method and the results from a language attitudes study. *Acta Linguistica Hafniensia* 37. 55–80.

Maegaard, Marie. 2007. *Udtalevariation og -forandring i københavnsk: En etnografisk undersøgelse af sprogbrug, sociale kategorier og social praksis blandt unge på en københavnsk folkeskole.* Danske Talesprog, Vol. 8. Copenhagen: Reitzel.

McCall, Leslie. 2005. The complexity of intersectionality. *Signs* 30(3). 1771–1800.

Microsoft. 2010, September 17. *LGBT diversity as a strategic business advantage.* Conference in Microsoft Development Center Copenhagen.

Møller, Janus Spindler. 2009. Stereotyping categorisations of speech styles among linguistic minority Danes in Køge. In Marie Maegaard, Frans Gregersen, Pia Quist, & Jens Normann Jørgensen (eds.), *Language attitudes, standardization and language change,* 231–254. Oslo, Norway: Novus.

Møller, Janus Spindler & Jens Normann Jørgensen. 2011. Enregisterment among adolescents in superdiverse Copenhagen. In Janus Spindler Møller & Jens Normann Jørgensen (eds.), *Language enregisterment and attitudes. Copenhagen Studies in Bilingualism,* Vol. 63, 99–121. Copenhagen: University of Copenhagen.

Nebeling, Michael. 2011. ". . . med et regnbueflag i hånden": Fortællinger om homoseksuelle inklusioner og homonationalisme. *Lambda Nordica.* 41–68.

Pharao, Nicolai, Marie Maegaard, Janus Spindler Møller, & Tore Kristiansen. 2014. Indexical meanings of [s+] among Copenhagen youth: Social perception of a phonetic variant in different prosodic contexts. *Language in Society* 43(1). 1–31.

Puar, Jasbir. 2007. *Terrorist assemblages: Homonationalism in queer times.* London: Duke University Press.

Quist, Pia. 2000. Ny københavnsk "multietnolekt." Om sprogbrug blandt unge i sprogligt og kulturelt heterogene miljøer. *Danske Talesprog* 1. 143–212.

Quist, Pia. 2008. Sociolinguistic approaches to multiethnolect: Language variety and stylistic practice. *International Journal of Bilingualism* 12(1+2). 43–61.

Schneider, David J. 2004. *The psychology of stereotyping.* New York: Guilford Press.

Stæhr, Andreas. 2010. *"Rappen reddede os": Et studie af senmoderne storbydrenges identitetsarbejde i fritids- og skolemiljøer.* Copenhagen Studies in Bilingualism, Vol. 54. Copenhagen: University of Copenhagen.

Tajfel, Henri.1969. Cognitive aspects of prejudice. *Journal of Social Issues* 25. 79–97.

Valocchi, Steve. 1999. The class-inflected nature of gay identity. *Social Problems* 46. 207–224.

Warner, Michael. 1999. *The trouble with normal.* New York: Free Press.

Yuval-Davis, Nira 2011. *The politics of belonging: Intersectional contestations.* London: Sage.

Zahn, Christopher J. & Robert Hopper. 1985. Measuring language attitudes: The Speech Evaluation Instrument. *Journal of Language and Social Psychology* 4. 113–123.

6

Nonstandard Plural Noun Phrase Agreement as an Index of Masculinity

Ronald Beline Mendes

Introduction

In spoken Brazilian Portuguese (BP), nominal number agreement (NP) is optional (*esses remos* or *esses remo* 'these oars'), but the nonstandard variant—a nonredundant plural (NRP—with the plural morpheme /-s/ only on the first element of the NP)—is negatively evaluated (Scherre 1997; Naro & Scherre 2003) and is generally not expected in the speech of well-educated or upper-class speakers. However, in the following transcribed conversation, almost all plural NPs are in the nonstandard NRP form. The conversation—among three male graduate students (MS)—was overheard by the author in a sports center locker room at the University of São Paulo (USP). The variability in NP number agreement is illustrated with a bold-faced capital "-S" (the plural morpheme) or with a "-Ø" (its omission) at the end of the NP elements:

1 MS1   *Cara, esse-S remo-Ø de fibra de carbono não presta*
        'Man, these carbon fiber oars are terrible'

2 MS2   *Como assim? Tá louco? Cê que não sabe remar...*
        'What do you mean? Are you nuts? It's you who don't know how to row. . .'

3 MS3   *Ah é? Quem é que ficou pra trás naquela-S duas corrida-Ø?*
        'Oh really? Who got behind in those two races?'

4   *Bom... eu já falei que prefiro o-S remo-S de fibra ... ô D. você*
5   *tem dois sabonete-S aí? Me empresta um?*
        'Well, I've already said that I prefer fiber oars. . . hey D. (at MS2) do you have two soaps there? Can you lend me one?'

6　MS2　*Nossa, F.! VOCÊ... ME pedindo sabonete? Tá tudo bem? (risos).*

'Wow, F.! YOU asking ME for soap? Everything alright? (laughter)'

7　MS3　*Esqueci, ué.*

'Come on. . . I forgot it.'

8　MS1　*Véio, cês viram aquele-S cara-Ø da Poli na raia? Que bando de zé ruela!*

'Dude, did you see those guys from the Poly-technical School? Such idiots!

9　MS3　*Pô primeira aula deles... dá um desconto ... Pô M. tira essa-S*
10　　　*roupa-Ø suja-Ø de cima da minha toalha, caralho! Que porco!*

'Come on. . . it was their first class. . . cut them some slack. . . Hey, M. . . . take those dirty clothes away from my towel, damn' it! You're such a pig!'

It may not be surprising that NRP is frequent in such an interaction among three men who are native BP speakers: In addition to the casualness of the conversation and the informality of the situation, it is well-known in Brazilian sociolinguistics that men generally tend to favor NRP relative to women (for a comprehensive list of references, see Oushiro 2015). Nevertheless, a couple of questions arise in relation to the previous conversation:

(1) could these male speakers be signaling "we are guys" when using NRP?

(2) when a male speaker doesn't employ NRP—that is, when he employs the standard plural NP form (STA)—would he sound less manly in a certain interaction?

The first question comes to mind when we consider that, given the conversational venue, MS1, MS2, and MS3 are likely graduate students (thus highly educated) and they are likely to be at least upper middle class (they arrive at the sports center in their cars, they have their own oars, and other pricy designer equipment and sportswear). If their linguistic performance is not mirroring expected data distribution in terms of class and education, is it gender that is at play? The second question complements the first. Standard plural NP forms rarely appear in the conversation, and when they do, they occur in MS3's speech (e.g., in line 4: *o-S remo-S* 'the oars' and *dois sabonete-S* 'two soap bars'). The conversation indicates that MS3 presents himself as "less of a pig" (who doesn't mix clean towels with dirty sports clothing), that he is careful and not forgetful (for his rowing mates, it is surprising that he had to ask one of them for a spare bar of soap), and that he can adopt a stance (Podesva 2007; Jaffe 2009) of a caring person (he defends the newbie rowers when MS1 mocks them). However, he does employ NRP (e.g., lines 3 and 9), when he gets mad at MS1. Could that be correlated with his briefly letting go of his "tidier" and more "proper" style?

Inspired by these questions, this chapter discusses production and perception data of variable NP agreement in São Paulo Portuguese. After reviewing relevant facts about NP number agreement in BP, the production study looks briefly at gay-sounding men's use of NRP in relation to straight-sounding men's and to women's. The perception study is more extensive, as it focuses on the effect of variable plural NP agreement on the perception of male speakers in terms of perceived effeminacy, education, class, formality, intelligence, friendliness, and gayness. This chapter argues that NRP indirectly indexes (Ochs 1992) masculinity in São Paulo and introduces a discussion about how this case of indexicality may be differently perceived by men and women.

NP Number Agreement in BP

Nominal number agreement has been extensively studied in BP, especially from a quantitative sociolinguistics perspective (Braga 1977; Scherre 1988, 1996, 1997; Dias 1993; Naro & Scherre 2003; Antonino 2007; Brandão & Vieira 2012; Oushiro 2015—among many others). The nonstandard variant is generally categorized as a "grammar mistake" at school, so there is stigma associated with it. Nevertheless, it is ubiquitous all over Brazil. Scherre (1996) has shown that there are differences between overall frequencies of NRP across different speech communities in Brazil, but the social and linguistic constraints on its use are similar. Most research has pointed to the fact that the NRP form is favored at lower levels of education and in men's speech. In terms of speakers' age, apparent time analyses (Bailey et al. 1991) provide no evidence of a change in progress, as younger and older speakers show similar tendencies to employ NRP, while speakers in the intermediate age group tend to show relatively lower frequencies of the form. In addition, these studies show that linguistic factors can be very significant—more so than certain social factors, including speaker's sex. One example of such factors is the morphological class of the leftmost element in plural NPs (definite and indefinite articles, possessives, numerals, indefinite quantifiers, etc.).

In São Paulo, multivariate analyses by Oushiro (2015) yield results that are not very different from those obtained in other communities. The analysis of plural NPs extracted from a sample of 118 interviews with *Paulistanos*—those born and raised in the city of São Paulo—shows that speaker's sex is a significant factor group (though not as significant as linguistic factors or other social factors such as level of education or class).[1] In contrast, when the interviewees in Oushiro's sample were asked what they thought of when they heard *dois pastel* 'two fritters' (without the -*s* on the second word), they never once mentioned anything regarding gender/sexuality. Different to what is observed for other variables for which we asked similar questions (such as coda /r/), the speakers analyzed by Oushiro (2015) always had something to say about NRP. A word cloud based on the speakers' responses highlights ideas such as "*Paulistano*," "mistake," "less educated," "Italianate," and "ignorance," among others—but never ideas such as "butch" or "masculine" (as the conversation transcribed in the introduction might lead one to believe). In other words, sex/gender-related meanings do not seem to be readily referred to by *Paulistanos* when it comes to NRP.

However, in an earlier perception study focusing on gay-sounding men's speech, NP plural agreement was in fact mentioned as a linguistic cue. Following Gaudio (1994), Mendes (2011) played previously recorded readings of a short text by five different men to 106 participants.[2] The participants were asked to place the readings on a scale from 1 to 5, with 1 being the least gay-sounding reading and 5 the most gay-sounding. Of the 106 participants, 101 attributed the grades 4 or 5 to the same two readings. When they were asked to justify their assessment, some of the participants mentioned, among other linguistic cues, that "gay guys talk very correctly. . . . They don't seem to make so many mistakes." When asked what they meant by "mistakes," they talked mostly about number agreement and gave examples of two-word NPs. It is of crucial importance to mention that there was actually no variation in NP plural marking in the text read by the five men. This means that the perception that there is a relationship between sounding more or less "gay" and speaking "correctly" was not based on the readings but was, rather, triggered by them, and imagined from daily life.

The facts briefly reviewed previously can then be summarized as follows:

- Men tend to favor nonstandard NRP (across communities, including São Paulo), but the significance of speaker sex as a factor group is smaller than that of other social or linguistic factors, and sex/gender differentiation does not come up when *Paulistano* people are invited to talk about the social meanings of NRP.
- When directly asked about linguistic cues for what makes men sound "gay," listeners mention correctness of grammar and freely comment on NP number agreement—regardless of the fact that the stimuli (five readings of a same text) included no instance of nonstandard NRP.

Together, these facts illustrate the need to (1) check whether a production analysis that includes sexuality (rather than sex) yields different results from those reviewed previously, and (2) test whether male speakers are perceived differently depending on their use of standard or nonstandard NP number agreement. Combined with the results in Mendes (2011), the metapragmatic discourse on NRP (as among the *Paulistanos* sampled in Oushiro 2015) suggests an indirect relationship between variable NP number agreement—"talking (in)correctly"—and ideas of effeminacy and masculinity in male speech. What we want to discuss then is the following: Would an effeminate, gay-sounding man be perceived as less effeminate if he used the nonstandard NRP form? And would a masculine, straight-sounding man be perceived as more effeminate (less masculine) if he used the standard NP plural marking (STA)?

Sexuality in NRP Production

In order to investigate whether there is a correlation between sexuality and variable NP number agreement in linguistic production, I analyzed the distribution of NRP in thirty-six sociolinguistic interviews with informants born and raised in the city of São Paulo: twelve masculine-sounding straight men, twelve effeminate-sounding gay men, and twelve women—stratified by three age groups (twenty-five to thirty-five years old, thirty-six to forty-five years old, and forty-six or older) and two levels of education (high school and college).

The interviews with the women and the masculine-sounding straight men are part of a larger sample recorded by different members of the Study Group in Sociolinguistics at USP in 2009 and 2010. The twelve effeminate-sounding gay men were all recorded by me in 2010. Although all thirty-six interviews followed the same general script (one hourlong conversation about similar topics), it is possible that the interviews with the gay men were somewhat more casual than the others, considering that the interviewer and the participants were either friends or acquaintances (as compared to the other twenty-four interviewees and their respective interviewers). We selected all twelve gay men from my social network as sounding particularly effeminate (not just in my own opinion but in the opinion of other friends), but we didn't inform any of them about the linguistic purposes of the interviews. We told all thirty-six informants that they were participating in a research project about the city of São Paulo.

From that sample, we extracted only two-word NPs (such as *os remos* 'the oars' and *aqueles cara* 'those guys,' in the conversation transcribed in the section "Introduction"). In NPs with more elements (e.g., *essas roupa suja* 'these dirty clothes') (cf. line 9 in the transcription), there are more than two ways of marking the plural—*-s* in all of the elements; *-s* in the first, but not in the other two; and *-s* in the first and in one of the other two. In addition, two-word NPs are much more frequent.[3] For our present purposes, the inclusion of three-word or longer NPs would unnecessarily complicate the quantitative analysis.

The relative weights in Table 6.1 are obtained from multivariate analyses (in Goldvarb) and indicate the differentiation between factors in a group, in terms of data distribution. The analysis included not only other social factor groups (such as which neighborhood in the city the informant lived the

TABLE 6.1
NRP distribution and weights (36 interviews)

	Factor Groups	NRP/Total 568/4,693	NRP% 12	Weight	Range
Sexuality	Masc. Straight Men	409/1,382	30	.83	
	Women	115/1,569	7.3	.48	60
	Effem. Gay Men	44/1,742	2.5	.23	
Education	High School	381/2,246	17	.63	40
	College	187/2,447	7.6	.38	
Age	25–35	151/1,522	10	.43	
	36–45	187/1,490	12.6	.52	11
	46+	230/1,681	13.7	.54	
Phonetic	casa-s, mão-s, etc.	528/3,985	13	.54	24
Salience	other (cor-es, etc.)	40/708	5.6	.30	

Input: 0.068; significance: 0.004

longest, and whether their parents were from the city of São Paulo or other places in Brazil) but also a number of linguistic factors (such as the phonetic salience between the singular and the plural forms; the morphological nature of the element to the left of the NP).

Sexuality was the first factor group selected as significant in the analysis, presenting a range that is even wider than that for level of education. In relation to the masculine-sounding straight men in the sample, women employ NRP more infrequently and the effeminate-sounding gay men even more infrequently. Considering that the interviews with gay men are likely more casual than the others, it is striking how much they avoid NRP (only forty-four tokens, in a total of 1,742 plural NPs). This differs from a great many studies of various speech communities in Brazil, in which linguistic factors are more significant and education is usually the first social factor group selected as significant in multivariate analyses, whereas sex/gender does not always appear among the significant factor groups.

Here, the only linguistic factor group selected as significant is the salience of the difference between plural and singular forms. As is evident in Table 6.1, there is a great difference in the data distribution between regular plurals, which are morphologically simpler (those formed with the mere addition of -s to the singular, such as *remo/remos* 'oars,' *casa/casas* 'houses,' *mão/mãos* 'hands') and irregular forms (*pão/p-ães, cor/cor-es, vez/vez-es,* etc.). Regular plurals are much more prevalent in this sample (as in any sample of spoken Portuguese) than irregular ones, and NRP is much more frequent in the morphologically simpler cases, relative to the others.

By no means should these results be taken to be deterministic—as in "gay men use NRP less frequently *because* they are gay." Instead, even though the sample analyzed here is not very large, the distribution leads us to an intriguing question: Why do effeminate-sounding gay men use NRP so infrequently (more infrequently than women)? Similarly: Why do the masculine-sounding straight men in the sample use NRP more frequently in their interviews? The distributional pattern itself might be an indication that NRP does in fact function as an index of sex/gender differentiation, but these results do not actually say much about how men (effeminate or masculine) operate with variable NP plural marking in the construction of gender-based styles. These results then require us to think about what social meanings NRP carries, and that is what the following perception study helps us to determine.

Perceptions of Male Speech

As a follow-up to the findings in Mendes (2011), Oushiro (2015) and the distributional patterns shown in Table 6.1, I address the relationship between the various social meanings of NRP. As established earlier, two perception questions are of special interest: Would an effeminate, gay-sounding man be perceived as less effeminate if he used the nonstandard NRP form, and would a masculine-sounding straight man be perceived as less masculine if he used the standard NP plural marking (STA)? Based on these questions and on perception work by Campbell-Kibler (2006, 2008), we designed a matched-guise perception experiment with excerpts from sociolinguistic interviews with two effeminate-sounding men (Jaime and Lucas) and two masculine-sounding men (Carlos and Robson), all in their late twenties or early thirties. Jaime and Carlos went to college, while Lucas and Robson did not (so there is a difference of both class and level of education between both the effeminate and the masculine speakers). "Gay marriage" is among the scripted conversation topics and all four men mention their sexual orientation during their respective interviews. These four interviews are part of a sample of current *Paulistano* Portuguese, collected at USP.[4] According to the researchers involved in the project, among all the men in this sample, Lucas sounds particularly effeminate (more than Jaime), while Robson sounds very masculine (more than Carlos).

We extracted two short passages (ten seconds on average) with at least three occurrences of plural NPs from each of these four interviews (all from conversational topics other than gay marriage). All plural NPs were originally in the standard STA form in the selected excerpts. We then digitally manipulated them in Praat (Boersma & Weenink 2014), in order to create alternative nonstandard NRP versions of each, with the removal of the right NP element final [s]. All target tokens are two-word regular plural NPs which, as Table 6.1 shows, are the most productive in Portuguese. The relevant NPs are indicated in the following transcriptions of every excerpt, with bold-faced (s/ø) added to the rightmost element of every underlined plural NP (the English translations are literal for the plural NPs).

(1) Jaime

a. family habits
bom a minha família assim eu meu pai e minha irmã ... e minha
sobrinha meu cunhado ... isso a gente se encontra sempre eu faço todas
as refeições com <u>meus pai</u>(s/ø) porque eles moram aqui do lado eu não
tenho nem fogão não sei cozinhar ... eh e assim dias <u>dos pai</u>(s/ø) dia
<u>das mãe</u>(s/ø) Natal <u>essas coisa</u>(s/ø) a gente sempre está junto mesmo ...

'well my family like me my father and my sister ... and my niece my
brother-in-law ... yes we always get together I have all meals with
<u>my parents</u> because they live right beside me and I don't have a cook
I don't know how to cook ... um and like <u>Father's Day</u> <u>Mother's Day</u>
Christmas <u>these things</u> we really are always together'

b. childhood and friends
é o que falo até com <u>meus amigo</u>(s/ø) a gente é de uma geração muito
privilegiada porque a gente viveu ... o analógico e agora o digital ...
pra lembrar <u>as brincadeira</u>(s/ø) que não tinha internet não tinha com-
putador não tinha nada e agora a gente vive plenamente a questão de
do da informática ... então é uma/ eu acho bem legal assim a gente
viu os <u>dois mundo</u>(s/ø) e é e é bem louco porque foi uma mudança
muito rápida né ...

'it's what I tell <u>my friends</u> we are from a very lucky generation because
we've lived ... the analog and now the digital ... to remember <u>the</u>
<u>games</u> because there was no internet no computer nothing and now
we live completely with information technology ... so it's a/ I think
it's very nice like we've seen <u>two worlds</u> and it's very crazy because it's
been a quite fast change, right ...'

(2) Lucas

a. São Paulo neighborhoods
às vezes eu vou <u>nos bairro</u>(s/ø) assim <u>nas casa</u>(s/ø) de <u>amigos</u>
<u>meu</u>(s/ø) que são em bairros tanto de zona Leste quanto a zona
Sul enfim qualquer ... zona co/ eu conheço muita gente assim por
São Paulo inteiro entendeu conheço ... bastante São Paulo todas <u>as</u>
<u>zonas</u>(s/ø) ... e e aí eu chego às vezes <u>naqueles bairro</u>(s/ø) que são
tudo casas assim que você vê que não é aquela realmente aquele essa
muvuca que tem no Centro meu eu falo "ai que delícia" né ...

'sometimes I go to <u>the neighborhoods</u> like <u>the homes</u> of <u>my friends</u>
that are in the East zone as well as in the South zone ... anyway ... any
zone ... I know a lot of people all over São Paulo you know ... I do
... all <u>the zones</u> of São Paulo ... and sometimes like I arrive in <u>those</u>

<u>neighborhoods</u> that are like all houses so you see it's really not like that mess you see in Central São Paulo and I go "ah, that's so nice" right . . .'

b. São Paulo's public transport system
você perde no mínimo <u>duas hora</u>(**s/ø**) do seu dia . . . assim isso eu estou falando o mínimo . . . porque no meu trabalho tinha pessoas que acordavam <u>quatro hora</u>(**s/ø**) da manhã pra estar no trabalho às oito . . . então perdem <u>duas hora</u>(**s/ø**) pra ir <u>duas hora</u>(**s/ø**) pra voltar se você multiplicar isso no dia já são <u>quatro hora</u>(**s/ø**) . . . se você multiplicar isso vezes <u>cinco dia</u>(**s/ø**) da semana s/ quatro vezes cinco vinte já são eh <u>vinte hora</u>(**s/ø**) . . .

'you spend at least <u>two hours</u> of your day . . . yes I mean as the minimum . . . because at my work there were people that would wake up at <u>four hours</u> in the morning so that they could be at work by eight . . . so it takes them <u>two hours</u> to go <u>two hours</u> to come back home which makes four hours a day . . . if you multiply that by <u>five days</u> a week four times five is already <u>twenty hours</u>'

(3)   Carlos

a. friends
os <u>meus amigo</u>(**s/ø**) do outro prédio nem tenho tanto convívio mais al/ <u>alguns pouco</u>(**s/ø**) de vez em quando ao telefone às vezes quando . . . eu faço alguma coisa aqui em casa eu chamo eles vêm mas os <u>meus amigo</u>(**s/ø**) mesmo são <u>os amigo</u>(**s/ø**) do colégio né que também são (xxx) . . . até por causa da escola né o pessoal acaba escolhendo <u>escolas próxima</u>(**s/ø**) né então o pessoal mora tudo na região também . . .

'<u>my friends</u> in the other building I don't see so frequently anymore <u>some few</u> sometimes on the phone when . . . I do something here at home I call them but <u>my friends</u> are really <u>the friends</u> from my high school time that are also (xxx) . . . because of the school you end up picking <u>nearby schools</u> right, so all of us live in the same region . . .'

b. social events
o pessoal costuma fazer <u>alguns evento</u>(**s/ø**) (por exemplo) tem festa junina tem . . . eh almoço do dia <u>das mãe</u>(**s/ø**) almoço do dia <u>dos pai</u>(**s/ø**) então . . . até porque tem um restaurante aqui então eles costumam promover <u>esses evento</u>(**s/ø**) até pra . . . pra lógico pra eles é interessante porque pra comercialmente também . . . mas até pra . . . promover essa integração entre <u>os condômino</u>(**s/ø**) assim então aqui costuma ter mais

'people usually organize <u>some events</u> (for example) there's the June party there's . . . um the lunch for the day of <u>the mothers</u> the lunch for

the day of <u>the fathers</u> so . . . because there's a restaurant here and they
usually organize <u>these events</u> . . . but also in order to motivate the integration among <u>the tenants</u> so here there's usually more (of such events)'

(4)   Robson

a. leisure
<u>os cara</u>(**s/ø**) tem lá o centro de treinamento tipo . . . uma rampona
de madeira . . . <u>uns esqui</u>(**s/ø**) <u>uns capacete</u>(**s/ø**) e tal o cara desce a
rampona e cai num monte de esponja faz <u>umas manobra</u>(**s/ø**) <u>umas
coisa</u>(**s/ø**) simples de fazer

'<u>the guys</u> have there the training center . . . like a big wooden ramp
. . . <u>a few skis</u> <u>a few helmets</u> and such the guy comes down the ramp
and falls onto a sponge mass and does <u>some moves</u> <u>some things</u> very
simple to do'

b. economy
eu tenho que pagar <u>minhas conta</u>(**s/ø**) e quem está me ajudando são/ o
meu pai de set/ que fez <u>setenta ano</u>(**s/ø**) ontem . . . e eu já fui um cara que
tive empresa <u>cinco funcionário</u>(**s/ø**) pagava tudo pros <u>meus amigo</u>(**s/ø**)
não tinha . . . eh um cara independente tinha minha casa tudo . . .

'I have to pay <u>my bills</u> and who is helping me are my father who just
turned <u>seventy years</u> old yesterday . . . and I was a guy who had a
company <u>five workers</u> and I used to treat <u>my friends</u> all the time . . .
there wasn't . . . um (I was) and independent guy I had my house
everything'

Each excerpt was extracted from a different conversational topic. Although the
topic itself is not directly analyzed, the fact that there are two different topics
for every speaker makes it possible to check whether the listeners' perceptions
of gender differentiation are triggered by the lack/presence of plural /-s/ when
the speakers talked about different subjects.

With two excerpts per speaker and two versions for each, there are sixteen stimuli, which were organized in four sets, as shown in Table 6.2. Each

TABLE 6.2
Sets of stimuli for the Perception Test

Set A	Set B	Set C	Set D
Jaime(a) -s	Jaime(a) Ø	Jaime(b) -s	Jaime(b) Ø
Lucas(a) Ø	Lucas(a) -s	Lucas(b) Ø	Lucas(b) -s
Carlos(a) -s	Carlos(a) Ø	Carlos(b) -s	Carlos(b) Ø
Robson(a) Ø	Robson(a) -s	Robson(b) Ø	Robson(b) -s

stimulus is identified by the speaker's name, the excerpt (a or b), and the variant being used (STA -*s* or NRP ø). Each set of stimuli contains two excerpts by effeminate-sounding male speakers and two by masculine-sounding ones—each pair (A-B or C-D) containing one excerpt with only standard plural NPs and one with only NRPs.

Each of these sets of stimuli was played for twenty-five survey participants, for a total of 100 different listeners. Given that each participant listened to four stimuli, the present data comprise 400 questionnaires. Listeners used a pair of earphones that blocked out most if not all external sounds.[5] After listening to each stimulus, the participants filled out a form (see an English version in Figure 6.1) describing the impression that they had constructed of the speaker. The forms contain six 6-point Likert scales (for perceived levels of education, friendliness, effeminacy, formality, intelligence, and social class) and a number of boxes for more generic traits (shy, hard-working, conservative, etc.). Participants could listen to a stimulus as many times as they liked before filling out the corresponding form, but only a few asked to listen a second time. In the case of the Likert scales, a selection had to be made for each, but the generic traits could be selected only if they matched the image that each participant had portrayed based on a certain stimulus (in other words, not checking a box is also a response: it means that the corresponding trait does not describe the portrayed image of the male speaker). In the last box, other traits could also be volunteered by the participants.

This guy sounds...

not educated at all	□	□	□	□	□	□	very educated
not friendly at all							very friendly
not effeminate at all	□	□	□	□	□	□	very effeminate
not formal at all							very formal
not intelligent at all	□	□	□	□	□	□	very intelligent
lower class	□	□	□	□	□	□	upper class

You think he is... (check as many boxes as you want)

□ shy	□ hard working	□ spoiled
□ cool	□ dishonest	□ conservatie
□ religious	□ helpful	□ country guy
□ family oriented	□ lazy	□ nerd
□ articulate	□ crass	□ sophisticated
□ irritating	□ funny	□ independent
□ stuck up	□ irresponsible	□ preppy
□ self confident	□ sincere	
□ simple	□ gay	

□ other(s): _____

FIGURE 6.1 Perception Test Form

For all of the 6-point Likert scales (from "not at all educated" to "very educated," from "not friendly at all" to "very friendly," from "not effeminate at all" to "very effeminate,, etc.), Welch Two-Sample T-tests were conducted in R (R Core Team 2014) for four datasets: (1) the combined responses given for both effeminate-sounding speakers, in relation to those for the masculine-sounding speakers; (2) the responses given per speaker (regardless of the set of stimuli); (3) the responses given per speaker for the sets of stimuli A and B; and (4) the responses given per speaker for the sets of stimuli C and D. For (5), the results for all Likert scales in the test are presented. For the other three datasets (2–4), the discussion is concentrated on the scale of effeminacy. The analysis then returns to dataset (1), but separates the responses given by male and female listeners, in order to check if their perceptions differ from one another. Finally, the responses for the "gay" box are also analyzed.

The following series of boxplots (Figure 6.2) depicts the responses given by the survey listeners (from 0 to 5, on the y-axis) for the effeminate-sounding speakers (Effem.—Jaime and Lucas together) and the masculine-sounding speakers (Masc.—Carlos and Robson together)—the dataset named in (1). On the x-axis, both effeminate- (Effem.) and masculine-sounding (Masc.) speakers appear according to the plural NP variant used in their excerpts—either NRP or the STA form. The asterisks in the boxplots indicate the significance of the difference between the NRP and STA guises: $p < 0.05^*$, $p < 0.01^{**}$, $p < 0.001^{***}$.

Except for "friendliness" (last distributional boxplots), t-tests verify a significant difference for all of the other scales, between perceptions of the male speakers in their NRP or STA guises, both for the effeminate- and the masculine-sounding speakers. In general, the male speakers were perceived as less effeminate, less educated, lower class, less formal, and less intelligent (but not less friendly) in their NRP guise.

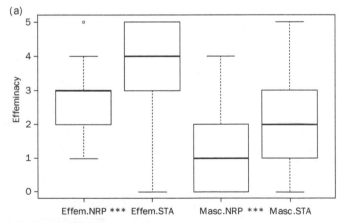

FIGURE 6.2 Data distribution for Gender.Variant

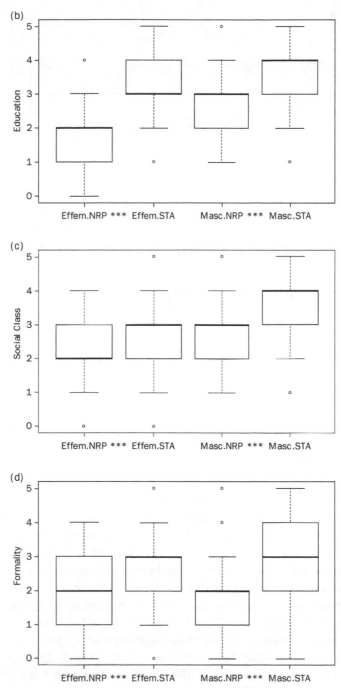

FIGURE 6.2 Continued

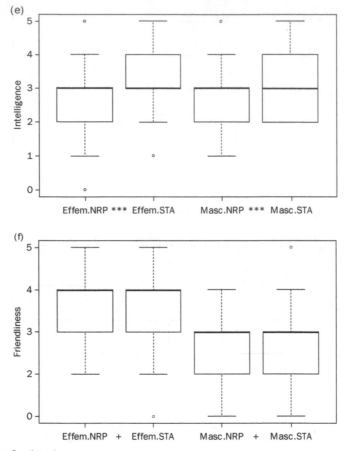

FIGURE 6.2 Continued

For effeminacy, the median lines for the masculine-sounding men show that, in general, they were perceived as less effeminate in comparison to the effeminate-sounding men: the listeners tended to check levels 1 and 2 for the masculine-sounding men, and levels 3 and 4 for the effeminate-sounding men. Some listeners also checked the first box (level zero) for both. There is a significant difference in how either effeminate- or masculine-sounding speakers were perceived whether in NRP or STA guise ($p = 4.64^{-10}$ and 6.17^{-8}, respectively). This shows that while effeminate-sounding men tend to be perceived as relatively more effeminate than masculine-sounding men in the sample, both groups of speakers are perceived as relatively more effeminate when they are in STA guise of plural NPs. The mean for masculine-sounding speakers in their STA guise is 2.5, which is equidistant from zero (not effeminate at all) and from 5 (very effeminate), which means that listeners actually tended to perceive these stimuli as "neutral." The whiskers at level 4 (for Masc. NRP) and level 5 (for Masc. STA) indicate that some survey participants did perceive these masculine-sounding speakers as effeminate-sounding, and it is interesting to note that the highest level was only checked when the masculine-sounding men were in STA guise. However, given the more general distribution, it seems that it is not the case that the masculine-sounding men sound more effeminate when in STA guise but rather that they sound *less* effeminate (more masculine) when in NRP guise.

That general pattern is maintained when we look at the distribution of responses for each speaker, shown in Figure 6.3. Each of the effeminate- and masculine-sounding speakers was perceived as significantly less effeminate when listened to in NRP guises. However, there are a few interesting specifics about Carlos (one of the masculine-sounding speakers). If we focus on the median lines for every speaker, we see that the difference between these values for NRP and STA is represented by 1 point in Figure 6.3 for all of them (3 to 4, for Jaime; 3 to 4, for Lucas; 1 to 2, for Robson), except for Carlos (1 to 3). As one of the masculine-sounding speakers, it is rather striking that Carlos would be perceived as "so much less" effeminate when listened to in his NRP guise—or "so much more" effeminate when listened to in his STA guise.

The results for Robson (the other masculine-sounding man) are also interesting. The difference between the means of perceived effeminacy for him is not as high as for Carlos, but it is still significant ($p < 0.05$ as compared to $p < 0.001$ for Carlos). However, the range of responses given for Robson is very wide, reaching from level 0 to level 5 (very effeminate) for his STA

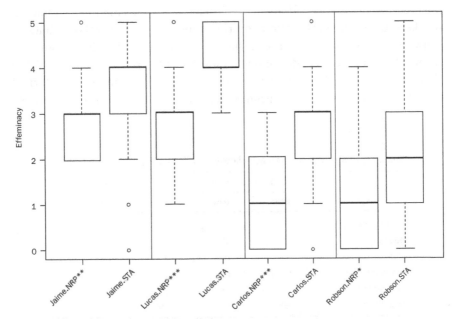

FIGURE 6.3 Data distribution for Speaker.Variant

stimuli. This was striking to the researchers building the corpus, as they themselves had perceived Robson as particularly masculine-sounding throughout his whole interview. These differences between how the two otherwise masculine-sounding men are perceived in terms of effeminacy may hypothetically be due to other masculinizing attributes that contribute to the impression that Robson sounds more masculine than Carlos.

The boxplots in Figure 6.3 also indicate that, in spite of the differences among the perceptions regarding the four individuals, there is more variation in responses for the masculine-sounding men (Carlos and Robson) than for the effeminate-sounding ones (Jaime and Lucas). The common perception among the sociolinguists who worked on the SP2010 sample was that both Lucas and Jaime sounded effeminate (Lucas particularly), so it is not surprising that most of the participants' responses for the scale on effeminacy range from 3 to 5 for these speakers. However, it is notable that there were responses at levels 2 and 1 for Lucas, when listened to in his NRP guise. In other words, even a very effeminate-sounding speaker was perceived as not as effeminate when using NRP. Therefore, the results presented so far make a good case for the correlation between NRP and sounding relatively less effeminate (or more masculine). I will return to this result later when I separate male and female listeners and examine how their perceptions differ.

In the interest of space, individual boxplots for the other scales are not presented by speaker. Table 6.3 summarizes these findings and indicates that, in addition to friendliness (which was not significantly differentiated for any speaker), there are a number of scales for which listeners reacted differently to the presence or absence of NRP across listeners. For the effeminate-sounding speakers, the responses for Jaime contribute more to the general distributions shown in the boxplots in Figure 6.2a, since Lucas (the very effeminate-sounding speaker) is not perceived, depending on whether he's listened to in his NRP or STA guise, as pertaining to a higher or lower class, as being more or less formal or as being more or less intelligent. As for the masculine-sounding speakers,

TABLE 6.3

Summary of significant differences between NRP or STA guises per speaker

	Effeminate-Sounding		Masculine-Sounding	
	Jaime	Lucas	Carlos	Robson
effeminacy	✓	✓	✓	✓
education	✓	✓	✓	✓
class	✓	no	✓	?
formality	✓	no	✓	✓
intelligence	✓	no	✓	no
friendliness	no	no	no	no

the question mark for Robson regarding the formality scale indicates that the *p* value in this case was close to 0.05. Instead of indicating lack of significance, I preferred to indicate lack of conclusiveness. What is important to attend to, though, is the fact that there is a significant difference between the perception of male speakers in NRP or STA guises for *all* speakers only for effeminacy and education. This could mean that there is an ideological relationship—in the sense of Irvine (2001) and Eckert (2008)—between perceived effeminacy and education. If we go back to Mendes (2011) and the opinion stated by some of his interviewees that "gay people talk correctly," and if we consider that the idea of sounding gay was generally associated with the image of an effeminate man, it is possible that these perceptions are built upon a cultural basis that is marked by stereotypes such as "boys are messy, good at Mathematics and sports" and "girls are organized, good at Portuguese and arts."[6] In other words, there seems to be an ideological link between "properness" and "femininity/effeminacy." This will be further explored when we separate responses given by men and women in the perception test.

Another analysis that is worth reporting here is the one that looks at the effeminacy-scale responses for the individuals but separates the sets of stimuli—A and B, on the one hand (Figure 6.4); C and D, on the other (Figure 6.5). From a statistical point of view, these datasets are each considerably smaller (since each pair has half of the total amount of responses), but they are worth looking at to see whether the survey participants' perceptions

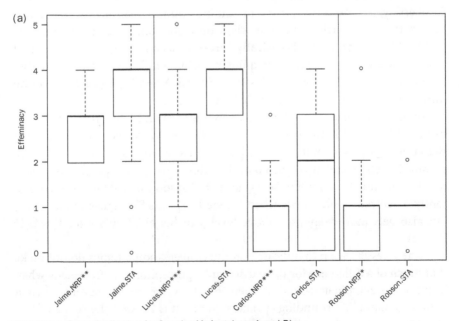

FIGURE 6.4 Data distribution for Speaker.Variant (sets A and B)

(b)

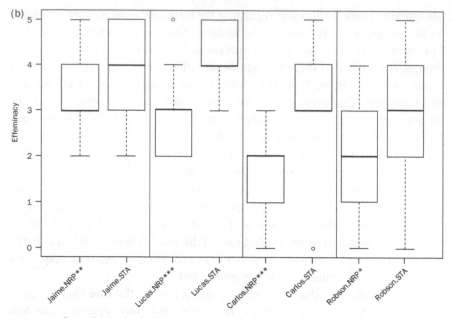

FIGURE 6.5 Data distribution for Speaker.Variant (sets C and D)

differ when the speakers talk about different topics. Once again, the range of responses for the effeminate-sounding speakers is not as wide as that for the masculine-sounding speakers, between levels 3 and 5 of effeminacy, and lower levels for NRP and higher levels for STA are observed across the board. Conversely, the responses for the masculine-sounding speakers vary quite a bit—both within each graph and when they are compared. For the sets C and D (Figure 6.5), Carlos is basically perceived as not effeminate in his NRP guise, whereas he is perceived as quite effeminate in his STA guise. The distribution of responses for Carlos's stimuli in sets A and B (Figure 6.4) is quite different, as there is not such a divide between the NRP and STA guises. Here, although Carlos is perceived as relatively more effeminate when listened to in his STA guise, he still gets responses as low as "zero level effeminacy" for the same guise. As for Robson, he is perceived as effeminate only once for the stimuli in sets A and B (Figure 6.4), but the participants' perceptions vary much more for the stimuli in sets C and D. Robson not only is more consistently perceived as effeminate when listened to in his STA guise in Figure 6.5 but also gets more responses above level 3 in his NRP guises for the C-D dataset.

These results seem to indicate that the conversational topics do not make that much of a difference for the participants' perceptions of effeminacy when it comes to effeminate-sounding men, but they are more relevant when it comes to masculine-sounding speakers. While it is beyond the scope of this chapter to explore this finding further, we need to remember that, aside from the topics the speakers are talking about, there may be other linguistic features that draw the listeners' attention. For example, Robson talks remarkably slowly in the excerpt that was used in sets C and D, and his pronunciation of -s is notably long. There is no research in Portuguese about the correlation between perceived gay talk and /s/ lengthening that corresponds to the work that has been done for English (Gaudio 1994; Podesva, Roberts, & Campbell-Kibler 2002; Rogers & Smyth 2003, and others) but that could well be a linguistic feature that made a difference in this test and these results in Figures 6.4 and 6.5.

Do Men's and Women's Perceptions Differ?

The results presented in Figure 6.2 indicate that, in general, both effeminate-sounding men and masculine-sounding men are perceived, when listened to in their NRP guise, as less effeminate, less educated, belonging to a lower social class, less formal, and less intelligent—but not as less friendly. Moreover, Figures 6.3, 6.4, and 6.5 show that, per speaker and in each pair of stimuli, there are significant differences for effeminacy in all cases, depending on the guise. When we separate the responses given by male and female listeners (whose numbers were balanced in the sample), the general picture remains the same (only the responses for the scale of friendliness were not significantly different, in terms of NRP and STA guises). There is, however, an interesting differentiation between the perceptions by male and female listeners in terms of the hierarchy of how significant the differences between NRP and STA guises were for the various scales. Table 6.4 organizes the scales in the order of such significance.

This table indicates that the difference between responses for "more or less educated" depending on the NRP or STA guises was the most significant for all speakers, regardless of the listener's sex. So, women and men agree that both the effeminate- and the masculine-sounding speakers sound like they have a lower degree of education when they listen to their NRP guise (and a higher degree of education when they listen to their STA guise excerpts). However, all

TABLE 6.4

Differences between female and male participants in the Perception Test

Female Participants		Male Participants	
Effem.-sounding	Masc.-sounding	Effem.-sounding	Masc.-sounding
education	education	education	education
intelligence	class	effeminacy	effeminacy
class	intelligence	intelligence	class
effeminacy	formality	formality	formality
formality	effeminacy	class	intelligence

other features vary in rank. With regard to effeminacy, while it comes in fourth or fifth place (respectively for effeminate- and masculine-sounding speakers) for female listeners, it comes in second for male listeners, right along with education, both for effeminate- and masculine-sounding speakers. In other words, the significance between the responses for effeminacy in terms of NRP and STA guises is the second highest in men's perceptions, but not in women's.

The order summed up in Table 6.4 suggests that men likely latch on to ideas of masculinity in relation to NRP more strongly than women. Therefore, for men, NRP contributes to a more masculine style of speaking—hence the NRP-filled conversation among highly educated, well-off male rowers in the sports center locker room, presented in the introduction to this chapter. The fact that those male rowers are known as "rich" graduate students actually enhances the aura of masculinity around plural NPs in the NRP form. For men, then, NRP is a useful resource in the expression of masculinity, while for women it may be perceived more directly as an index of lower social class or intelligence. Of course, this does not mean that women will always "dislike" or disapprove of NRP in a man's speech—after all, NRP is certainly not the only linguistic tool available for men interested in being perceived as more masculine. In addition, it is possible that men are not always invested in a masculine style just to attract the interest of women but also to negotiate a clearer divide between more masculine and less masculine men.

This discussion is also supported by a distributional analysis of the responses for the "gay" box in the second part of the perception form (cf. Figure 6.1). Figures 6.6 and 6.7, respectively, show how many times the "gay"

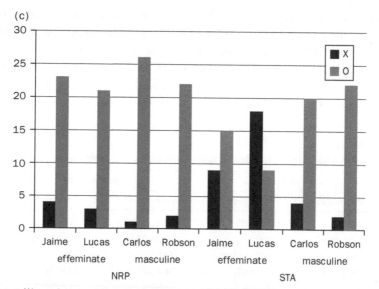

FIGURE 6.6 Women's responses in the "gay" box

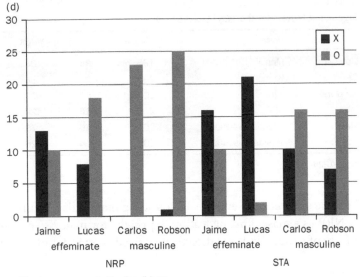

FIGURE 6.7 Men's responses in the "gay" box

box was checked (x) or not (o) by men and women, for each effeminate- and masculine-sounding speaker, when they were listened to in both their NRP and their STA guises. Both men and women check the "gay" box more times for the effeminate-sounding speakers (Jaime and Lucas, when they are listened to in both their NRP and their STA guises). However, men check the "gay" box more often than women when the speakers are listened to in their STA guise. Compare, for example, one of the effeminate-sounding men, Jaime—who was checked as "gay" sixteen times by male listeners, but only eight times by females; or one of the masculine-sounding speakers, Carlos, who was checked as "gay" ten times in his STA guise by male listeners, as opposed to four times by female ones.

A multivariate analysis was run in R, taking "x" ("gay" box checked) and "o" ("gay" box not checked) as dependent variants. It included the participants' sex, their age, their origin (born and raised in the city of São Paulo or not), the guise (NRP or STA) and the overall masculinity/effeminacy of the four speakers as fixed effects, and listener and speaker as random effects. The model also tested for two-way interaction effects between all possible combinations of the listener's sex, NRP/STA variants, and whether the speaker was effeminate- or masculine-sounding. None of these interactions was selected as significant, which means that the important predictors in the model displayed in Table 6.5 are truly independent of one another. Listener sex is selected as significant even with the inclusion of listener as a random effect in the model, which means that sex overcomes the intraparticipant variation and possible idiosyncrasies, and seems to have a real effect on how many times the "gay" box is checked: more often by men than by women, more often in the STA guise, and more often

TABLE 6.5

Significant factors for the "gay" box responses

	Factors	Total Tokens	x %	Weight
Listener's	Men	196	39	.64
Sex	Women	204	22	.36
NP plural	STA	200	44	.72
form	NRP	200	16	.28
Male	Effeminate-sounding	200	46	.73
Speaker	Masculine-sounding	200	14	.26

Input: 0.226

when the male speaker is an effeminate-sounding man. This is a further argument for NRP as a masculinizing feature, especially for male listeners (even if the STA form of plural NPs is not directly perceived as an index of effeminacy).

Conclusion

For speakers of BP, it might sound dubious to state that we hear effeminacy in a man's speech when his plural NPs are in the STA form. The data discussed in this chapter show that there must be a relationship between perceptions of effeminacy versus masculinity in the speech of men and ideas of level of education, class, formality, and intelligence.

The data indicate that people in São Paulo consistently perceive male speakers as less effeminate when listened to in their NRP guise. In relation to both Mendes (2011) and Oushiro (2015), the analyses presented here constitute a further step in the study of social meanings of the variable NP plural agreement. Considering that, on one hand, the speakers in Oushiro's study never mention gender or sexuality in their metapragmatic discourse about NRP, and that, on the other hand, when NRP/STA forms of plural NP are isolated in the speech of men they are perceived as more masculine or more effeminate, we have a first piece of evidence that this is a case of indirect indexicality (Ochs 1992). In addition, we have the result, presented in Table 6.4, that effeminacy comes second in male listeners' perception in a rank of social meanings associated with the variable. For female listeners, though, ideas of class and intelligence are more significant (after education) in their perception of male speakers. Aside from the discussion around how NRP can be useful for men who are invested in the practice of masculine styles, the analyses reported here offer a possible path for an explanation of the indirect ideological link between perceptions of masculinity and forms that are generally taken as an index of a lower level of education. Beyond this specific case of Brazilian Portuguese spoken in São Paulo, such an explanatory path illustrates a way to discuss indirect indexicality in more general terms. Furthermore, the fact that the link between perceived masculinity/effeminacy and perceived lower/higher level of education is less indirect for male than it is for female listeners calls for an investigation of whether there are other ideological links related to masculinity that are more or less strongly established for men than for women.

Acknowledgments

I am indebted to Livia Oushiro for her key participation in designing the perception experiment as well as running the statistical analysis and interpreting results. Special thanks to Kathryn Campbell-Kibler, for her invaluable help in the design of the perception experiment and the questions it attempts to answer, and to Keith Lewis and Erez Levon for their multiple readings of this chapter. The remaining errors and mistakes are, of course, my own.

Notes

1. Those who are born in the state of São Paulo, but outside the capital city, are differently identified, as *Paulistas*.

2. For the original short text in Portuguese, see Mendes (2011). All of these five men identify themselves as gay, but that information was not shared with the survey participants.

3. In Oushiro (2015), for example, 17,866 plural NPs were extracted from 118 interviews, of which 84% were represented by two-word NPs, whereas 15% were represented by three-word NPs, and 1% by four- and five-word NPs.

4. The entire sample can be accessed at projetosp2010.fflch.usp.br. The sixty interviews are stratified by sex, age, and level of education and were collected by *GESOL—Grupo de Estudos Sociolinguísticos* at USP. There are twelve sociolinguistic profiles, with five informants each (one from each of the five urban zones of São Paulo). The collection of this sample was funded through a generous grant from *FAPESP* (*Fundação de Amparo à Pesquisa do Estado de São Paulo*).

5. This experiment utilized Sennheiser HMD-26 headphones.

6. This is sometimes talked about in magazines that discuss education in Brazil. Cf. http://revistaescola.abril.com.br/crianca-e-adolescente/comportamento/coisa-menino-co isa-menina-sera-431455.shtml (February 10, 2015).

References

Antonino, Vivian. 2007. A concordância nominal em predicativos do sujeito e em estruturas passivas no português popular do interior do estado da Bahia. Salvador, Brazil: Universidade Federal da Bahia MA thesis.

Bailey, Guy, Tom Wikle, Jan Tillery, & Lori Sand. 1991. The apparent time construct. *Language Variation and Change* 3. 241–264.

Boersma, Paul & David Weenink. 2014. Praat: Doing phonetics by computer (version 5.3.52), http://www.fon.hum.uva.nl/praat/.

Braga, Maria Luiza. 1977. A concordância de número no sintagma nominal no triângulo mineiro. Rio de Janeiro, Brazil: Pontifícia Universidade Católica do Rio de Janeiro MA thesis.

Brandão, Silvia & Silvia Vieira. 2012. Concordância nominal e verbal: Contribuições para o debate sobre o estatuto da variação em três variedades urbanas do português. *Alfa* 56(3). 1035–1064.

Campbell-Kibler, Kathryn. 2006. Listener perceptions of sociolinguistic variables: The case of (ING). Palo Alto, CA: Stanford University PhD dissertation.

Campbell-Kibler, Kathryn. 2008. I'll be the judge of that: Diversity in social perceptions of (ING). *Language in Society* 37(5). 637–659.

Dias, Maria Clara Alves Correa. 1993. A variação na concordância nominal: Um contraste entre o urbano e o rural na fala brasiliense. Brasília: Universidade de Brasília MA thesis.

Eckert, Penelope. 2008. Variation and the indexical field. *Journal of Sociolinguistics* 12. 453–476.

Gaudio, Rudy. 1994. Sounding gay: Pitch properties in the speech of gay and straight men. *American Speech* 69. 30–57.

Irvine, Judith T. 2001. Style as distinctiveness: The culture and ideology of linguistic differentiation. In Penelope Eckert & John Rickford (eds.), *Style and sociolinguistic variation*, 21–43. Cambridge: Cambridge University Press.

Jaffe, Alexandra. 2009. Introduction: The sociolinguistics of stance. In Alexandra Jaffe (ed.), *Stance: Sociolinguistic perspectives*, 3–28. Oxford: Oxford University Press.

Mendes, Ronald Beline. 2011. Gênero/sexo, variação linguística e intolerância. In Diana Luz Pessoa de Barros (ed.), *Preconceito e intolerância: Reflexões linguístico-discursivas*, 171–192. São Paulo, Brazil: Editora do Mackenzie.

Naro, Anthony Julius & Maria Marta Pereira Scherre. 2003. Estabilidade e mudança linguística em tempo real: A concordância de número. In Maria da Conceição Paiva & Maria Eugênia Lamoglia Duarte (eds.), *Mudança linguística em tempo real*, 47–62. Rio de Janeiro, Brazil: Contra-capa/FAPERJ.

Ochs, Elinor. 1992. Indexing gender. In Alessandro Duranti & Charles Goodwin (eds.), *Rethinking context: Language as an interactive phenomenon*, 335–358. New York: Cambridge University Press.

Oushiro, Livia. 2015. *Identidade na pluralidade: Avaliação, produção e percepção linguística na cidade de São Paulo*. São Paulo, Brazil: Universidade de São Paulo PhD dissertation.

Podesva, Robert. 2007. Phonation type as a stylistic variable: The use of falsetto in constructing a persona. *Journal of Sociolinguistics* 11. 478–504.

Podesva, Robert, Sarah Roberts, & Kathryn Campbell-Kibler. 2002. Sharing resources and indexing meanings in the production of gay styles. In Kathryn Campbell-Kibler, Robert Podesva, Sarah Roberts, & Andrew Wong (eds.), *Language and sexuality: Contesting meaning in theory and practice*, 175–189. Stanford, CA: CSLI.

R Core Team. 2014. R: A language and environment for statistical computing. R Foundation for Statistical Computing, Vienna, Austria, http://www.R-project.org/. Last accessed: April 14, 2014.

Rogers, Henry & Ron Smyth. 2003. Phonetic differences between gay- and straight-sounding male speakers of North American English. In Maria-Josep Solé, Daniel Recasens,

& Joaquin Romero (eds.), *Proceedings of the 15th International Congress of Phonetic Sciences*, 1855–1858. Barcelona: Universitat Autònoma de Barcelona.

Scherre, Maria Marta Pereira. 1988. Reanálise da concordância nominal em português. Rio de Janeiro, Brazil: Universidade Federal do Rio de Janeiro PhD dissertation.

Scherre, Maria Marta Pereira. 1996. Sobre a influência de três variáveis relacionadas na concordância nominal em português. In Giselle Machline de Oliveira e Silva & Maria Marta Pereira Scherre (eds.), *Padrões sociolinguísticos: Análise de fenômenos variáveis do português falado na cidade do Rio de Janeiro*, 85–118. Rio de Janeiro, Brazil: Tempo Brasileiro.

Scherre, Maria Marta Pereira. 1997. Concordância nominal e funcionalismo. *Alfa* 41. 181–206.

7

Phonetic Variation and Perception of Sexual Orientation in Caribbean Spanish

Sara Mack

Introduction

While the study of language variation and sexuality has garnered considerable attention in many language varieties, there has been less work to date in Spanish-speaking contexts. The majority of investigations have been from the perspective of discourse analysis, lexicography, and literary studies. For example, Sívori (2005) analyzes the verbal interactions of the gay male community of Rosario, Argentina, highlighting the community's practice of code-switching and manipulation of lexical gender markers. Similarly, Peña's (2003) study of the gay male bilingual community of Miami examines the lexical strategies used by community members to express identity and in-group status. Documentation of phonetic variation associated with gay male speakers has been predominantly accomplished through anecdotal accounts, most of which rely on allusion to effeminacy rather than overt mention of sexual orientation.[1] Sowards's (2000) interview data from Mexico links "a high pitched voice" to effeminate behavior (146), while Zentella (2003) notes an association between male effeminacy and /s/ epenthesis known as *habla fisna* in Dominican Republic Caribbean Spanish. The term is a play on *habla fina* ('fine speech'); *habla fisna* is characterized by hypercorrective /s/-epenthesis at syllable end. While this pattern of variation is often associated with formality, higher socioeconomic status (SES), or "posh speech" (Roca 2005: 38), it is associated with male effeminacy in some contexts as well. While this anecdotal evidence gives some insight into which phonetic variables are linked to a gay male speech stereotype, there has been little systematically gathered data on the topic in any variety of Spanish.

This chapter details an experimental protocol designed to increase our understanding of the relationship between the perception of male sexuality and phonetic variation in Spanish. Specifically, the study examines how phonetic variables are related to the perception of sexual orientation (PSO) in male speech in Puerto Rican Caribbean Spanish.[2] This perspective on variation and sexual orientation is organized around the concept of indexicality. In the most general terms, indexicality refers to the idea that certain patterns in speech communicate, or index, social information (Ochs 1992; Foulkes & Docherty 2006). In recent years, studies examining indexicality, especially in the context of phonetic variation, have increasingly been used to gain a deeper theoretical understanding of how languages are acquired and how they change over time, as well as to explore complex relationships between identity and language (see Foulkes & Docherty 2006).

Since there are few data upon which to posit hypotheses, the study protocol presented here provides an exploratory view of what indexes PSO from multiple perspectives. First, an explicit measures perception task examines uniformity of listener evaluations and explores if PSO correlates to perceptions of height, age, and social class as well as acoustic cues such as vowel characteristics, speaker vocal tract length, and average vowel space expansion. In addition, a voice recognition task assesses the interaction between PSO and syllable-final /s/. As mentioned previously, anecdotal evidence points to a possible connection between PSO and distinctive patterns of /s/ production resulting from a phonological weakening process that occurs in Caribbean Spanish (Cedergren 1978; López Morales 1980, 1983; Lafford 1986; Alba 1990). The process, known as aspiration and deletion, occurs syllable- and word-finally and yields three traditionally recognized variants: the sibilant [s], a fully retained variant; the [h], commonly known as the aspirated variant; and the phonetic zero, also known as the deleted or elided variant.[3] Patterns of aspiration and deletion are closely correlated with social variables; studies document correlations between production of the syllable-final /s/ and speaker gender, social class, and attitudes. Documentation of the variable production of syllable-final /s/ corresponding to social variables is plentiful, and, as Terrell (1979) notes, its variable production has been shown time after time to be correlated to social variables. In general, findings of studies across aspirating and deleting dialects indicate a continuum of socially stratified variation. The use of sibilant [s], on one end, is correlated with higher SES, the speech of women, and careful speech, while the use of the deleted variant, on the other end, is correlated with lower SES, the speech of men, and casual speech. The aspirated variant is documented in the middle in many dialects. However, since the weakening process is at different stages in different varieties, the relative positions of the variants on the continuum vary. In addition, the dynamic nature of language variation means that variants' socioindexical properties may change according to local context.

Methods

We carried out all data collection at a large public university in the San Juan metropolitan area. We based the choice of location on the prevalence of aspiration and deletion in the linguistic profile of the community, as well as the availability of local linguists who served as consultants and university-level students who could serve as study participants. All participants were native speakers of Puerto Rican Spanish and undergraduate or master's-level students at the university. We recruited participants using fliers, bulletin board postings (both on paper and online), and word of mouth. We made no reference to sexual orientation in the fliers or postings. The specific purpose of the study was referred to as "an experiment on speech perception" on the informed-consent form. All participants were paid US$10. Participants completed a short interview on speech and stereotypes in order to establish that there is a conscious speech stereotype associated with PSO in general, and to explore the extent to which individual participants were cognizant of it. I have reported the data from the short interviews separately (Mack 2010b), but it is relevant to note that all of the participants in the study were aware of speech stereotypes in general and all participants reported an awareness of a speech stereotype for gay males, although the opinions of what individual elements that stereotype entailed varied. Both study tasks were designed and delivered via computer using E-Prime experiment management software (Schneider, Eschman, & Zuccolotto 2002).

EXPLICIT MEASURES PERCEPTION TASK METHOD OVERVIEW

The explicit measures perception task served two purposes. As a stand-alone experiment, it examined the uniformity of listener evaluations of PSO; explored how PSO is correlated with perceptions of speaker height, age, and social class; and investigated which acoustic cues correlate with perceptions of a speaker as gay-sounding or straight-sounding. In terms of the larger study protocol, its purpose was to evaluate stimuli for use in the voice recognition task.

Speaker Participants and Stimuli

Twenty speakers were recruited to produce the study stimuli; their mean age was twenty-three years. Local informants helped to identify and recruit several stereotypically gay-sounding speakers, but it was assumed that the variation occurring in a group of twenty speakers would provide enough natural variation for two subsets, one of more stereotypically gay-sounding speakers and one of more stereotypically straight-sounding speakers, to be identified for the voice recognition task.

We recorded the speakers as they read a list of article-noun combinations. The combinations included nouns among the top 175 highest-frequency words in Spanish (Davies 2006). There were equal numbers of masculine and feminine article-noun combinations. The list included three of the five vowels present in the Spanish vowel system in stressed position (/e/, /i/, and /u/) and /a/ in pretonic position. The fifth vowel, /o/, occurred only in post-tonic, phrase-final position. Since one role of the explicit measures task was to evaluate stimuli to be used in the voice recognition task (investigating the relationship between /s/ realization and PSO), stimuli for the explicit measures task did not include any instances of /s/. The article-noun combinations were the following (frequency ratings appear in parentheses):

(1) *el día*
    'the day' (71)

(2) *la vida*
    'the life' (88)

(3) *el tiempo*
    'the weather' or 'the time' (68)

(4) *la gente*
    'the people' (158)

(5) *el mundo*
    'the world' (118)

(6) *la manera*
    'the manner' (152)

We based the decision to use short-duration stimuli partially on the success of similar methods in Munson et al. (2006). That study and subsequent studies using the same type of stimuli (Munson, Jefferson, & McDonald 2006; Munson 2007) demonstrated that speaker social attributes were established in the minds of listeners after exposure to short, single-word stimuli. Article-noun combinations were used rather than single words to increase the naturalness of the stimuli, as article-noun combinations are more common in Spanish than are single nouns.

In the same recording session in which speakers recorded the article-noun combinations, they also recorded additional stimuli used only in the voice recognition task. Recording sessions for the speakers lasted from twenty to forty minutes, and each speaker was paid US$10 for his participation.

Listener Participants

This portion of the study included twenty-three participants (five male, eighteen female; henceforth "listeners"). All were native speakers of Spanish who had grown up in Puerto Rico and were undergraduate or master's-level students at a large public university in the San Juan metro area. Their mean age was twenty-two years. All listeners completed a demographic questionnaire that included questions about their age, region of origin within Puerto Rico, level of education, and linguistic background. All reported at least basic knowledge of English; six spoke an additional language (other than Spanish or English); and six spoke more than one additional language.

Procedures

In the task, listeners listened to audio stimuli and reported evaluations of speaker age, height, social class, and sexual orientation. Each of the twenty speakers' recordings was presented four times, each time with a question addressing speaker age, height, social class, or sexual orientation, resulting in eighty trials total.

In each trial, listeners heard the six article-noun combinations produced by the same speaker. The phrases appeared onscreen as the recordings played. After they heard the six phrases, we presented listeners with a question addressing one of the four perceived speaker characteristics (age, height, social class, or sexual orientation). For age, listeners provided direct magnitude estimates of age in years. For height, social class, and perceived sexual orientation, we presented listeners with a 5-point scale and they entered the whole number (1 through 5) that corresponded to their evaluation. We developed each scale in conjunction with trained linguists from the study community. For perceived height, "1" corresponded to much taller than average and "5" corresponded to much shorter than average; for perceived social class, "1" equaled higher social class and "5" equaled lower social class. In the scale for perceived sexual orientation "1" corresponded to gay, "2" corresponded to very gay, "3" corresponded to more or less gay, "4" corresponded to straight/heterosexual, and "5" corresponded to neither gay nor straight/heterosexual. This scale was selected as the most appropriate for local norms, and after the data were gathered the scale was normalized to be comparable with the height and social class scales. The presentation order of speakers and questions was randomized (i.e., the experiment was not blocked by question).

Analysis and Results

The first set of analyses explored to what extent listeners were uniform in their ratings of speaker PSO. The first analysis was a matrix of Spearman's rho correlations between the twenty-three listeners' ratings and the twenty speakers' perceived sexual orientation. Approximately half of the listener pairs' correlations did not achieve statistical significance at the < 0.05 level, suggesting that different listeners were rank-ordering speakers differently. Second, we performed a factor analysis (Gorsuch 1983) on the listeners' ratings of the speakers' PSO. A factor analysis helps to describe variation in variables by identifying potential interdependencies; in this case, the factor analysis grouped listeners using their ratings of PSO for all speakers. An examination of individual listeners' loadings on the six factors showed that there were seven listeners on the first factor; five on the second; three on the third, fourth, and fifth factors; and two on the sixth. Listener clusters in this analysis were the same as those groups that were significantly correlated in the correlation analysis. Two Kruskal-Wallis tests (Kruskal & Wallis 1952) showed that these groupings were not due to differences across listeners in either the mean score that they gave to the twenty speakers or in the standard deviation of their scores. It is also possible that external factors could account for the clustering patterns, so we examined the demographic data for each listener to see if there were links between speakers that might provide an explanation. However, there were few differences between clusters in terms of the demographic information that we collected. The five males who took part in the study were spread throughout the clusters (two in one cluster, and the other three in separate clusters). Listeners in each cluster were similar in terms of language background, age, and level of education. This suggests that there are distinct patterns of listener performance. In the analysis section below, I look at the question of listener consistency and variation further with an examination of the connections between listener clusters and acoustic parameters of the stimuli.

The next analysis was a correlation examining the relationship between listener judgments of PSO and the other perceived characteristics (height, age, and social class). There was a significant relationship between perceived sexual orientation and height, $r = -.461$, p (two-tailed) $< .041$, with speakers rated as gay-sounding more likely to be rated as shorter than speakers rated as straight-sounding. There were no significant relationships between perceived sexual orientation and perceived age or perceived social class.

We measured acoustic properties of the stimuli using Praat signal-processing software (Boersma & Weenink 2003). Vowel characteristics measured included individual and mean F1 (Bark), individual and mean F2 (Bark), and individual and mean F0 of each stressed vowel (/e/, /i/, /u/) and the pretonic /a/ in *la manera*. Estimates of speaker vocal tract length in cm were also calculated by measuring the F3 of pretonic /a/ in *manera*, treating it as if it had been produced by an unmodified vocal tract, and deriving vocal-tract length using the odd-quarter formula (Fant 1966). We also calculated average vowel space expansion, using the bark-scaled F1 and F2 values (according to the formula found in Bradlow, Torretta, & Pisoni 1996).

A correlation analysis assessed the relationship between PSO and individual vowel acoustic characteristics. There was a significant correlation between PSO and F2 frequencies of two tokens of mid front vowels: /e/ in *la manera* ($r = -.478$, $p < .05$) and /e/ in *el tiempo* ($r = -.456$, $p < .05$), with speakers with higher F2 more likely to be perceived as more gay-sounding. There were no significant correlations between PSO and individual F1 frequencies, individual F0 values, estimated vocal tract length, average dispersion, or for the F2 frequencies of the other vowels. Since this is an exploratory study, it is useful to note there was one relationship approaching significance, the F2 frequency for the remaining midfront token, /e/ in *la gente* ($r = -.412$, $p = .071$).

We also analyzed the relationships between mean acoustic characteristics and mean listener ratings of PSO, perceived height, perceived age, and perceived social class. Correlation analyses showed that PSO was significantly correlated with mean F2 measures, $r = -.572$, p (two-tailed) $< .05$. As with the individual acoustic analysis, speakers with higher F2 frequencies were perceived as more gay-sounding; it seems likely that this is carried by /e/. There were no significant correlations between PSO and mean F1, mean F0, mean vowel space expansion or estimated vocal tract length.

As discussed previously, an examination of listener consistency and variation in ratings showed distinct patterns of listener evaluations of PSO, but the differences were not due to differences in mean ratings or standard deviations of the ratings. One potential explanation is that specific acoustic cues provoked different reactions for different listener groups. To test this hypothesis, we conducted a Spearman rho correlation analysis of perceptions of sexual orientation and the mean acoustic characteristics of the stimuli. The listeners were separated according to the clusters derived in the factor analysis. The correlation analysis showed that there were listeners whose ratings were significantly correlated to mean F2 values in all but one cluster. In addition, five individual listeners in three clusters had significant correlations between ratings and mean F1 values, while two listeners' ratings (in two unique clusters) were significantly correlated with estimated vocal tract length. Just one listener had scores significantly correlated with mean F0, and one listener had ratings significantly correlated with average vowel space dispersion. In other words, the predominant acoustic cue appears to be mean F2 values, as it was significantly correlated with ratings in all but one cluster. However, listeners in different cluster groups attended to other acoustic cues (mean F1 values and estimated vocal tract length) as well.

VOICE RECOGNITION TASK METHOD OVERVIEW

As mentioned previously, the tasks described here are part of an experimental protocol with several different components. The explicit measures task was the first step in investigating the relationships between phonetic variation and perceptions of sexual orientation, and it provided important information on listener uniformity, correlation among identity categories, and acoustic cues. However, the method is not without drawbacks. For one thing, the task required listeners to classify speakers in terms of set social categories, often with dualistic constructs, that may or may not have existed in the mind of the listener before completing the task. Consequently, it is not exactly certain what is being measured: an existing, independent belief of the kind of variation related to a social category (sexual orientation, social class, etc.) or one that develops in the study itself (see, e.g., Wilson, Lindsey, & Schooler 2000; Schwarz & Bohner 2001). Another potential drawback is that the method depends on a cognitive processing model that is straightforward and more or less sequential: first, listeners hear a stimulus and then an accurate reflection of perception is reported as a result. However, this is not necessarily the case. Accuracy and veracity of the evaluation may be impacted by social desirability concerns (see Fazio & Olson 2003). In addition, processing may not occur in a simple sequence. A growing number of studies have shown that if listeners believe that they are listening to variation associated with a specific social identity (i.e., stereotypical speech; see Strand 1999), it affects how they process sounds (see Niedzielski 1999; Strand 2000;Hay, Nolan, & Drager 2006; Hay, Warren, & Drager 2006; Hay & Drager 2010). In other words, the explicit measures task described in the previous section is useful to gain an initial view of the relationship between phonetic variables and PSO in Spanish, but it could be complemented by a method that relies less on overt activation of social identity categories.

In an attempt to address these methodological issues, I included a timed voice recognition task exploring the relationship between /s/ variation and PSO as part of the larger experimental protocol. Rather than asking listeners to evaluate speakers in terms of a certain characteristic, a timed voice recognition task examines relationships between variables by using priming experiment methodology, measuring listeners' response time for recognizing a voice they have heard earlier. Priming experiments set up an expectation in the priming phase and then measure how a given variable is affected by that expectation in a test phase. Early priming experiments considered semantic associations between lexical items, measuring latency effects in associated and nonassociated objects (Fazio 2001). More recently, priming methods have been extended to investigate the automatic activation of sociocultural identity and sociocultural value judgments, such as racial and gender stereotypes (see, e.g., Nosek, Greenwald, & Banaji 2010). Priming techniques also have been used to examine low-level speech processing, social stereotypes, and variable phoneme production. Congruence (or lack thereof) is the key factor in priming tasks: Congruent objects elicit faster response times, while objects that are not congruent are responded to slower. In other words, when listeners hear a voice, a set of associations for a specific social identity is activated. When presented with the same voice later, listeners respond faster if the variant used is one that closely corresponds to the identity that has been activated. In the context of this study, the prediction was that there would be more congruency (and therefore less latency in responses) when the [s] variant was paired with voices previously evaluated as gay-sounding.

Listener Participants

There were fifty-four listener participants who completed this task. Because of technical issues, we had to discard eleven of these participants' results, leaving forty-three participants whose data we used in the final analysis.[4] The mean age of listeners was 22.8 years. As in the explicit measures task, all listeners completed a demographic questionnaire that included questions about their age, level of formal education, region of origin, the amount of time they have spent in the San Juan metropolitan area, and their linguistic background.

Stimuli

We used two sets of stimuli in this task. The first set, used in the priming phase, was made up of the same six article-noun combinations used in the explicit methods perception task (described earlier).

The second set, used in the test phase, was produced using an adaptation of a matched-guise design (Lambert et al. 1960). Speakers produced three variations of the stimuli containing the variable of interest, the /s/ pronunciation. The test phase stimuli included two phrases:

(1) *Estos chicos no vienen.*
    'These boys aren't coming.'

(2) *Estos coches no van.*
    'These cars don't run/don't go.'

The speakers were instructed to read the phrase several times pronouncing each /s/ several times as [s], as [h], and by eliding all /s/. This method resulted in more natural sounding tokens as compared to digitally manipulated stimuli.

Using the mean scores from the explicit measures perception task, we identified the seven speakers evaluated as the most stereotypically straight-sounding and the seven speakers evaluated as the most stereotypically gay-sounding. We used these speakers' stimuli as the test items in the voice recognition experiment; we used the stimuli that had been recorded by speakers who were not in either one of these groups as practice and distracter items.

Procedure

The experiment began with instructions that the listeners read through at their own pace, pressing any key on the keyboard to advance. In order to encourage the listeners to make evaluations of the speakers according to social categories, they were told that they would listen to a stimuli from individual speakers who varied in how stereotypically gay or straight-sounding they were (PSO priming, Condition One) or how stereotypically upper-, middle-, or lower-class sounding they were (SES priming, Condition Two). The choice to inform listeners that the voices varied in terms of SES was made based on the strong associations between /s/ production and social class. The benefit of including this condition was that it would provide comparison data that would verify whether or not advising listeners in Condition One that the voices varied in terms of PSO had an effect on listener responses. The groups for each condition were of similar size, with twenty-one listeners (fourteen female, seven males) in Condition One and twenty-two listeners (nineteen females, three males) in Condition Two.

The data collection procedure was made up of a series of trials. Listeners first completed a practice block of ten trials to become familiar with the task. After the practice block, the experimental trials began. Upon completion of all the trials, text appeared that informed listeners that the experiment was complete and thanked them for their participation.

Each trial included a priming phase, a distracter phase, and a test phase. In the priming phase, listeners were instructed to listen to the speaker and attempt to remember his voice. Listeners heard the six priming phase noun-article combinations, all produced by the same speaker. An orthographic display of the words was presented on the computer monitor at the same time the recording was heard. Again, the goal of this priming phase was to activate stereotypical notions of social identity in the mind of the listener, and establish an idea of the speaker's social identity in the mind of the listeners.

In the distracter task, listeners solved simple mental math problems or completed counting exercises. After the distracter task was completed, the listeners began the test phase. There was a labeled middle button on the keyboard, and listeners were instructed to press it as soon as the computer screen turned from red to green. This action activated a short beep that corresponded to the start of the stimulus audio recording for the test phase. The stimulus for the test phase was auditory only; it was not accompanied by an orthographic display of the phrase. The test phase stimulus was made up of one phrase that included the syllable-final /s/ in one of its three variations: sibilant [s], aspirated [h], or deleted [o] (phonetic zero). The listeners were instructed to press the leftmost button (labeled "same") if the speaker was the same as in the prime phase and the rightmost button (labeled "different") if he was a different speaker. The listeners were instructed to press the appropriate button as quickly as possible without compromising accuracy. In the next trial, the sequence was repeated with the next stimuli set.

All trials appeared in random order. Each listener heard each of the fourteen speakers during six trials throughout the experiment: with each of the three /s/ types ([s], [h], phonetic zero) in two different test phrases. This resulted in eighty-four responses made by each listener, plus the practice block of ten trials and fourteen distracter trials. The complete experiment protocol took approximately one hour to complete.

Again, the underlying logic of this type of task is that when study participants are exposed to a stimulus, the exposure activates a set of associations related to that stimulus. Thus, when listeners hear what they believe to be a gay-sounding voice, it activates a set of beliefs about gay-sounding speakers (i.e., stereotypes). The response times gathered in the test phase, then, were a measure of the strength of the association between the variable of interest and those stereotypes. Variants that are more closely associated with (or more congruent to) the speech stereotype will be processed faster than those that are not (or that are less congruent). This technique follows methods in Fazio, Sanbonmatsu, Powell, & Kardes (1986), Banaji & Hardin (1996), Blair & Banaji (1996), and Kawakami, Young, & Dovidio (2002) that document the pervasiveness of automatic stereotyping, the influence of priming on response time to stimuli, and the lack of conscious control over evaluative judgments.

Analysis and Results

A d-prime (d') analysis was conducted to examine listeners' overall performance in the task. D-prime (Macmillan & Creelman 2005) analyses are used as an alternative to conventional percentage correct measures; in this case, the analysis measured the detection of whether a voice changed between the priming phase and the test phase. The d' value indicates whether the listener exceeded a threshold of detection, and whether she or he was biased to providing a particular response. For example, if a listener was unsure of an answer, he or she might tend to respond with "same" more often than "different." In that case, the percentage values may not be an accurate reflection of how well listeners performed in the detection task. A higher absolute d' value means that there is more sensitivity to the difference between when the talker is the same and when the talker is different, which translates to a subject's higher sensitivity, while a d' value near zero is a reflection of chance performance (Macmillan & Creedman 2005; Claremont Graduate University 2009). In terms of this experiment, if we observe similar d' values for all stimuli types across both gay- and straight-sounding speakers, it would indicate that listener sensitivity is relatively stable and is not influenced by differences in the type of /s/ listeners hear or by perceived sexual orientation. If we observe d' prime values close to zero, it indicates that the listeners are performing at about chance level and that the signal is not strong. Higher d' prime values will mean that the signal is stronger, and that listeners are more sensitive to it.

In this experiment, d' analysis was conducted for [s] and deleted variants.[5] This resulted in the following possible combinations:

(1) [s] + straight-sounding voice
(2) deleted + straight-sounding voice
(3) [s] + gay-sounding voice
(4) deleted + gay-sounding voice

The mean d' values were highest for cases where gay-sounding speakers produced the [s] variant and lowest for cases where gay-sounding speakers produced the deleted variant. In order to assess the statistical significance of these results, the d' data was analyzed in a two-factor repeated-measures ANOVA (analysis of variance). The two factors were PSO (gay- or straight-sounding) and /s/ type (sibilant [s], aspirated [h], or the deleted variant). There was a significant main effect of PSO, $F_{(1, 42)} = 7.15$, $p < .005$. There was also a significant main effect of /s/ type, $F_{(1, 42)} = 42.61$, $p < .005$, and a significant combined effect $F_{(1, 42)} = 10.91$, $p < .005$. A paired-sample t-test showed a significant difference between the two phrases containing the deleted variant as well as between the phrases containing deleted variant phrases and [s] variant phrases, but not between the two [s] variant phrases ([s] + gay-sounding voice and [s] + straight-sounding voice). These results indicate that there was a difference in listeners' sensitivity based on PSO and /s/ type. The signal was strongest and listeners were most sensitive to differences in the case of speakers producing the [s] variant. When listeners heard the deleted variant produced by speakers who were stereotypically gay-sounding, their sensitivity to the signal was lower than in any other combination, suggesting a mismatch between PSO and the type of /s/ produced. In other words, /s/ appears to be part of the stereotype in listeners' minds.

The response time data were analyzed in a three-factor mixed ANOVA. There were two within-subjects' factors, PSO (gay-sounding or straight-sounding) and /s/ type (sibilant [s], aspirated [h], or the deleted variant), and one between-subjects factor, condition (Condition One, PSO priming, or Condition Two, SES priming). There was a significant main effect of perceived sexual orientation, $F_{(1, 41)} = 6.47$, $p < .05$, with responses to gay-sounding speakers faster than to straight-sounding ones. This was the only statistically significant main effect, and there were no statistically significant interactions. In other words, listeners responded more quickly to the speakers who had been previously rated as gay-sounding and slower to the speakers who had previously been rated as straight-sounding, and this difference was statistically significant. Since the earlier statistical analysis had shown that stimuli recorded by the gay-sounding speakers were shorter in duration, we carried out a linear mixed-effects model analysis to examine whether stimuli length was a significant factor in response times; we found no significant effect.

Since this was an exploratory investigation, we conducted a separate analysis of the data by condition in order to assess if there were distinct trends in the data depending on the priming condition (Condition One, PSO priming; Condition Two, SES priming). For each condition, a two-factor within-subjects ANOVA was carried out, with PSO and /s/ type as the two factors. In Condition One, the analysis showed a non-significant main effect of /s/ type, $F_{(2, 21)} = .430$, $p = .65$. It also showed a non-significant main effect of PSO $F_{(1, 21)} = 1.57$, $p = .22$, as well as a non-significant interaction effect between PSO and /s/ type on response times, $F_{(2, 42)} = .098$, $p = .91$.

In contrast to Condition One, the two-factor within-subjects ANOVA for Condition Two did show a significant main effect of PSO, $F_{(1, 21)} = 5.25$, $p < .05$, $n2 = .2$, with faster responses for gay-sounding speakers. There was not a statistically significant main effect of /s/ type, but the result was suggestive, $F_{(2, 21)} = 2.86$, $p = 0.068$, $n2 = .12$, with faster responses for the [s] variant. There was no significant combined effect $F_{(2, 42)} = .056$, $p = .945$, $n2 = .003$. In other words, when listeners were led to believe that the speakers varied in terms of their social class, there was an observable effect of perceived sexual orientation on response times. However, these results should be understood within the limits of the study design, which relied on a previous task with different listener participants to categorize the voices as gay or straight-sounding. This design relies on the assumption that all listeners share the same perceptions, which the explicit measures task suggests may not be the case.

In addition, it is important to note that the voice recognition task, while utilizing priming experiment techniques, was accompanied by an interview task in which listeners reported their opinions on speech stereotypes related to speaker identity, including whether or not there was a stereotype of gay male speech. It is possible that the discussion of stereotypes in the interview activated a set of associations that affected performance on the voice recognition task. Future investigations using similar methods should improve upon existing methodology to minimize the activation of associations to the social identity category in question.

Discussion and Conclusions

There are several significant findings of the study protocol, relevant to both the general study of perception and identity as well as to the study of phonetic variation in the Hispanic linguistics subfield. First, the explicit measures task analysis showed that rather than a shared pattern of evaluation of sexual orientation among all listeners, there are distinct patterns of evaluations shared among clusters of listeners. Furthermore, within those clusters, there is variation among individuals in terms of which acoustic cues significantly correlate to evaluations. It may be that patterns of evaluations are triggered by an aggregate of factors (Eckert 2000; Levon 2007 and others) that vary significantly by individual. This has implications for the larger study of language and identity, as it indicates that simply considering a mean score fails to take advantage of a more nuanced, detailed view of observable variation that variable listener evaluations provide, especially in overt tasks such as the one presented here. It also suggests that identifying correlations between specific acoustic cues and social identity is more problematic than currently conceptualized; the differences in patterns of evaluations among individuals and groups suggest that evaluations are reliant on individual lived experience as well as community- or cultural-based shared beliefs. In the case of Puerto Rican Spanish, the study has clearly shown that while there are shared conscious stereotypes of speech and sexual orientation, the acoustic cues to which listeners respond cannot be generalized across the listener populations as a whole, and it is necessary to examine differences across individuals as well as groupwise patterning.

The explicit measures perception task also adds to the study of phonetic variation and social identity in terms of correlation among evaluations of distinct social identity categories. The results showed that perceptions of sexual orientation were correlated with perceptions of height, but not with perceived social class or perceived age. The significant relationship between perceived height and PSO replicates findings from Munson et al. (2006), which showed a similar correlation in English. It is somewhat intriguing that there was no correlation between perceived sexual orientation and perceived social class (cf. Maegaard & Pharao, Chapter 5, and Mendes, Chapter 6, this volume). One possible explanation for this is that the task stimuli did not include any instances of /s/, whose variable use is well documented as a correlate of social class in production studies of Caribbean and other varieties of Spanish (Fontanella de Weinberg 1973; Cedergren 1978; López-Morales 1983; Lafford 1986; Alba 1990 and others). In the absence of a variable strongly correlated with social class (such as /s/), it is possible that the remaining cues did not carry enough socioindexical impact to reveal relationships that might exist. Especially since /s/ realization is so highly correlated with social factors from a production standpoint, future studies are needed to assess the impact of /s/ in perception studies using overt methods such as this one. What is clear from the current study is that in Puerto Rican Spanish, as in other language varieties, listener evaluations of social identity are sensitive to differences present in an audio-only signal.

Perhaps most notably, the explicit measures task found a significant correlation between individual acoustic measures and evaluations of male sexual orientation in Puerto Rican Spanish, with PSO significantly correlated with F2 values of two midfront vowel (/e/) tokens. Speakers with higher F2 values (more fronted [e]) were more likely to be rated as gayer-sounding, and those with lower F2 values (more back [e]) as more straight-sounding. This contributes to a cross-linguistic understanding of acoustic cues and identity, as this role of F2 is somewhat parallel to findings reported in Munson et al. (2006), in which the investigators found that judgments of sexual orientation in English were correlated with F2 frequency of back vowels. This cross-linguistic comparison suggests that although there may be similarities in the type of phonetic factors (e.g., F2 frequencies) that contribute to evaluations of sexual orientation across languages, the linguistic context in which those factors are relevant (e.g., in front or back vowels) depends on local interpretations. This corresponds to Johnson's (2006) cross-linguistic analysis of relationships between height, gender, and vowel production. Data from the context of Puerto Rican

Spanish presented here provide cross-linguistic data that are key to establishing a taxonomy of which acoustic factors affect perception of social identities across languages. At the same time it documents, for the first time, a variable relevant in the perception of male sexual orientation in Spanish.

The fact that F2 frequencies of two tokens of /e/ in stressed position were correlated to listener evaluations of sexual orientation also has significant implications for the study of the Spanish vowel system. This apparent socio-indexical capacity of /e/ suggests a degree of variability in the Spanish vowel system rarely explored in traditional analyses. Vowel variation has not been considered a robust indicator of social identity, most likely because of the historical stability of the Spanish vowel system. Dalbor (1980) notes, "Spanish vowels are quite uniform from dialect to dialect. In fact, the Spanish vocalic system is simpler, more uniform, and more symmetrical than that of any other language commonly studied ..." (148–149). More recently, Schwegler & Kempff (2007) maintain: "*Las vocales en español son, generalmente, muy estables; la variación en su pronunciación, sobre todo al compararla con la de las consonantes, es poca*" ('Vowels in Spanish are, generally, very stable; variation in their pronunciation, especially in comparison with that of consonants, is little') (30). While some variation according to contextual and social factors has been reported (see Harmegnies & Poch-Olivé 1992; Holmquist 2008; Oliver Rajan 2007; Santoro 2007), overall there are few studies documenting variation in stressed or unstressed contexts, and few data that link this variation to social attributes. The explicit measures task in this study protocol, however, clearly demonstrates that the variation in F2 observed in a particular stressed vowel (/e/) is significantly correlated to PSO in Puerto Rican Spanish; this indicates that vowel variation can, indeed, be a relevant socioindexical cue in Spanish varieties. This finding highlights the need for acoustic studies of the Spanish vowel system that examine variation and social meaning from different perspectives, looking at differences beyond those which can be captured in narrow phonetic transcription.

The findings of the voice recognition task show that there is some indication that stereotypes of speech and social identity interact with speech processing in Puerto Rican Spanish. First, the d' data showed a significant main effect of PSO and /s/ type, as well as a significant combined effect. Sensitivity to the signal was lowest when listeners heard the deleted variant produced by speakers who had been previously evaluated as stereotypically gay-sounding. A possible interpretation is that there was a lack of congruency in those cases; listeners did not expect to hear deletion after receiving the prime of a gay-sounding speaker. In addition, the signal was strongest and listeners were most sensitive to differences in the case of speakers producing the [s] variant. The most likely interpretation of this finding is that [s] tokens were more easily processed than deleted tokens. There are numerous studies that document that speech clarity influences ease of processing (see Ernestus, Baayen,

& Schreuder 2002; Tucker & Warner 2007). With [s] tokens, there was more phonetic information available to process the signal than with the deleted variants. Therefore, ease of processing could translate to a stronger signal and more sensitivity to [s] tokens. This could account for the statistically significant differences between the [s] and deleted variant, but there is also a statistically significant difference between gay- and straight-sounding speakers, as well as a significant combined effect. A possible interpretation is that there is an interaction between speech clarity and prototypical gender. That is, it is possible that the voices previously rated as more gay-sounding may be less gender prototypical. Studies have shown that processing is affected by gender prototypicality (Strand 1999, 2000). In the d' data, there are four possible combinations of perceived sexual orientation and /s/ type:

(1) [s] + straight-sounding voice
(2) deleted + straight-sounding voice
(3) [s] + gay-sounding voice
(4) deleted + gay-sounding voice

From what we know about the effects of gender prototypicality and speech clarity on speech processing, we would expect the strongest signal to appear in case 1 ([s] + straight-sounding voice), since this combination is the strongest both in terms of gender prototypicality and speech clarity. This prediction is not contradicted by the data. Next, we would expect case 4 (deleted + gay-sounding voice) to have the weakest signal, since it is weakest in terms of both gender prototypicality and speech clarity. The data are consistent with this prediction as well. We would expect case 2 (deleted + straight-sounding voice) to be an intermediate case, since it is made stronger by its gender prototypicality but weaker by its lower speech clarity. This is indeed the case. Finally, we would also expect case 3 ([s] + gay-sounding voice) to be intermediate, as it is weaker in terms of gender prototypicality but stronger in terms of speech clarity. This, however, is not the case. In fact, it is as strong as the other [s] variant. I hypothesize that the strength is a reflection of the strength of association between the sibilant [s] variant and the perception of the speakers as gay-sounding. Accuracy in the task, as measured by d', is affected not only by gender prototypicality and speech clarity but also by whether or not the sibilant [s] variant corresponds with speaker PSO. We need future studies to further understand the relationship between accuracy and socially stratified variation using d', especially studies that include the aspirated variant as a potential socioindexical cue.

The second statistically significant finding in this task was that there was an effect of perceived sexual orientation on response times, with voices perceived as gay-sounding eliciting faster responses than voices that are perceived as straight-sounding. This finding is problematic in light of the proposed explanation for the d' results. I proposed that gender prototypicality had an influence on accuracy, and assigned straight-sounding speakers as those with most prototypically male voices. If we follow the same line of reasoning, we would expect quicker responses for the more prototypically male voices (again, the straight-sounding speakers). One possible explanation is that measures of accuracy and speed of voice recognition are not necessarily comparable measures. The question is complicated by the results of a pilot test of the same methods in English (reported in Mack & Munson 2012) that found the reverse: Listeners responded more quickly to straight-sounding speakers than to gay-sounding ones, and the difference was statistically significant. These results have implications for speech processing, as they suggest that socially stratified variation affects processing in different ways in different languages. However, there is no way to specifically account for why and how these differences occur until more quantitative and qualitative cross-linguistic data are available.

Acknowledgments

Data from the study protocol reported in this chapter were also reported in Mack 2010a, 2010b, 2011, & 2013.

Notes

1. While it is outside the focus of this chapter, it bears noting that patterns of variation associated with gay or lesbian female speakers have received even less attention, with a dearth of even anecdotal accounts.

2. We use the term *PSO* is for convenience; it underscores that the focus of the study is on listeners' perceptions of speakers in terms of how straight- or gay-sounding they are. That is, listener perception, rather than a speaker's self-identified sexual orientation, is the variable of interest.

3. Although the three variants mentioned are traditionally recognized, a fourth variant, the glottal stop, is documented in Spain (Cortés Gómez 1979), Argentina (Fontanella de Weinberg 1973), the Philippines (Lipski 2001), and Puerto Rico (Valentín-Márquez 2006).

4. The technical issues were related to an error made in the setup of the software, with "random with repeat" inadvertently selected rather than "random with replacement."

5. Aspirated tokens were not used for the stimuli in which the test talker did not match the prime talker, so it was not possible to calculate d' for aspirated tokens.

References

Alba, Orlando. 1990. *Variación fonética y diversidad social en el español dominicano de Santiago.* Santiago, Chile: Pontificia Universidad Católica.
Banaji, Mahzarin & Curtis Hardin. 1996. Automatic stereotyping. *Psychological Science* 7(3). 136–141.

Blair, Irene V. & Mahzarin Banaji. 1996. Automatic and controlled processes in stereotype priming. *Journal of Personality and Social Psychology* 70. 1142–1163.

Boersma, Paul & David Weenink. 2003. PRAAT v. 4.1.7 (computer software). Amsterdam: Institute of Phonetic Sciences.

Bradlow, Ann, Gina Torretta, & David Pisoni. 1996. Intelligibility of normal speech: Global and finegrained acoustic-phonetic talker characteristics. *Speech Communication* 20. 255–272.

Cedergren, Henrietta. 1978. En torno a la variación de la s final de sílaba en Panamá: Analysis Cuantitativo. In Humberto Morales (ed.), *Corrientes actuales en la dialectología del caribe hispánico*, 37–50. Rio Piedras, Puerto Rico: Editorial Universitaria.

Claremont Graduate University. 2009. Web Interface for Statistical Education (WISE): Signal Detection Theory Tutorial, http://wise.cgu.edu/sdtmod/index.asp. (January 15, 2009.)

Corés Gómez, Eugenio. 1979. *El habla popular de Higuera de Vargas*. Badajoz, Spain: Diputación Provincial.

Dalbor, John. 1980. *Spanish pronunciation: Theory and practice*. New York: Harcourt Brace Jovanovich.

Davies, Mark. 2006. *A frequency dictionary of Spanish*. New York: Routledge.

Eckert, Penelope. 2000. *Linguistic variation as social practice: The linguistic construction of social meaning in Belten High*. Oxford: Blackwell.

Ernestus, Mirjam, Harold Baayen, & Rob Schreuder. 2002. The recognition of reduced word forms. *Brain and Language* 81. 162–173.

Fant, Gunnar. 1966. A note on vocal tract size factors and non-uniform F-pattern scalings. *Speech Technology Laboratory: Quarterly Progress and Status Report* 4. 22–30.

Fazio, Russell. 2001. On the automatic activation of associated evaluations: An overview. *Cognition and Emotion* 15(2). 115–141.

Fazio, Russell & Michael Olson. 2003. Implicit measures in social cognition research: Their meaning and use. *Annual Review of Psychology* 54. 297–327.

Fazio, Russell, David Sanbonmatsu, Martha Powell, & Frank Kardes. 1986. On the automatic activation of attitudes. *Journal of Personality and Social Psychology* 50(2). 229–238.

Fontanella de Weinberg, Beatriz. 1973. Comportamiento ante -s de hablantes femenninos y masculinos del español bonarense. *Romance Philology* XXVII(1). 50–58.

Foulkes, Paul & Gerard Docherty. 2006. The social life of phonetics and phonology. *Journal of Phonetics* 34. 409–438.

Gorsuch, Richard. 1983. *Factor analysis*. Hillsdale, NJ: Lawrence Erlbaum Associates.

Harmegnies, Bernard & Dolors Poch-Olivé. 1992. A study of style-induced vowel variability: Laboratory versus spontaneous speech in Spanish. *Speech Communication* 11. 429–437.

Hay, Jennifer & Katie Drager. 2010. Stuffed toys and speech perception. *Linguistics* 48. 865–892.

Hay, Jennifer, Aaron Nolan, & Katie Drager. 2006. From fush to feesh: Exemplar priming in speech perception. *The Linguistic Review* 23(3). 351–379.

Hay, Jennifer, Paul Warren, & Katie Drager. 2006. Factors influencing speech perception in the context of a merger-in-progress. *Journal of Phonetics* 34(4). 458–484.

Holmquist, Jonathan. 2008. Gender in context: Features and factors in men's and women's speech in rural Puerto Rico. In Maurice Westmoreland & Juan Tomás Testa (eds.), *Selected proceedings of the 4th Workshop on Spanish Sociolinguistics*, 17–35. Somerville, MA: Cascadilla Proceedings Project.

Johnson, Keith. 2006. Resonance in an exemplar-based lexicon: The emergence of social identity and phonology. *Journal of Phonetics* 34(4). 485–499.

Kawakami, Kerry, Kenneth L. Dion, & John Dovidio. 1998. Racial prejudice and stereotype activation. *Personality & Social Psychology Bulletin* 24(4). 407–416.

Kawakami, Kerry, Heather Young, & John Dovidio. 2002. Automatic stereotyping: Category, trait and behavioral activations. *Personality and Social Psychology Bulletin* 28(1). 3–15.

Kruskal, William & W. Allen Wallis. 1952. Use of ranks in one-criterion variance analysis. *Journal of the American Statistical Association* 47. 583–621.

Lafford, Barbara. 1986. Valor diagnóstico-social del uso de ciertas variantes de /s/ en el español de Cartagena, Colombia. In Rafael Núñez-Cedeño, Iraset Páez, & Jorge Guitart (eds.), *Estudios sobre la fonología del español del Caribe*, 53–75. Caracas, Venezuela: La Casa de Bello.

Lambert, Wallace E., R. C. Hodgson, Robert C. Gardner, & S. Fillenbaum. 1960. Evaluational reactions to spoken language. *Journal of Abnormal and Social Psychology* 60(1). 44–51.

Levon, Erez. 2007. Sexuality in context: Variation and the sociolinguistic perception of identity. *Language in Society* 36. 533–554.

Lipski, John. 2001. The place of Chabacano in the Philippine linguistic profile. *Estudios de Sociolingüística* 2(2). 119–163.

López-Morales, Humberto. 1980. Pluralidad nominal, elisión de -/s/ y ambigüedad en los sociolectos de San Juan. *Homenaje a Ambrosio Rabanales, Número especial de Boletín de Filología* 32. 851–863.

López-Morales, Humberto. 1983. *Estratificación social del español de San Juan de Puerto Rico*. México City, México: Universidad Nacional Autónoma de México.

Mack, Sara. 2010a. A sociophonetic analysis of perception of sexual orientation in Puerto Rican Spanish. *Laboratory Phonology* 1(1). 41–64.

Mack, Sara. 2010b. Perception and identity: Stereotypes of speech and sexual orientation in Puerto Rican Spanish. In Claudia Borgonovo, Manuel Español-Echevarría, & Philippe Prévoste (eds.), *Selected proceedings of the 12th Hispanic Linguistics Symposium*, 136–147. Somerville, MA: Cascadilla Proceedings Project.

Mack, Sara. 2011. A sociophonetic analysis of /s/ variation in Puerto Rican Spanish. In Luis Ortiz-López (ed.), *Selected proceedings of the 13th Hispanic Linguistics Symposium*, 81–93. Somerville, MA: Cascadilla Proceedings Project.

Mack, Sara. 2013. Explicit and implicit methods in quantitative analyses of sociophonetic variation. *Studies in Hispanic and Lusophone Linguistics* 6(1). 165–178.

Mack, Sara & Benjamin Munson. 2012. The influence of /s/ quality on perception of men's sexual orientation: Explicit and implicit measures of the "gay lisp" stereotype. *Journal of Phonetics* 40(1). 198–212.

Macmillan, Neil & C. Douglas Creelman. 2005. *Detection theory: A user's guide*. Mahwah, NJ: Lawrence Erlbaum Associates.

Munson, Benjamin. 2007. The acoustic correlates of perceived masculinity, perceived femininity, and perceived sexual orientation. *Language and Speech* 50(1). 125–142.

Munson, Benjamin, Sarah Jefferson, & Elizabeth McDonald. 2006. The influence of perceived sexual orientation on fricative identification. *Journal of the Acoustical Society of America* 119. 2427–2437.

Munson, Benjamin, Elizabeth McDonald, Nancy DeBoe, & Aubrey White. 2006. Acoustic and perceptual bases of judgments of women and men's sexual orientation from read speech. *Journal of Phonetics* 34. 202–240.

Niedzielski, Nancy. 1999. The effect of social information on the perception of sociolinguistic variables. *Journal of language and Social Psychology* 18(1). 62–85.

Nosek, Brian, Anthony Greenwald, & Mahzarin Banaji. 2007. The Implicit Association Test at age 7: A methodological and conceptual review. In J. A. Bargh (ed.), *Social psychology and the unconscious: The automaticity of higher mental processes,* 265–292. New York: Psychology Press.

Ochs, Eleanor. 1992. Indexing gender. In A. Duranti & C. Goodwin (eds.), *Rethinking context: Language as an interactive phenomenon,* 336–358. Cambridge: Cambridge University Press.

Oliver Rajan, Julia. 2007. Mobility and its effects on vowel raising in the coffee zone of Puerto Rico. In Jonathan Holmquist, Augusto Lorenzino, & Lofti Sayahi (eds.), *Selected proceedings of the 3rd Workshop on Spanish Sociolinguistics,* 44–52. Somerville, MA: Cascadilla Proceedings Project.

Peña, Susana. 2003. Pájaration and transculturation: Language and meaning in Miami's Cuban American gay worlds. In William Leap & Tom Boellstorff (eds.), *Speaking in queer tongues,* 231–250. Champaign, IL: University of Illinois Press.

Roca, Iggy. 2005. Saturation of parameter setting in Spanish stress. *Phonology* 22. 345–394.

Santoro, Maurizio. 2007. Puerto Rican Spanish: A case of partial restructuring. *Hybrido: Arte y literatura* 10(9). 47–57.

Schneider, Walter, Amy Eschman, & Anthony Zuccolotto. 2002. *E-Prime user's guide.* Pittsburgh, PA: Psychology Software Tools, Inc.

Schwarz, Norbert & Gerd Bohner. 2001. The construction of attitudes. In Abraham Tesser & Norbert Schwarz (eds.), *Blackwell handbook of social psychology: Intraindividual processes,* 436–457. Malden, MA: Blackwell.

Schwegler, Armin & Juergen Kempff. 2007. *Fonética y fonología españolas.* Hoboken, NJ: Wiley.

Sívori, Horacio. 2005. *Locas, chongos, y gays: Sociabilidad homosexual masculina durante la década de 1990.* Buenos Aires: Editorial Antropofagia.

Sowards, Stacey. 2000. Juan Gabriel and audience interpretation: Cultural impressions of effeminacy and sexuality in Mexico. *Journal of Homosexuality* 39(2). 133–158.

Strand, Elizabeth. 1999. Uncovering the role of gender stereotypes in speech perception. *Journal of Language and Social Psychology* 18(1). 86–99.

Strand, Elizabeth. 2000. *Gender stereotype effects in speech processing.* Columbus: The Ohio State University dissertation.

Terrell, Tracy. Final /s/ in Cuban Spanish. *Hispania* 62(4). 599–612.

Tucker, Benjamin & Natasha Warner. 2007. Inhibition of processing due to reduction of the American English flap. In Jürgen Trouvain & William Barry (eds.), *Proceedings of the 16th International Congress of Phonetic Sciences,* 1949–1952. Saarbrucken, Germany: Universität des Saarlandes.

Valentín-Márquez, Wilfredo. 2006. La oclusión glotal y la construcción lingüística de identidades sociales en Puerto Rico. In Nuria Sagarra & Almeida Jacqueline Toribio (eds.),

Selected proceedings of the 9th Hispanic Linguistics Symposium, 326–341. Somerville, MA: Cascadilla Proceedings Project.

Wilson, Timothy D., Samuel Lindsey, & Tonya Y. Schooler. 2000. A model of dual attitudes. *Psychological Review* 107. 101–126.

Zentella, Ana Celia. 2003. José, can you see: Latin@ responses to racist discourse. In Doris Sommer (ed.), *Bilingual aesthetics,* 51–66. New York: Palgrave Press.

8

Percepts of Hungarian Pitch-Shifted Male Speech

Péter Rácz and Viktória Papp

Introduction

The aim of this chapter is to report on the results of an online study on the perception of male pitch in Hungarian. Respondents listened to either a male voice with raised pitch or the same male voice with lowered pitch, and they rated the voice on a number of attribute scales (such as short–tall). The main result is that, contrary to the expected outcome based on the Western socio-linguistic literature, the voice with the lowered pitch was rated as significantly more *feminine*. Principal components analysis of the ratings shows a correlation of ratings on the straight–gay dimension with other scales. These correlations provide evidence on an overwhelmingly negative implicit attitude toward gay men among the respondents.

The next section reviews the literature on pitch variation to show that pitch is not merely an acoustic correlate of body size but, rather, shows complex, structured variation depending on a larger scale of social than biological factors. This is underpinned by results on pitch perception—the judgments of speaker attributes based on pitch show a pattern of structured variation. At the same time, these judgments match the actual traits of these speakers rather poorly.

We then go on to discuss the methods used in our experiment, before turning to a detailed exposition of our results. The section "Discussion" focuses on the difference between our results and those reported in the Western socio-linguistic literature.

Review of Literature

This section gives a brief overview of the biological versus cultural factors that play a role in the production and perception of voice pitch among young

151

men. As readers are likely aware, the mean (reading) pitch values reported in the literature differ cross-culturally among comparably aged speakers of the same gender and as such they are at least in part culturally determined. The fact that "normative" values reported in sociolinguistic and clinical literature are borrowed and traded between dialects and languages belies the underlying essentialist assumption in these fields. This assumption is that the mean (reading) pitch value is predominantly a result of biological forces only. If pitch variation were truly defined by sheer biology, we would also expect speakers to produce it and listeners to evaluate and relate to it homogeneously across the board. While this is not a new concept, a brief survey of the evidence is in order to lay out the assumptions that formed the basis of our hypotheses. We will give an overview of the perception of the speaking pitch and show evidence of how listeners are ready to attribute identity traits and often voluntary, agentive use to the gendered pitch. These uses are strongly embedded in the societal use of language, so the mechanistic interpretation of speech/speaker perception results does not acknowledge the intersectional nature of speaker identity. In this chapter, we use the term *pitch* with the understanding that the Hertz (Hz) values we report are in fact measures of the fundamental frequency which is the main, but not the only, acoustic correlate of pitch.

A frequently made assumption used to be that the pitch level of speech is physiologically determined and that it serves as a reflection of body size. However, a large number of studies noted an absence of any correlation between overall pitch level and the speaker's body dimensions such as height, weight, size of larynx, and so on (Künzel 1989; van Dommelen & Moxness 1995; Collins 2000; González 2004). Studies since have found effects of the speaker's biological age (e.g., Nishio & Niimi 2008; Torre & Barlow 2009), language (e.g., van Bezooijen 1995; Yamazawa & Hollien 1992), and dialects/ethnolects spoken (e.g., Awan & Mueller 1996; Deutsch et al. 2009) and between monolingual and bilingual speakers of the same language (e.g., Abu-Al-Makarem & Petrosino 2007; Ullakonoja 2007). All these strongly indicate that pitch is subject to sociocultural forces.

To give a few examples of the importance of cultural background, let's take the physiological comparisons (Kahane 1982; Hirano, Kurita, & Nakashima 1983) that found shorter vocal folds in Japanese adult males and females than in Caucasian Americans. This would predict higher-speaking fundamental frequency for the Japanese speakers. However, we have ample evidence that Japanese females have systematically higher pitch than US females, while Japanese males typically display lower fundamental frequency than US males (cf. Yuasa 2008 and references therein). Conversely, in children the lack of sexual dimorphism or gendered difference in the available frequency range until about age seven (e.g., Böhme & Stuchlik 1995; Lee, Potamianos, & Narayanan 1999; Vorperian et al. 2005) is paired with pitch and tune/tone usage that is shaped toward gendered norms before this age (e.g., Local 1982; Ferrand & Bloom 1996; Vorperian & Kent 2007). Finally, even the pitch of a community can change over time, as demonstrated in studies about Australian women over fifty years of age (Russell, Penny, & Pemberton 1995; Pemberton, McCormack, & Russell 1998) and when we compare US men's values across the studies, from Hollien & Shipp (1972) and Hollien & Jackson (1973) to Torre & Barlow (2009). The absence of clear correlations between pitch and biological attributes, the degree of structured pitch variation across and within speaker groups, and, most important, the presence of pitch variation among children prior to biological differentiation all indicate the importance of sociocultural factors in determining pitch variation not only in English but in other languages as well.

Now we turn our attention to the forces that shape the perception of pitch. While listeners are fairly bad at estimating speaker characteristics, they are also fairly consistent in their misjudgments such as systematically assuming that (natural or synthesized) low-pitched male speakers are tall (van Dommelen & Moxness 1995; González 2004), are more attractive, are older and heavier, are more likely to have a hairy chest, have a more muscular body type, and pose a higher risk of infidelity (Collins 2000; Feinberg et al. 2005; O'Connor, Re, & Feinberg 2011; Simmons, Peters, & Rhodes 2011)—but only by female listeners. In Pisanski & Rendall (2011) and Pisanski, Mishra, & Rendall (2012), listeners evaluated size, masculinity, and attractiveness of male and female voices whose speaking pitch was shifted either up or down. Body size, masculinity, and attractiveness were all rated in the predictable direction between low and high natural male voices by female listeners. Male listeners, on the other hand, showed no distinction in the attractiveness ratings between the low and high male voice conditions.

Vukovic et al.'s (2010) work branches out from analyzing the speaker's pitch in a vacuum and highlights the correlation between the pitch of the listener and his or her pitch preferences as a listener. They report that women's own pitch predicts their preference for masculinity in men's voices: the lower the women's pitch, the more likely they were to prefer the lower pitch-shifted condition in men. It is, however, not uncommon for women to prefer more feminine male voices. In Puts (2005), women prefer more feminine English male voices as long-term partners and in O'Connor, Fraccaro, & Feinberg (2012) as partners are significantly more likely to invest time and effort and to be financially generous.

To date, Apicella & Feinberg (2009) is the only work on non-Western pitch perception, carried out on the Tanzanian Hazda. In their sample, both men and women viewed lower-pitched voices in the opposite sex as being better at acquiring resources (i.e., hunting and gathering). While men preferred higher-pitched women's voices as marriage partners, women showed no overall preference for voice pitch in men. To the best of our knowledge, there is no literature on the pitch perception of Hungarian listeners or on the broader East-Central European languages.

In sum, pitch shows structured variation based on a wide variety of factors beyond body size and biological gender. This is reflected by perception as well—people have a low accuracy in determining speaker characteristics based on pitch alone. Furthermore, while general patterns are undoubtedly observed, the social evaluation of pitch can also widely vary. This makes the scarcity of data from languages other than English all the more regrettable.

In the rest of this chapter, we report on our experiment on the perception of modulated male pitch in Hungarian. The findings are, we believe, highly relevant in extending our knowledge on the perception of structured pitch variation in the world's languages (though limited by the complete lack of data on Hungarian male pitch from production studies).

Methods

OVERVIEW

We conducted our experiment online. All respondents were Hungarian speakers, age eighteen or above. After receiving written instructions, respondents listened to a minute-long voice clip, which they could listen to multiple times. Afterward, they were given twelve-attribute Likert scales (ranging from 1 to 5) to rate the person whose voice they had just heard. Then, in turn, they had to rate themselves using the same twelve scales. Finally, they had to fill in a background questionnaire on general details such as their age, gender, and education.

The experiment was an across-subject design with four conditions. This means that each respondent was only in one condition and the effect of the conditions on the responses is gauged by comparing respondents to each other. The experiment had four conditions, varying along two dimensions. Half the respondents listened to a clip of a male Hungarian voice with a raised pitch, and the other half listened to a clip of a voice with a lowered pitch. Half the respondents received written instructions which contained a reference to language and sexuality, and the other half had this reference omitted from the instructions. We discuss this in detail in the following sections. We will refer to the first dimension as sound (raised/lowered) and to the second as prime (prime/no prime).

We had three main hypotheses. First, we expected that respondents rate voice clips differently if these clips differ in pitch, in line with the results we see in the literature discussed previously. Second, we expect various ratings to correlate with each other, indicative of the types of linguistic stereotypes of male speakers of Hungarian that we might find among our respondents. There is no previous work on these linguistic stereotypes in Hungarian, making any results especially exciting. Finally, we also expected that mentioning *language* and *sexuality* in the instructions of the experiment amplifies the aforementioned two effects—that is, that stereotyping works stronger if it is primed.

STIMULI

The voice clip was recorded with a twenty-seven-year-old male native speaker of Hungarian in a sound booth. It is a fifty-eight-second reading of a neutral-sounding Hungarian text that contains no voiceless sibilants (cf. Appendix). In order to create the input stimuli, the pitch of the clip was shifted up and down, respectively, with one semitone, so that the distance between the raised clip and the lowered clip was two semitones. The original clip was not used in the experiment. We used the SoundTouch Audio Processing Library (Parviainen 2014) implemented in Audacity (v2.0.4). Our method shifts the entire sound band, so that the relative positions of the formants remain the same compared to the fundamental frequency. The advantage of this method is that the percept of the formants remains the same relative to the pitch, so that a voice clip with a raised or lowered pitch will sound like a person with a higher or lower pitch, rather than a person modulating his or her pitch in different ways.

We presented the two modified clips, along with the original recording, to a focus group of native speaker linguists and laypersons both to assess whether there is a perceptual difference between the clips and to determine the degree to which these clips sound natural. The group agreed that the main percept of the difference was a difference in pitch, and that the two modified clips sounded "normal"—that is, within the assumed pitch range of Hungarian males. We relied on these results, as well as our intuitions, in using the voice clips in the experiment.

Whether a given respondent heard the stimuli with the raised or with the lowered pitch is set by the *sound* condition. One respondent only heard one sound clip.

RESPONDENTS

The experiment was hosted on Qualtrics, an online survey platform, for five days in December 2013. Respondents were recruited through Facebook, Tumblr, Twitter, and mailing lists. No incentives were offered. In all, 921 people participated, all Hungarian speakers, age eighteen or above. Forty-nine respondents indicated that they recognized the speaker, and they were excluded from the experiment. From the remaining 872 respondents, 821 gave complete answers (i.e., did not miss a single response). The across-subject design allowed us to include partial answers in the statistical analysis, so we report results based on 872 respondents: 521 of the respondents are women, 322 are men, and 29 did not provide an answer. Twenty-eight respondents self-identified as gay.

Respondent age ranged from eighteen to seventy-two, with a mean age of thirty-three. Finally, years spent in education ranged from six to thirty-one, with a mean of seventeen. (School is officially obligatory until the age of sixteen, the tenth grade, in Hungary, with a high school leaving exam following after twelve years. Fifteen years in education suggest a bachelor's degree, seventeen a master's degree.)

The sample is not representative of Hungary's population. It is younger (the population's median age is 40.8, the sample's is 30) and more educated; 19% of the population has a college diploma, which implies at least fifteen years in education—in comparison, fifteen is the first quadrant of our sample. The sample has more female than male respondents (the population's male to female ratio is 0.91, the sample's is 0.61), and it has a skewed geographical distribution (17% of the population lives in Budapest, 31% of the respondents do). (All data come from the 2011 census of the Hungarian Central Statistical Office.) In brief, the sample is generally skewed toward young, educated women living in cities.

The respondents were divided evenly across conditions. In the *sound* condition, 443 heard the raised pitch clip, 429 the lowered one. In the *prime* condition, 438 were primed, and 434 were not. Ratings on the stimuli have a mean of 2.72, ratings on self have a mean of 2.83 (on 1–5 scales). If scores are standardized across respondents, the standardized scores highly correlate with the nonstandardized ones ($r = 0.97$). Due to this and to the sample size, we used nonstandardized scores.

DESIGN

We conducted the experiment in Hungarian. Respondents completed the experiment in their own web browsers. After giving consent, they were given a set of instructions telling them that the experiment is part of a study on attitudes toward speech and speech styles. In the prime condition, we prefaced this instruction with a sentence stating that the study is about language and sexuality. Following this screen, respondents were instructed to listen to a voice clip (either raised or lowered, depending on the *sound* condition) and picture the person they heard. They could listen to the voice clip multiple times while at this screen, but they were warned that they could not go back to it later.

In the next screen, they were given twelve attribute scales. The scales ran 1–5 and are the following:

- *dumb–clever*
- *masculine–feminine*
- *straight–gay*
- *emphatic–indifferent*

- *extroverted–introverted*
- *fake–natural*
- *sober–passionate*
- *rich–poor*
- *short–tall*
- *handsome–ugly*
- *faithful–unfaithful*
- *friendly–unfriendly*

The scales were largely based on Levon (2006). The ordering of the scales was random. The ordering of attributes within the preceding pairs reflects the ordering in the experiment, which was fixed and was based on the alphabetic order of the attributes in Hungarian. We emphasized this in the instructions.

The next screen showed the same scales in a different random order, and the respondents were asked to rate themselves. In this chapter, we use one piece of information from this scale, self-ratings on the *straight–gay* scale. Participants had a clear bimodal distribution of ratings, with an overwhelming majority rating themselves as 1, or *completely straight*. We interpreted ratings of 5 as *self-reported gay* in our analysis.

Self-rating was followed by a screen with a general background question-naire asking about the respondent's gender, age, years spent in education, place where the respondent went to high school, and whether the respondent knows the male they just heard in person.

Predictions

As we established previously, we had three main hypotheses. Hypothesis I is that the voice clip with the lower pitch would be rated differently from the voice clip with the higher pitch. Specifically, it would be *taller*, more *masculine*, and more *straight*. Hypothesis II is that these ratings are correlated—a voice that is rated as more *straight* is also rated as more *masculine*, for instance. Hypothesis III is that mentioning *language* and *sexuality* in the instructions of the experiment amplifies the preceding two effects—stereotyping working stronger if it is primed.

As seen in our review earlier, there is overwhelming evidence for the social/indexical use of pitch in English and other languages. Given no previous work on Hungarian, our starting assumption was that pitch differences will be evaluated in the same way as elsewhere—the voice with the lower pitch will be rated as more *masculine, straight,* and *tall* than the voice with the higher pitch. Based on Levon (2006), who reports similar correlations, we also expected ratings to correlate with each other. Our predictions on these correlations are more arbitrary and are mainly based on anecdotal evidence of sexual stereotypes in Hungary. As such, these correlations more readily lend themselves to *post hoc* interpretations.

We have the following predictions for our results:

(1) There are correlations between the conditions and the ratings.
   a. The raised voice receives lower ratings on the *short–tall* scale, because a higher pitch is associated with smaller height.
   b. The raised voice receives higher ratings on the *masculine–feminine* scale, because a higher pitch is associated with femininity.
   c. The raised voice receives higher ratings on the *straight–gay* scale, because Hungarian gay males are perceived as more feminine.
   d. Priming of sexuality increases these effects.

(2) When it comes to rating the stimuli, there are correlations amongst the ratings themselves.
   a. A masculine, straight man is a more positive stereotype than a feminine, gay man, so that "positive" ratings (like that of *friendliness*) will correlate positively with low ratings on *masculine–feminine* and *straight–gay*.
   b. This effect is more pronounced for male respondents than for female ones.
   c. This effect is more pronounced for straight respondents than for gay ones.
   d. Priming of sexuality increases these effects.

Results

OVERVIEW

We tested the set of predictions under (1) using linear regression with the individual scales as dependent variables and the two conditions and respondent information as predictors (we elaborate on this later). Predictions (1)a–(1)d are not supported by our results. However, we found a significant difference in ratings on the *masculine–feminine* scale depending on the *sound* condition; the raised clip is rated as less feminine ($p < 0.5$). We return to this result in the discussion. It is worth noting, however, that respondents reacted differently to the raised and the lowered clip on this scale, even if the direction of the effect is the inverse of what was predicted. Priming did not have any effect on the ratings for the entire respondent set. Respondents who self-identified as gay ($n = 28$) were significantly more likely to give both clips a higher rating on the *straight–gay* scale if they were primed ($p < 0.5$).

The set of predictions under (2) cannot be straightforwardly tested. Essentially, they are assumptions on the shape of the response set, that is, the way the responses on the individual scales correlate with each other (we elaborate on this later). It is possible, however, to say whether the predictions are confirmed by the shape of the response set. Prediction (2)a is supported by our results. Higher ratings on *straight–gay* and *masculine–feminine* pattern together, and these also pattern together with higher ratings on positive-negative scales like *rich–poor* and *handsome–ugly*. This remains true irrespective of respondent background. For instance, women and men pattern together in their responses. Gay respondents are even less forgiving—their high ratings on *straight–gay* and *masculine–feminine* pattern together with higher ratings on even more positive–negative scales. This relates to the fact that these respondents are more perceptible to priming.

EFFECTS OF CONDITIONS

We analyzed the effect of condition on ratings in the following way. We looked at individual scales (like *masculine–feminine*) and used stepwise linear regression to determine whether the information we have about the listener (age, gender, and background; which clip he or she listened to, whether he or she was primed) affects the result. For a given scale, the dependent variable was the score on the scale, and the predictors were the condition, the age, gender, and years of education of the respondent, as well as the town in which the respondent went to high school.

We had predictions for three scales, so we report results that have a significance value smaller than 0.5, following standard practice. Since we had no hypotheses for the other scales, we would have only reported effects that are twelve times stronger (since there are twelve scales)—any effect smaller than that we attribute to chance alone.

Pitch has an effect on ratings on the *masculine–feminine* scale (but not on the *short–tall, straight–gay* scales). The direction of this effect is, however, the opposite of what we expected: the raised clip is perceived as more *masculine* ($p < 0.5$). The only relevant predictor is *sound* (i.e., the pitch difference). Figure 8.1 shows a density plot of the answers.

If we focus on the gay respondents (n = 28), we find that sound had no effect on their ratings. The prime, however, did—gay respondents gave higher ratings on the *straight–gay* scale if they were primed. The only relevant predictor is *prime*. Figure 8.2 shows a density plot of the answers. We must note, however, that the sample size is much smaller for gay respondents (28 respondents vs. 873 overall), which affects the strength of the predictors (though the effect remains significant).

CORRELATIONS OF RATINGS

The second hypothesis relates not to the correlation of the scores with the conditions but rather to the correlation of the scores with each other. These

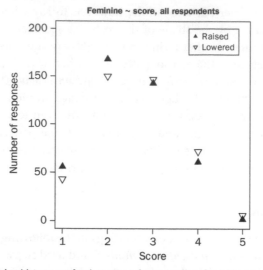

FIGURE 8.1 Overlapping histogram of rating scores for *masculine–feminine*, all respondents

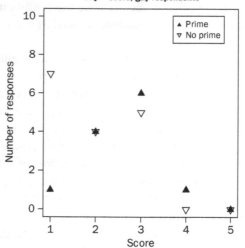

FIGURE 8.2 Overlapping histogram of rating scores for *straight–gay*, gay respondents

correlations are informative of how respondents perceived a male voice. While the correlations can be influenced by the conditions (and the other predictors), this is less relevant here.

In order to visualize correlations between ratings, we first look at the correlation matrices in the data set. Respondents gave two kinds of ratings—they rated the stimulus (the sound clip) on twelve scales, and they used the same twelve scales to rate themselves. We will focus on ratings on the stimulus.

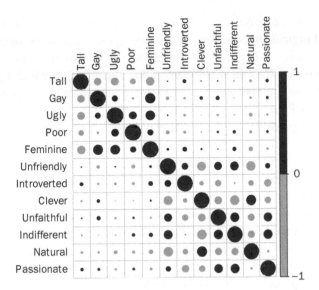

FIGURE 8.3 Correlations of ratings on the sound clip with each other, all respondents

Figure 8.3 shows the correlations of the stimuli ratings with each other for all respondents. The size of the circle in each cell indicates the strength of the correlation between the scale indicated in the first column and the scale indicated in the column headers. Only the second attribute of each scale is shown (so that *masculine–feminine* is feminine). Positive correlations are black, negative correlations are gray. We can see strong patterns in the responses. *Tall* has a strong negative correlation with feminine. In turn, feminine has a strong positive correlation with *gay, ugly,* and *poor,* whereas unfriendly has a positive correlation with *unfaithful, indifferent,* and, curiously enough, *passionate.* (Recall that the respondents were rating a male voice.)

Though Figure 8.3 sheds some light on the correlation patterns, the way they cluster together is far from evident. Furthermore, this figure says nothing about the effect of the conditions and the other predictors (like respondent gender or sexual orientation) on these correlations.

We used principal components analysis (PCA) to address these issues. PCA takes a dataset consisting of interrelated variables (like our ratings) and turns it into a dataset consisting of the same number (in this example) of independent variables. These variables are set up in such a way that the first variable explains the most amount of variation in the dataset, the second variable the second largest amount of variation, and so on. These new, independent variables (the principal components) can be input to the original dataset to see how they pattern together with the variables they are based on (our ratings) as well as the subject-level predictors (like the age and gender of the listeners).

A principal components analysis of the stimuli ratings of our respondents yields a set of principal components reflecting the correlations of the original ratings. The first two of these components are responsible for 24% of the variation. They set up the two main dimensions according to which the data are structured. We can visualize these two main dimensions by the means of a biplot (Figure 8.4).

Figure 8.4 shows that ratings pattern together very strongly on two main dimensions. First, component 1 pits *indifferent, unfriendly,* and *passionate* against *natural* and *clever*. To put it simply, according to the respondents, the person they heard is either typically the former (*indifferent, unfriendly,* etc.) or the latter (*natural* and *clever*). Component 2 shows us something we have seen in the correlation matrix—tall ratings are contrasted with *feminine, ugly, gay,* and, to a lesser extent, *poor* ratings (i.e., high ratings on these scales). The *introverted* scale does not do much on these two dimensions. Our predictors (*sound* and *prime,* as well as respondent age, gender, etc.) do not affect these patterns much. If we plot the principal components for female and male respondents, we get almost the same picture. Independently from the stimuli, the prime, and their backgrounds, respondents all agreed on a response pattern that invokes the image of a clever, natural Hungarian man, compared to an *unfriendly, passionate, indifferent*

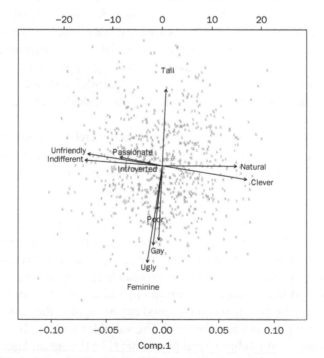

FIGURE 8.4 Principal components analysis of stimuli ratings, all respondents

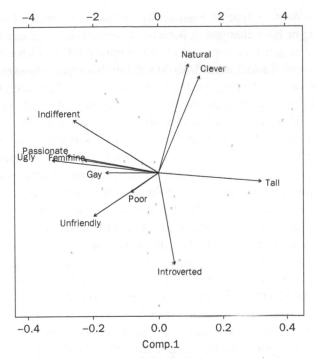

FIGURE 8.5 Principal components analysis of stimuli ratings, gay respondents

one, and that of a tall and rich Hungarian man, compared to a *feminine, gay, ugly*, and *poor* one.

One notable exception for the indifference of subject-level variables is the respondents' sexual orientation. Gay respondents present a different correlation pattern, shown in Figure 8.5. The two dimensions that are typical of all the respondents are less distinct here. Basically, *feminine* and *gay* pattern together with not just *ugly* and *poor*, but all the negative attributes.

Discussion

This study produced two main results. First, respondents rate the lower-pitched voice as *more feminine* than the higher pitched voice. Second, ratings on the *straight–gay* scale correlate with ratings on other scales. High ratings on *gay* indicate negative ratings of other attributes such as *short, poor,* and *ugly*, and so on.

Gay participants rated the stimuli as more *gay* if they were primed. Their high ratings on *gay* indicate more negative ratings on other attributes than those of the rest of the sample.

We expected that respondents would rate the higher-pitched voice as more *feminine*. On the one hand, the result that respondents found the higher-pitched voice more *masculine* can be understood as a sign that Hungarian listeners prize a non-Western type of masculinity or that the norms of masculinity are changing or have changed. It is certainly remarkable that our result goes against what is generally reported in the literature (cf. Feinberg et al. 2005; Pisanski & Rendall 2011; Pisanski, Mishra, & Rendell 2012), although, as we saw in the earlier review, the situation is not this clear-cut (cf. Puts 2005; O'Connor, Fraccaro, & Feinberg 2012). At the same time, significant results in the literature (see above) tend to come from female listeners, whereas our result did not show a gender effect. On the other hand, it is also possible that masculine pitch in Hungarian is located above the low-condition pitch in the experiment (cf. Re et al. 2012), effectively making one voice in the sound dimension an outlier uninterpretable to listeners within their known reference framework, even though the responses of our pretest focus group suggest otherwise.

The fact that high *gay* ratings correlate with negative ratings on other attribute scales can be compared to the results of a similar study by Levon (2006). Levon found that high ratings on *gay* correlated with high ratings on *neat* and *friendly*, two positive attributes. Our study found that high ratings on *gay* correlated with high ratings on negative attributes, like *poor* and *ugly*. If we interpret this as an indicator of the difference in the attitudes of the two samples (college undergraduates in Manhattan vs. predominantly female and predominantly highly educated Hungarians), this could correspond to a general difference in attitudes toward homosexuality in Eastern Europe and the West (Lipka 2013). At the same time, the two studies are not directly comparable due to the difference in the samples, as well as the difference in the scales (Levon does not have *ugly* or *poor*, for instance, while the *friendly–unfriendly* dimension was orthogonal to the *straight–gay* dimension in our PCA).

Nevertheless, both the respondents' reaction to pitch differences and the correlations of their ratings are markedly different from reports on Anglo societies, which serves to re-emphasize the cultural situatedness of any exploration of linguistic variables. Western concepts of masculinity and their linguistic manifestations cannot be treated as the sole paradigm of sociolinguistic inquiry.

Appendix

Stimulus Text

Aligha látogat úgy Budára külföldi vendég, hogy ne látogatna el a Budai Várba. A már majdnem negyven éve kiemelt hagyatékként kezelt területen látogatók ezrei fordulnak meg évente. Lenyűgöző épületei, a középkorból eredő történelme rengeteg felemelő pillanatot jelent minden idetévedőnek. A mai várnegyedet már IV. Béla idejében megemlíti egy oklevél. Méltó pompáját azonban a palota a Hunyadiak idején nyerte el. Nem kellett rengeteg időnek eltelnie ahhoz, hogy a várat, ugyanúgy, ahogy a királyi palotát, a törökök ármánnyal foglalják el. A Vár nyugati haderők jóvoltából menekült meg a török iga alól, de itt nem értek véget a kemény idők. Történelme folyamán még jónéhány alkalommal került idegen kézre, legutóbb a világháború végén. Ennek ellenére, ha egy külföldi ma a Várba látogat, nem talál ott majd egyebet, mint egy lenyűgöző múlt halhatatlan emlékeit.

'It's hard to visit Buda without visiting Buda Castle. The area, which has been a prime heritage site for more than forty years, has thousands of visitors every year. Its breathtaking architecture, along with its medieval history, has a lot to offer to these visitors. Today's Castle is first mentioned in a charter by Béla IV. It reached its present form under the Hunyadis. As the rest of the country, the Castle was captured by the Turks, and later escaped Turkish occupation with help from the West. It has been occupied by foreign troops a number of times since then, such as during the Second World War. However, when a foreigner visits the Castle today, they will only find the mementos of a glorious past.'

References

Abu-Al-Makarem, Ali & Linda Petrosino. 2007. Reading and spontaneous speaking fundamental frequency of young Arabic men for Arabic and English languages: A comparative study. *Perceptual and Motor Skills* 105(2). 572–580.

Apicella, Coren L. & David R. Feinberg. 2009. Voice pitch alters mate-choice-relevant perception in hunter–gatherers. *Proceedings of the Royal Society: Biological Sciences* 276. 1077–1082.

Awan, Shaheen N. & Peter B. Mueller. 1996. Speaking fundamental frequency characteristics of white, African American, and Hispanic kindergartners. *Journal of Speech and Hearing Research* 39(3). 573–577.

Böhme, Gerhard & Gisela Stuchlik. 1995. Voice profiles and standard voice profile of untrained children. *Journal of Voice* 9(3). 304–307.

Collins, Sarah A. 2000. Men's voices and women's choices. *Animal Behaviour* 60(6). 773–780.

Deutsch, Diana, Jinghong Le, Jing Shen, & Trevor Henthorn. 2009. The pitch levels of female speech in two Chinese villages. *Journal of the Acoustical Society of America* 125(5). 208–213.

Feinberg, David R., Benedict C. Jones, Anthony C. Little, D. Michael Burt, & David I. Perrett. 2005. Manipulations of fundamental and formant frequencies influence the attractiveness of human male voices. *Animal Behaviour* 69(3). 561–568.

Ferrand, Carole T. & Ronald L. Bloom. 1996. Gender differences in children's intonational patterns. *Journal of Voice* 10(3). 284–291.

González, Julio. 2004. Formant frequencies and body size of speaker: A weak relationship in adult humans. *Journal of Phonetics* 32(2). 277–287.

Hirano, Minoru, Shigejiro Kurita, & Terujuki Nakashima. 1983. Growth, development, and aging of human vocal folds. In Diane Bless & James Abbs (eds.), *Vocal fold physiology: Contemporary research and clinical issues*, 22–43. San Diego, CA: College-Hill Press.

Hollien, Harry & Bernard Jackson. 1973. Normative data on the speaking fundamental frequency characteristics of young adult males. *Journal of Phonetics* 1. 117–120.

Hollien, Harry & Thomas Shipp. 1972. Speaking fundamental frequency and chronological age in males. *Journal of Speech and Hearing Research* 15(1). 155–159.

Kahane, Joel 1982. Growth of the human prepubertal and pubertal larynx. *Journal of Speech and Hearing Research* 25(3). 446–455.

Künzel, Hermann 1989. How well does average fundamental frequency correlate with speaker height and weight? *Phonetica* 46(1–3). 117–125.

Lee, Sungbok, Alexandros Potamianos, & Shrikanth Narayanan. 1999. Acoustics of children's speech: Developmental changes of temporal and spectral parameters. *Journal of the Acoustical Society of America* 105(3). 1455–1468.

Levon, Erez. 2006. Hearing gay: Prosody, interpretation, and the affective judgments of men's speech. *American Speech* 81(1). 56–78.

Lipka, Michael. 2013, December 12. Eastern and Western Europe divided over gay marriage, homosexuality. *Factank: News in the numbers* (blog), *Pew Research Center*. Retrieved from http://www.pewresearch.org.

Local, John. 1982. Modelling intonational variability in children's speech. In Suzanne Romaine (ed.), *Sociolinguistic variation in speech communities*, 85–103. London: Edward Arnold.

Nishio, Masaki & Seiji Niimi. 2008. Changes in speaking fundamental frequency characteristics with aging. *Folia Phoniatrica et Logopaedica* 60(3). 120–1127.

O'Connor, Jillian, Daniel Re, & David R. Feinberg. 2011. Voice pitch influences perceptions of sexual infidelity. *Evolutionary Psychology* 9(1). 64–78.

O'Connor, Jillian, Paul Fraccaro, & David Feinberg. 2012. The influence of male voice pitch on women's perceptions of relationship investment. *Journal of Evolutionary Psychology* 10(1). 1–13.

Parviainen, Olli. 2014. Soundtouch audio processing library. Available at http://soundtouch.surina.net.

Pemberton, Cecilia, Paul McCormack, & Alison Russell. 1998. Have women's voices lowered across time? A cross sectional study of Australian women's voices. *Journal of Voice* 12(2). 208–213.

Pisanski, Katarzyna & Drew Rendall. 2011. The prioritization of voice fundamental frequency or formants in listeners' assessments of speaker size, masculinity, and attractiveness. *Journal of the Acoustical Society of America* 129(4). 2201–2212.

Pisanski, Katarzyna, Sandeep Mishra, & Drew Rendall. 2012. The evolved psychology of voice: evaluating interrelationships in listeners' assessments of the size, masculinity, and attractiveness of unseen speakers. *Evolution and Human Behavior* 33(5). 509–519.

Puts, David Andrew 2005. Mating context and menstrual phase affects women's preferences for male voice pitch. *Evolution and Human Behavior* 26(5). 388–397.

Re, Daniel, Jillian O'Connor, Patrick Bennett, & David R. Feinberg. 2012. Preferences for very low and very high voice pitch in humans. *PLoS ONE* 7(3). e32719.

Russell, Alison, Lynda Penny, & Cecilia Pemberton. 1995. Speaking fundamental frequency changes over time in women: a longitudinal study. *Journal of Speech and Hearing Research* 38(1). 101–109.

Simmons, Leigh, Marianne Peters, & Gillian Rhodes. 2011. Low pitched voices are perceived as masculine and attractive but do they predict semen quality in men? *PLoS ONE* 6(12). e29271.

Torre, Peter, III & Jessica A. Barlow. 2009. Age-related changes in acoustic characteristics of adult speech. *Journal of Communication Disorders* 42. 324–333.

Ullakonoja, Riikka 2007. Comparison of pitch range in Finnish (L1) fluency and Russian (L2). In Jürgen Trouvain & William Barry (eds.), *Proceedings of the XVIth International Congress of Phonetic Sciences*, 1701–1704. Saarbrücken, Germany: Universität des Saarlandes.

van Bezooijen, Renée. 1995. Sociocultural aspects of pitch differences between Japanese and Dutch women. *Language and Speech* 38(3). 253–265.

van Dommelen, Wim & Bente Moxness. 1995. Acoustic parameters in speaker height and weight identification: Sex-specific behaviour. *Language and Speech* 38(3). 267–287.

Vorperian, Houri & Ray Kent. 2007. Vowel acoustic space development in children: A synthesis of acoustic and anatomic data. *Journal of Speech, Language, and Hearing Research* 50(6). 1510–1545.

Vorperian, Houri, Ray Kent, Mary Lindstrom, Cliff Kalina, Lindell Gentry, & Brian Yandell. 2005. Development of vocal tract length during early childhood: A magnetic resonance imaging study. *Journal of the Acoustical Society of America* 117(1). 338–350.

Vukovic, Jovana, Benedict Jones, Lisa DeBruine, David Feinberg, Finlay Smith, Anthony Little, Lisa Welling, & Julie Main. 2010. Women's own voice pitch predicts their preferences for masculinity in men's voices. *Behavioral Ecology* 21(4). 767–772.

Yamazawa, Hideko & Harry Hollien. 1992. Speaking fundamental frequency patterns of Japanese women. *Phonetica* 49(2). 128–140.

Yuasa, Ikuko Patricia. 2008. *Culture and gender of voice pitch: A sociophonetic comparison of the Japanese and Americans*. London: Equinox.

9

/s/exuality in Smalltown California

GENDER NORMATIVITY AND THE ACOUSTIC REALIZATION OF /S/

Robert J. Podesva and Janneke Van Hofwegen

Introduction

Previous sociophonetic research has established that, in some communities, the realization of /s/ may correlate with a speaker's gender (Strand 1999; Stuart-Smith 2007; Stuart-Smith, Timmins, & Tweedie 2007; Fuchs & Toda 2010; Hazenberg 2012; Zimman 2012; Levon & Holmes-Elliott 2013; Pharao et al. 2014), sexuality (Linville 1998; Munson et al. 2006; Levon 2007; Campbell-Kibler 2011; Hazenberg 2012; Zimman 2013; Pharao et al. 2014), or rurality (Campbell-Kibler 2011). While past research has tended to zero in on one of these dimensions, this chapter examines how ideologies about the country, gender, sexuality, and their inter-relations play out in the same community. We find it fruitful to consider these connections because communities where rurality constitutes an important axis of social distinction are likely to subscribe to traditional norms regarding gender and sexuality. This chapter examines the acoustic realization of /s/ among residents of Shasta County, a community just north of California's San Joaquin Valley. Drawing on a series of comparisons within the local community, we show that country-identified speakers exhibit different patterns from speakers who orient to the town, and also that members of a tight-knit LGBT (lesbian/gay/bisexual/transgender) community exhibit somewhat different patterns from community members who do not identify as sexual minorities. We further contrast our findings with patterns previously observed for speakers in urban areas and find that in spite of significant differences between straight and LGBT speakers in Redding, both groups of speakers produce more normatively gendered patterns than their counterparts in cities. Our primary claim is that the realization of /s/ is heavily constrained by dominant local ideologies about gender and sexuality. Specifically, the sociopolitical conservativism characteristic of this country community polarizes gender distinction and pressures sexual minorities to adhere to normative gender patterns.

Before describing the community under consideration in greater detail, we review a number of social factors that have been found to correlate with the acoustic realization of /s/. One of the most robust factors established in the previous literature is sex, stemming in part from gross physiological differences between women and men. Given generally larger vocal tracts and disproportionately larger lips relative to the vocal tract, the cavity in front of the constriction for /s/ is typically larger for men, yielding relatively lower-frequency concentrations of energy for fricatives—which is most frequently observed to effect the acoustic measures of center of gravity (lower for men) and skewness (higher for men).

While it cannot be denied that a sex-based anatomical difference influences sibilant frequencies, physical size merely sets the limits for what is possible, and numerous studies have found that women and men alike play within these limits to fashion a variety of gendered selves. This is possible in large part because the place of articulation for /s/ is highly variable, with the fronting and retraction of the tongue producing shorter and longer front cavities, respectively. For example, Stuart-Smith, Timmins, & Tweedie (2007) find that men in Glasgow retract the tongue to produce /s/, which in effect enhances the sex-based physiological difference. Such sex-based difference can also be counteracted, which was observed in the same Glaswegian English-speaking community, where Stuart-Smith (2007) reports that young working class women's /s/ is acoustically similar to that of men in the community. The intersectionality of gender and class can also be seen in Levon & Holmes-Elliott's (2013) study of two British reality television programs. They find, for example, that working-class women (on *The Only Way Is Essex*) produce higher peak frequencies of /s/ (which generally correlate with fronter articulations) when talking with other women than when talking in mixed-sex interactions, while upper-middle-class women (on *Made in Chelsea*) do not exhibit such contextual differences. Levon & Holmes-Elliott (2013) argue that the way women on *The Only Way Is Essex* perform gender "is grounded in what is essentially a class-based understanding of self" (117).

Transgender individuals offer another lens through which the gendered indexical potential of /s/ can be viewed. In his study on gender construction in Ottawa, Hazenberg (2012) finds that trans women and men pattern with members of their own gender group, rather than with members of the sex class assigned to them at birth. This pattern suggests that trans men and women develop new norms regarding the frequency of /s/ while transitioning. Direct evidence for this longitudinal change can be observed in Zimman's (2012) yearlong study of trans men, in which increasingly lower centers of gravity for /s/ were documented over time. While medical interventions like testosterone therapy likely influenced speech patterns in a number of ways, they were unlikely to have influenced speech articulators that directly bear on the realization of /s/.

The acoustic realization of /s/ also represents well-chartered territory in studies of language and sexuality. Much of the earlier work on /s/ concentrated on its temporal dimensions of variability. Gay men were found by some to produce longer /s/ than their straight counterparts (e.g., Linville 1998), and subsequent perception studies have verified that listeners may draw on durational cues when assessing how gay speech samples sound. Levon (2007) systematically altered the duration of /s/ in matched guise samples while covarying the samples' pitch properties. He found that small durational manipulations were insufficiently salient to significantly affect gayness ratings on their own, but that samples with both lengthened /s/ and widened pitch ranges were perceived as gayer-sounding. The spectral properties of /s/ have also been found to be correlated with sounding gay. Munson et al. (2006), for example, find that /s/ produced by gay men exhibits a more negatively skewed spectrum, and Campbell-Kibler (2011) has verified that listeners are likely to perceive /s/ with higher centers of gravity and lower skewness values as sounding gay, regardless of the linguistic style in which such realizations of /s/ are embedded.

Although much of the previous work on the spectral properties of /s/ centers on fronted articulations (which are generally characterized by high centers of gravity and low skewness), retracted variants of /s/ are also indexically rich. In addition to their prevalence among male Glaswegians and working-class women in a variety of UK contexts, as discussed earlier, retracted variants have been associated with regional variation in the United States. In particular, retracted /s/ is a feature prevalent in southern US speech styles. For example, Campbell-Kibler (2011) used the matched-guise paradigm to assess listener evaluations of speech containing retracted variants of /s/ and found that speakers whose stimuli contained these variants were judged as sounding more southern than the same speakers when their stimuli contained fronter realizations of /s/. Given that southern identity is tightly intertwined with rural identity in the United States, retracted variants also have the potential to be perceived as sounding rural. As Hall-Lew & Stephens (2012) show in their work on country talk, users of the register often characterize their speech as regionally southern.

To recap the range of indexical values associated with the phonetic realization of /s/, fronter realizations are typically linked to traditional forms of femininity and gay male identity, while more retracted variants index hegemonic forms of masculinity, working-class instantiations of femininity, and country or southern identity. That speakers exhibit intraspeaker variation in the realization of /s/ (Levon & Holmes-Elliott 2013) as well as longitudinal change (Zimman 2013) underscores the feature's salience as a resource for constructing a variety of identities. To proponents of what Schilling (2013) terms *speaker design* approaches to style, sociolinguistic features are resources with which speakers construct identities, as well as stances toward interlocutors or topics of discussion as discourse unfolds.

While it is important to understand the initiative elements of identity construction, it is also crucial to consider the ways in which speakers are not entirely free to construct identities at will (i.e., how agency is constrained). Ahearn (2001) defines agency as "the socioculturally mediated capacity to act." This capacity to act is highly constrained by the sociocultural context in which linguistic variation is produced, as communities may place limitations on the range of practices that its members can engage in as well as the kinds of identities that can be performed. As Moore (2010) illustrates in her study of *was/were* variation in Bolton, even though the social practices in which community members engage are the strongest social predictor of the variation in question, the members of some communities of practice are so strongly constrained by their social class positions that they may lack the agency to produce nonstandard variants at all. In this chapter, we argue that in relatively small communities, the same kinds of sociopolitical stances that make a speaker's orientation to the country a salient dimension of social distinction privilege heteronormative scripts for gender performance. That is, ideologies about rurality are tied up with ideologies about gender, and they work together to constrain patterns of linguistic variation, in this case the realization of /s/.

The community under consideration here is an inland Northern California community—Shasta County, of which the town of Redding is the county seat. In the following two sections, we provide a description of the community and our methods for analyzing the data collected there. We then present the results of our acoustic analysis, first identifying gender- and sexuality-based differences internal to the community under consideration, and then reconsidering those patterns in light of patterns previously observed in urban communities. We end by offering our interpretations of the results, suggesting directions for future investigation and revisiting the central themes of the analysis: constraints on variation, indexical ambiguity, and the connection between sociopolitical ideology and linguistic variation.

The Community

This study constitutes part of a collaborative research project at Stanford University called Voices of California. The department-wide project aims to address the dearth of dialectological research on non-coastal, non-urban areas parts of California, given that most work on California dialectology describes patterns in San Francisco, Los Angeles, and Santa Barbara. Each year, project researchers—consisting mainly of graduate students and faculty from the Department of Linguistics—visit a field site for two weeks in early autumn and conduct audiorecorded sociolinguistic interviews with up to 140 speakers in each location. At the time of this writing, data have been collected in Bakersfield, Merced, and Redding, the last of which is the current chapter's focus.

Shasta County, and its largest town, Redding, lie just north of the northern edge of the San Joaquin Valley, more commonly called the Central Valley, as shown in Figure 9.1. In many ways, people in Redding identify with and feel they have more in common with inhabitants of the Central Valley (such as Merced and Bakersfield, where data have also been collected for the Voices of California project) than the geographically closer inhabitants of cities in the northern parts of the state. The Central Valley is a particularly interesting site because of its settlement history. The Dust Bowl in the 1930s brought a number of people west from Oklahoma, Texas, and other southern states to the southernmost point of the Central Valley near Bakersfield, where they settled

FIGURE 9.1 Map of California depicting location of Redding relative to the Central Valley and other cities to which Redding positions itself

communities that utilized the region's fertile land to produce agriculture, raise livestock, and eventually drill for oil. Many of the migrants continued up the Central Valley, some reaching as far north as Shasta County. Due to the rather different landscape there, settlers pursued other industries tied to the land—such as logging and ranching. These migration patterns have important linguistic ramifications, since the "Okies" who settled or significantly populated many of the Central Valley communities brought a number of southern linguistic features with them, including the pin-pen merger, extensive vowel mergers preceding laterals, and, as will be discussed here, retracted /s/.

Another distinctive characteristic about Shasta County is the community's political and social conservatism. In the 2012 US presidential election, Shasta County had the third-highest percentage of supporters for Mitt Romney, the politically conservative Republican candidate, of the fifty-eight counties in the state. This contrasts sharply with cities in the northern half of the state, like San Francisco and Sacramento, which heavily supported Obama. While this could be characterized as a political divide in the state, it also constitutes a divide between the urban and the non-urban, and the contrasting social ideologies that typify the non-urban versus urban places. Redding residents rather uniformly experience a strong sense of alienation from urban areas. This feeling of disenfranchisement stems in part from the state's largely liberal policies that restrict how community members live their lives and use their land. One of our interviewees describes this perspective in example (1):

(1)   One of the biggest problems is the laws are made to fit a city, and they don't fit here, and they try to run it like a city, and it ain't a city, you know, I mean, and a lot of the laws, you can't even make 'em fit here but yet they still want you to go by 'em. Pretty ridiculous anymore.

It is partly due to anti-urban sentiment that community members as a whole locate cities outside of the region they would call Northern California. The same speaker continues in example (2):

(2)   San Francisco ain't Northern California even though they keep callin' it Northern California.

In fact, we found striking differences across field sites regarding where interviewees believed the border between the north and south of the state lay. Whereas Merced residents generally located this border south of Merced, Shasta County residents placed the border considerably farther north, some putting the border north of even Chico. Crucially, for nearly all interviewees, Northern California excludes cities like San Francisco and Sacramento. It is partly on the basis of widespread acrimony between the residents of Redding and cities that some community members continue to voice support for a secessionist movement that would result in the creation of a fifty-first state, the State of Jefferson, which would also include parts of southern Oregon. According to the original proposal, Redding was to be the state capital.

This anti-urban stance plays out recursively within the town of Redding. So even though the community as a whole positions itself in opposition to cities, within the town some people are more oriented to the town while others are more oriented to the country. This distinction was not in our initial sampling strategy, but it emerged as a salient distinction over the course of fieldwork. We categorized interviewees as country-oriented if they lived outside the Redding town limits, expressed preferences for a country lifestyle and/ or disdain for city life, or make their living from agriculture, ranching, or other rural pursuits. All other speakers were categorized as town-oriented. We want to emphasize that even though some people were more oriented to the town, no one should be considered particularly urban-oriented.

In addition to the community's political conservatism, Redding is also socially conservative, and we can perhaps best see evidence of this when we consider the experiences of our LGBT community members. Redding differs substantially from the liberal cities in Northern California that have long welcomed sexual minorities in that Redding LGBT community members have experienced rather extreme policing of the expression of gender and sexuality. We were first clued into this fact by the challenges we faced when trying to find LGBT community members to interview. This difficulty was echoed by one of the community members who moved to Redding from elsewhere and joked about how difficult it was for her to find other LGBT individuals upon her arrival. She recounts the day that she located an LGBT support group by saying, "Finally, I found the gay people! They were under a rock . . . at Planned Parenthood!" *Planned Parenthood* is where support group meetings take place, which is where we made our initial contacts with the community. Kate Greenberg, Jeremy Calder, and Rob Podesva have made a handful of follow-up visits, during which we have conducted short-term participant observation by attending gatherings like a rally for National Coming Out Day, an evening of coming-out stories, and more informal social events, like barbecues. In the end, we managed to interview sixteen of the group's participants, which is a nearly exhaustive sample of people who were willing to be interviewed. The community is internally diverse, consisting of gay men, lesbians, and transgender men and women. This contrasts with urban LGBT communities of practice, which tend to be more segregated along the lines of age and gender.

One of the factors contributing to the cohesion of this disparate group is their reliance on one another for support in what is often a hostile environment for sexual minorities. On July 1, 1999, Gary Matson and Winfield Mowder, a local gay couple, were murdered by white supremacists, who later confessed to killing the couple because they were gay. Violence directed at LGBT individuals is strikingly frequent in this community, as nearly all of our participants shared stories of harrowing abuse. Several LGBT community members' lives have been endangered, as exemplified in example (3), taken from an interview with a twenty-five-year-old trans man:

(3)   So, the driver goes, opens the back door to the car, to the station wagon, and pulls out a baseball bat, and then the other sober guy comes over and got a golf club. And I'm like, "What the fuck are we doing?" Like, "This is random," you know, next thing you realize everyone is kinda looking at me funny. And I went, "Oh: shit," and I just turn around and haul ass. They caught up to me. Beat the bloody fuck out of me. And left me there.

Others report extreme violence even in institutional settings that should provide community members with safety. Consider in example (4) the following narrative told by a nineteen-year-old gay man who recounted a violent attack on school grounds. According to the interviewee, the school captured the incident on video recordings but chose not to pursue legal action because the attackers' faces were covered.

(4)   I was the only one that was open saying, "I'm gay, yeah, I'm gay, whatever." And uh that actually caused a lot of problems for me. Um, I was held down by four guys in the boy's locker room and while one of them carved, or, the fifth one had a knife and carved it into my chest, "fag," backwards so every time I look into a mirror, it was actually right there on my chest completely diagonal backwards, so if I looked into a mirror it said, "fag."

While many LGBT community members experience violence, others feel strong pressure from religious organizations to keep their sexuality private. As one forty-six-year-old gay man put it in example (5):

(5)   But yeah, you know, and I've I've got status in my, not that status is important, but, at both churches, and uh, you know, just a part of me that doesn't want to be judged.

Nevertheless, other community members view being out in a sometimes hostile community as an important political statement and precondition for social change.

We offer these snapshots of abuse and community pressure not to present a sensationalistic characterization of the community but rather to accurately reflect the experiences of our interviewees. The lived experience of most LGBT community members in Shasta County is unfortunately one characterized by verbal and physical violence. At the same time, there are signs that the community is evolving in its views toward LGBT identity. While community members are often confronted with ignorance (the support group's T-shirt reads, "LGBT is not a sandwich!"), some straight-identified community members have begun to voice support for LGBT rights. At a roadside demonstration on

National Coming Out Day, for example, several community members honked their car horns to demonstrate their approval of LGBT visibility, and very few passersby expressed disapproval.

Methods

Given Redding's ethnic profile of roughly 90% white inhabitants, this analysis includes only white-identified speakers (incorporating speakers of color is a priority for future work). In all, of the 130+ sociolinguistic interviews conducted for the Redding field site, fifty-one are used in this analysis. Fifteen speakers identified as LGBT and were active participants in Redding's LGBT community. The remaining thirty-six speakers (eighteen female; eighteen male) did not self-identify as LGBT, and for simplicity's sake we refer to them as "straight" henceforth. We further classified the straight speakers as either "country-oriented" or "town-oriented" based on the criteria discussed previously. We did not categorize LGBT speakers in this way because none of them were country-oriented. Among the LGBT speakers, seven were gay/bi men, four were lesbians, two were trans men, and two were trans women. These numbers reflect the overall composition of support group attendees.

As the purpose of this analysis was to gauge the relative retraction or frontness of /s/ in the community of Redding, we utilized similar acoustic measurements used by other sociophonetic studies of /s/ that focus on gender, sexuality, and/or region. These measures include highest peak frequency (e.g., Stuart-Smith 2007; Levon & Holmes-Elliott 2013) as well as the first four spectral moments: center of gravity (e.g., Stuart-Smith 2007; Campbell-Kibler 2011; Hazenberg 2012; Zimman 2012, 2013), standard deviation (e.g., Stuart-Smith 2007; Campbell-Kibler 2011), skewness (e.g., Zimman 2012, 2013), and kurtosis (e.g., Stuart-Smith, Timmins, & Wrench 2003). In terms of these measures, a relatively fronter /s/ is characterized by higher peak frequency, higher center of gravity (COG), higher standard deviation, higher kurtosis values, and lower (often negative) skewness values, and vice versa for retracted /s/.

In preparation for analysis, the interviews were first orthographically transcribed and time-aligned. Word and phone segments were then obtained using the Penn forced alignment software package FAVE (Rosenfelder et al. 2011). Forced alignment enabled the automated extraction of nearly 113,000 tokens of /s/ across all three of the field sites (Redding, Merced, and Bakersfield). Figure 9.2 illustrates both a wide-band spectrogram and a spectral slice of one forced-aligned token of /s/ from the word "sixteen." Tokens from all three field sites were analyzed together to determine the relevant internal linguistic factors predicting /s/ variation in a broader California population. We included significant linguistic factors in the statistical analysis presented, but we will not discuss them at length in this chapter.

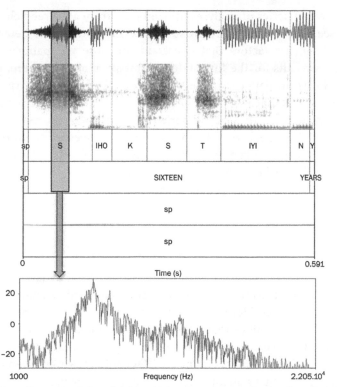

FIGURE 9.2 Acoustic representation of /s/ in wideband spectrogram (top) and spectral slice (bottom)

After extraction, each token was then band-pass filtered to retain frequencies between 1,000–22,050 Hz, after which spectral measurements were taken at the midpoint of a 40 millisecond Hamming window. The duration of each token was also recorded and log-transformed to ensure a more normal distribution of duration values. Finally, tokens with adjacent sibilants were removed from the analysis, since boundaries between such sounds cannot be determined systematically, leaving a total of 63,851 /s/ tokens from Redding alone. Prior to statistical analysis, a subset of these tokens was checked for alignment reliability, in terms of whether the 40 millisecond Hamming window was indeed contained inside the /s/ segment. In the course of reliability testing, a very small proportion of the total number of tokens (3.25%) were determined to be misaligned. Moreover, further investigation into the misaligned tokens revealed that two-thirds of them were still likely to lead to reliable spectral measures.

We used multilevel mixed-effects regression modeling in an effort to determine the predictive linguistic and social factors for relative fronting/ retraction of /s/. Because there were so many response variables (i.e., the spectral measures) to consider, we conducted regression modeling in three series. The first series of analyses utilized data from all three field sites, not only to see how the data were broadly patterning but also to determine the relevant linguistic factors that constrain the observed patterns. We will not discuss results for the first series of statistical analyses here, given our primary focus on patterns in Redding. Nevertheless, we incorporated the linguistic factors that we found to be significant in the first series into all subsequent models. The second series of models considered patterns for straight Redding speakers only, to examine the effects of town or country orientation on the realization of /s/. Finally, a third series of models incorporated LGBT speakers alongside the straight speakers, to examine patterns according to sexuality and gender identity.

Results

Separate mixed-effects regression models for COG, peak frequency, and skewness, revealed that nearly identical predictors emerged as significant across the spectral measures. Moreover, comparable studies of /s/ and gender/sexuality in urban communities (Hazenberg 2012; Zimman 2013) primarily report results for COG. Thus, for the sake of brevity as well as comparability, we report here on the factors that influence COG only. However, given that previous work suggests that sibilant duration is another important cue for signaling gay-sounding speech (Linville 1998; Levon 2007), we also present results for log duration in this section.

CENTER OF GRAVITY

Given this study's primary concern with the social factors predicting /s/ fronting and retraction in the community of Redding, this section focuses mainly on the significant social factors that affect COG. However, as mentioned in the previous section, we considered the effects of linguistic factors alongside social factors in all regression models, so we begin with a brief summary of linguistic factors that influenced COG values. Factors that emerged as significant were the preceding and following sound (both of which exerted a coarticulatory influence on the realization of /s/), stress, phrase position, and log duration. We observed significant fronting effects (i.e., higher COG was occasioned) when /s/ was preceded by front vowels, appeared in stressed syllables, and occurred in phrase- and/or syllable-initial position, and fronter realizations also correlated with longer duration. We also observed significant retraction when /s/ was preceded or followed by /r/ and occurred in phrase- and/or syllable-final position.

In the second series of regression models—which analyzed /s/ tokens from the straight Redding speakers—three social factors emerged as

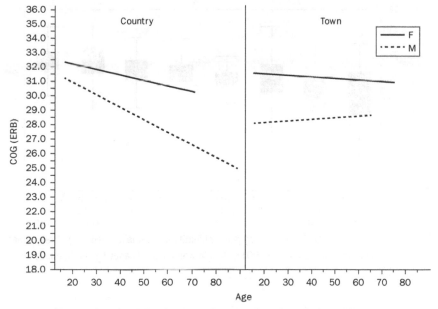

FIGURE 9.3 Center of gravity (ERB) of /s/ as a function of age for women (solid) and men (dashed), for speakers oriented to the country (left) and town (right) (straight-identified speakers only)

significant. Figure 9.3 shows how these three factors pattern in the community. First of all, gender is a significant predictor of COG ($p < 0.001$) in Redding, in that females have higher COG than males. Age likewise is a significant factor ($p < 0.0096$); there appears to be a change in progress afoot in which younger speakers have a generally fronter /s/ than their elders. However, upon closer examination, we see that age plays a more important role for country-oriented speakers than for town-oriented speakers. A significant interaction effect of age crossed with orientation ($p < 0.0113$) illustrates that the age effect is strongest with country-oriented individuals (particularly men). Thus, from these findings, we can deduce that country orientation in straight speakers plays an important role in /s/ variation in Redding, in that the older country speakers produce a more retracted /s/, but younger country people appear to have adopted the town norm: a relatively more fronted realization of /s/.

The last part of the analysis incorporated data from the fifteen LGBT speakers in the sample. Figure 9.4 shows COG for each gender and sexuality group, ordered from lowest to highest. In terms of how LGBT speakers compare to their straight counterparts, gay men in the community produce /s/ with a significantly higher COG than do the straight men, which is consistent with previous literature on other communities. Lesbians show significantly lower COG values than the straight women in this community, a pattern

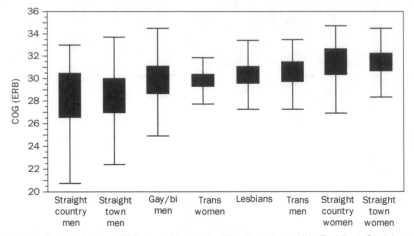

FIGURE 9.4 Center of gravity (ERB) of /s/ by gender identity and sexuality (Redding). Straight men significantly lower than gay men ($p < 0.0001$); straight women significantly higher than lesbians ($p < 0.0001$)

among women that has not been shown in previous studies on other communities. There was no difference between gay men and lesbians. As for the trans speakers, their numbers were too sparse to incorporate into the statistical models, even though the two trans men and two trans women included in our study constitute all four of the trans participants in the LGBT support group. Nevertheless, we find it fruitful to discuss their overall patterning on the descriptive statistic level. Recall that previous research shows that trans men and women exhibit patterns consistent their gender group (Hazenberg 2012; Zimman 2013), rather than with members of their sex classes assigned at birth. This is not quite the case here, as trans women exhibit a somewhat low COG and trans men produce a rather high COG for their gender group. Thus, in terms of COG, trans speakers in the Redding sample do not have appreciably different /s/ (in terms of COG) than do members of their biological sex class assigned at birth.

The trend in Figure 9.4 reveals with some clarity that straight men and women form the poles of the continuum in Redding, with LGBT speakers in the middle. The extreme gender polarization in Redding becomes more noteworthy when we compare the Redding findings with those from urban communities. Figure 9.5 compares patterns observed for men in Redding with those observed for men in San Francisco (Zimman 2013). Because Zimman's (2013) study quantifies COG in Hz, we depart from our previous analyses, which examine COG in equivalent rectangular bandwidth (ERB), by considering COG in Hz and thereby make our values directly comparable to Zimman's. Figure 9.6 compares patterns observed for women in Redding with those observed for women in Ottawa, as reported

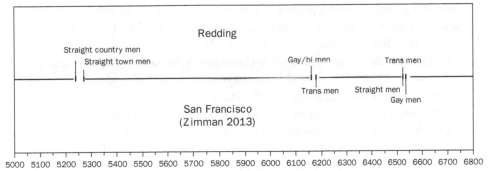

FIGURE 9.5 Mean center of gravity (Hz) of /s/ by gender identity and sexuality for male-identified speakers in Redding (top), compared to San Franciscans (Zimman 2013) (bottom)

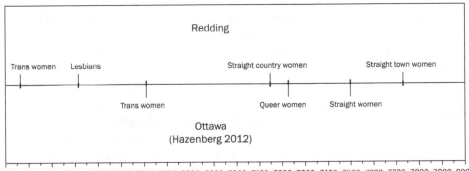

FIGURE 9.6 Mean center of gravity (Hz) of /s/ by gender identity and sexuality for female-identified speakers in Redding (top), compared to Ottawans (Hazenberg 2012) (bottom)

in Hazenberg (2012); data from Californian, or even US, contexts were unavailable. Like Zimman (2013), Hazenberg (2012) quantifies COG data in Hz, so we follow the same practice. Finally, since Hazenberg's analysis is based only on the lexical item "so," the Redding values reported in Figure 9.6 likewise are based only on "so" tokens. Compared to straight speakers in Ottawa (Hazenberg 2012) and the San Francisco Bay Area (Zimman 2013), Redding straight men and women sit on the extreme poles of the frequency continuum for /s/ COG. That is, Redding straight men exhibit more retracted /s/ than the straight men of Zimman (2013) (see Figure 9.5), and Redding straight women exhibit more fronted /s/ than the straight women of Hazenberg (2012) (see Figure 9.6).

How do the LGBT speakers in Redding compare to LGBT speakers in urban centers? Figure 9.4 shows us that gay men in Redding have significantly higher COG values than do Redding straight men, but they have lower COG values than gay men in urban areas. In fact, they exhibit an even lower COG than do straight men in San Francisco. Does this mean that everyone in Redding has a low COG, regardless of gender group? When we compare the Redding women with Hazenberg's (2012) Ottawa women, we fail to see an across-the-board lower COG pattern for all Redding women. However, lesbians in Redding notably have a lower COG than do lesbians in Ottawa, and country-oriented straight women in Redding have a lower COG than do straight women in Ottawa. Such patterns notwithstanding, it is important to note that town-oriented women from Redding have the highest COG levels for any group in any study. So, with respect to gay men, we see Redding speakers exhibiting more retracted variants of /s/ than gay or straight men in urban communities. But Redding lesbians are, by contrast, not as differentiated in COG levels from straight Redding women (at least not the country-oriented women).

Another useful way of thinking about the data is to look at individual patterns. The regression results indicated that Redding gay men are significantly higher than the straight men as a whole, but when we look at individual patterns, we see that they are somewhat evenly distributed across the range of all the male speakers. The trend for individual female speakers is perhaps even more illuminating. Figure 9.7 shows the mean COG for straight town-oriented (in white), straight country-oriented (in gray), and lesbian (in black) women. Here, country-oriented women form the poles of the continuum: They have both the lowest COG values as well as the highest COG values, depending on age. Age plays an integral role in this pattern because women with the highest values are the younger country women, while those with the lowest are the older country women. Clustered along with these older country women

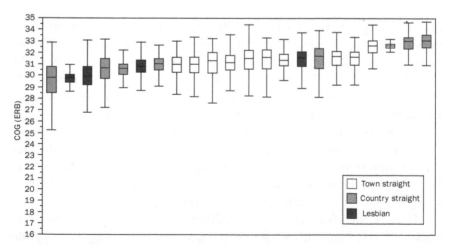

FIGURE 9.7 Center of gravity (ERB) of /s/ by individual for lesbian (black), straight country-identified (gray), and straight town-identified (white) women

are three of the four lesbians. So, the women in Redding who produce the lowest COG values (or most retracted /s/) are lesbians and older straight country women.

DURATION

Before moving on to a general discussion, we briefly report results for the social factors influencing the duration of /s/. Considering the findings of studies like those of Linville (1998) and Rogers, Smyth, & Jacobs (2000), where sibilant duration is significantly correlated with gay-sounding speech, log duration was incorporated into a statistical model of its own for all Redding speakers. No significant social factors emerged as predictors in the model for log duration of /s/. In fact, for gender in particular, there were no significant differences between men and women in Redding. Additionally, it is notable that gay men exhibit the same duration patterns as the straight men, and lesbians showed the same pattern as straight women. As Figure 9.8 shows, the medians for each gender/sexuality category were nearly numerically identical across all groups of people—except for two of the groups.

For log duration, trans men and women form the poles of the continuum. The trans men exhibit the shortest /s/ duration and the trans women, the longest. Remarkably, while trans speakers did not quite match the patterns of their gender groups with respect to the spectral measures of /s/ discussed earlier, here we see them producing gender-polarized patterns, and in the direction predicted by their gender identities, in terms of the duration of /s/. This raises the question of whether the duration of /s/ may be easier to control when performing gender than its spectral properties.

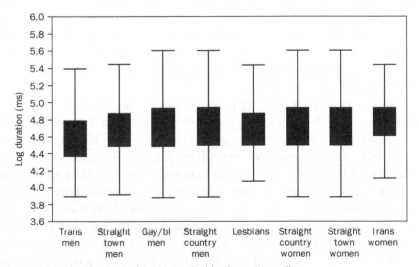

FIGURE 9.8 Log duration (ms) of /s/ by gender identity and sexuality

Discussion

In this section, we call attention to four of the most significant patterns reported in the previous section and offer our interpretation of these findings. First, the degree of retraction correlates with speaker age, but only for speakers who are oriented to the country. That town-oriented speakers exhibit no age patterns suggests that their production of /s/ is stable. By contrast, older country-oriented speakers produce a more retracted /s/, while younger country-oriented speakers produce a relatively more fronted /s/. We interpret this pattern to mean that the /s/ that was once retracted among country-oriented speakers, and perhaps brought into the community in the Dust Bowl Migration, is now leveling to a fronted standard. This finding is not surprising, given that the community is undergoing urbanization. Given that environmental legislation has all but shut down the once thriving logging industry, the community is relying on other industries located in the town proper to sustain the economy. And even as the economy has suffered, the town's population has continued to grow, as the community attracts retirees from other communities, as well as new members of the influential local Bethel Church.

Second, when compared to speakers in urban communities, straight men in Redding exhibit a more retracted /s/, while (town-oriented) straight women exhibit a relatively fronted /s/. The gender-polarized realizations of /s/, we argue, stem from community pressure to adhere to traditional gender norms. These patterns of gender polarization are reminiscent of Stuart-Smith's (2007) Glasgow findings, as well as Levon & Holmes-Elliott's (2013) findings for British reality shows. In both of these cases, ideologies of gender are mediated by the ways that speakers understand other aspects of their identity, such as class. In the present study, we see that gender ideologies, particularly normative ideologies according to which women and men should be maximally distinct from one another, are influenced by conservative sociopolitical ideologies that privilege a country lifestyle, which is crucially characterized as standing in opposition to city life.

Third, we found that Redding gay men exhibit more retracted /s/ than gay or straight men in San Francisco. This pattern suggests that gay men experience the same pressure to adhere to gender norms as their straight male counterparts. Given the extreme and often violent policing of gender and sexuality in Redding, it is unsurprising that non-heteronormative realizations of /s/ are not more common among gay men. Although fronted realizations of /s/ have been characterized as resources for the construction of gay identity in other research, in the context of Redding, one must also consider the potentially harmful consequences of their production. While gay men do exhibit a higher mean COG for /s/ than straight men, they do so while staying within the strict confines of normatively gendered patterns. So the realization of /s/ appears to participate in constructing sexuality only insofar as the construction of sexuality does not stand in the way of constructing normative gender.

The final pattern that we would like to discuss here is that even though lesbians were variable in their patterns, three of the six women who produced the most retracted variants of /s/ in the corpus were lesbians; the other three were older country-oriented women. We argue that lesbians can retract /s/ more than straight women without violating gender norms because there exists a competing local index of retracted /s/—country. Figure 9.9 spells this proposal out a little more explicitly. If we consider the indexical space for /s/, we can think of the linguistic forms of /s/ as constituting a continuum, ranging from fronted on one side to retracted on the other. On the one hand, there is a set of gender- and sexuality-based meanings, with fronted /s/ indexing femininity, non-normative masculinity, and gayness. Campbell-Kibler's (2011) study shows that speech containing fronted /s/ is consistently perceived as sounding gay, regardless of the style in which it is embedded. She likens /s/ to a red-heeled stiletto, since the meaning of this sign object can travel from one context to another—the stiletto is always perceived as sexy, just as fronted /s/ is always perceived feminine or gay. On the other end of the continuum, retracted /s/ can index masculinity, non-normative femininity, and perhaps a lesbian identity. However, even though retracted /s/ can be interpreted in terms of gender and sexuality, the indexical space is more expansive, such that retracted variants can also be interpreted as sounding country or southern. It is because of these additional readings of retracted /s/ that a lesbian's use of the variant need not be viewed as a transgression of gender norms. Although we have located non-gendered meanings of retracted /s/ in a different space, we do not mean to suggest that country speech and southern speech are not gendered—if anything, they are gendered as masculine in this community. But crucially, these gendered meanings are indirect, and are far from being unambiguously masculine.

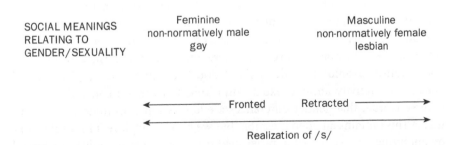

FIGURE 9.9 Indexical space for realizations of /s/ in Redding

Conclusion

To conclude, we revisit a few of the central themes of our analysis and offer our ideas for important directions for future study. First, we have advanced an analysis that attends to the ways in which variation patterns are *constrained* by the community's sociopolitical landscape. While speakers surely exercise agency—we see evidence of agency in gay men's use of fronter /s/ than their straight counterparts in Redding—they do so within a system of constraints. When gay men produce /s/ in Redding, they do so under strong pressure to retract the sound. The agency that they exercise operates on a smaller scale, so that gay men can (but need not) produce slightly less retracted /s/ variants than straight men, thus maintaining some distinction between themselves and straight men (if such distinction is important) without explicitly violating the gender norms that are so heavily surveilled in Redding. Without denying that speakers have agency, it is crucial to note that individuals are not free to produce whatever linguistic variants they want.

Nevertheless, we also suggest that speakers may be bestowed with greater agency in situations characterized by greater ambiguity. The social meaning of linguistic variation is never fully determinate, and in cases where indeterminacy is greater, speakers may be relatively free to exploit ambiguity. When lesbians produce /s/ in Redding, their retracted variants could in principle be interpreted as non-heteronormative, but so too could such variants be interpreted as sounding country (or as indicating that their speakers align with the ethos of a country lifestyle). And it is worth mentioning that country readings of retracted /s/ may be especially likely when listeners are themselves oriented to the country. In sum, the indeterminacy of social meaning may afford speakers the freedom to produce a wider range of linguistic variants without fear of sanctions.

Finally, we have emphasized the connection between sociopolitical ideology and linguistic variation. The field of sociolinguistics is only beginning to understand the nature of this connection. In their work on the pronunciation of *Iraq* among members of the US House of Representatives, Hall-Lew, Coppock, & Starr (2010) report that liberals favor [a] in the final syllable of the word, while conservatives favor [æ]. Here, we have argued that, in Redding, conservatism promotes gender polarization between women and men, and gender normativity among sexual minorities. But can we conclude that the reverse is true, that gender differences are less extreme, in more liberal contexts? This remains an open question, but we hope to explore it in future work by analyzing data collected in other field sites that are more politically liberal than Redding.

We aim to expand our investigation in a number of other ways. First, we plan to consider the patterns for speakers of color. Since our focus was on Redding, we limited our investigations to speakers who identify as white, which is the overwhelming majority of Redding's inhabitants. But as we proceed with examining other communities in greater detail, we plan to also consider ethnic groups that are well represented in those communities—particularly Hispanic speakers in our Bakersfield sample. The variant under consideration here—/s/—would be particularly interesting in this context because of its status as a locus of variation in many varieties of Spanish (cf. Mack, Chapter 7, this volume). We hasten to add that expanding the data set in this way may be facilitated by using the methods advanced here. The acoustic robustness of /s/ has given rise to largely accurate forced alignments, which expedite the analysis of sibilants across large datasets. Finally, we issue a call for continued work on the linguistic practices of sexual minorities in rural, or at least less urban, contexts. Most of what we know about the linguistic practices of sexual minorities in the United States, and indeed all over the world, is based on research conducted with sexual minorities who live in cities. As we have shown here, the ways in which speakers experience gender and sexuality can be very different in rural contexts, and differences in experience yield strikingly divergent variation patterns. Failing to consider the particularities of how gender and sexuality play out in specific communities like the one under investigation here, as well as across a variety of communities like the range exemplified in this volume, may give rise to impoverished understandings of how linguistic variation figures in the construction of sexuality.

Acknowledgments

Many thanks to the Richard A. Karp Foundation, Penny Eckert, the Department of Linguistics, and the School of Humanities and Sciences for funding data collection; Jeremy Calder and Kate Geenberg for their fieldwork with the LGBT community; and audiences at Stanford Sociotea, NWAV 42, Pomona College, UCLA, and Cornell University for helpful feedback. Any errors are our own.

References

Ahearn, Laura M. 2001. Language and agency. *Annual Review of Anthropology* 30. 109–137.
Campbell-Kibler, Kathryn. 2011. Intersecting variables and perceived sexual orientation in men. *American Speech* 86(1). 52–68.
Fuchs, Susanne & Martine Toda. 2010. Do differences in male versus female /s/ reflect biological or sociophonetic factors? In Susanne Fuchs, Martine Toda, & Marzena Żygis (eds.), *Turbulent sounds: An interdisciplinary guide*, 281–302. Berlin: Mouton de Gruyter.
Hall-Lew, Lauren, Elizabeth Coppock, & Rebecca L. Starr. 2010. Indexing political persuasion: Variation in the Iraq vowels. *American Speech* 85(1). 91–102.
Hall-Lew, Lauren & Nola Stephens. 2012. Country Talk. *Journal of English Linguistics* 40(3). 256–280.

Hazenberg, Evan. 2012. *Language and identity practice: A sociolinguistic study of gender in Ottawa, Ontario*. St. Johns, NL: Memorial University of Newfoundland MA thesis.

Levon, Erez. 2007. Sexuality in context: Variation and the sociolinguistic perception of identity. *Language in Society* 36. 533–554.

Levon, Erez & Sophie Holmes-Elliott. 2013. East end boys and west end girls: /s/-fronting in Southeast England. *University of Pennsylvania Working Papers in Linguistics* 19(2). 111–120.

Linville, Sue Ellen. 1998. Acoustic correlates of perceived versus actual sexual orientation in men's speech. *Folia Phoniatrica et Logopaedica* 50. 35–48.

Moore, Emma. 2010. Interaction between social category and social practice: Explaining *was/were* variation. *Language Variation and Change* 22. 347–371.

Munson, Benjamin, Elizabeth C. McDonald, Nancy L. DeBoe, & Aubrey R. White. 2006. The acoustic and perceptual bases of judgments of women and men's sexual orientation from read speech. *Journal of Phonetics* 34. 202–240.

Pharao, Nicolai, Marie Maegaard, Janus Spindler Møller, & Tore Kristiansen. 2014. Indexical meanings of [s+] among Copenhagen youth: Social perception of a phonetic variant in different prosodic contexts. *Language in Society* 43(1). 1–31.

Rogers, Henry, Ron Smyth, & Greg Jacobs. 2000. *Vowel and sibilant duration in gay- and straight-sounding male speech*. Paper presented at the first International Gender and Language Association Conference, Stanford, CA.

Rosenfelder, Ingrid, Josef Fruehwald, Keelan Evanini, & Jiahong Yuan. 2011. FAVE (Forced Alignment and Vowel Extraction) Program Suite.

Schilling, Natalie. 2013. Investigating stylistic variation. In Jack K. Chambers & Natalie Schilling (eds.), *Handbook of language variation and change*, 2nd edn., 327–349. Somerset, NJ: Wiley.

Strand, Elizabeth. A. 1999. Uncovering the role of gender stereotypes in speech perception. *Journal of Language and Social Psychology* 18(1). 86–99.

Stuart-Smith, Jane. 2007. Empirical evidence for gendered speech production: /s/ in Glaswegian. In Jennifer Cole & José Ignacio Hualde (eds.), *Laboratory phonology*, Vol. 9, 65–86. New York: Mouton de Gruyter.

Stuart-Smith, Jane, Claire Timmins, & Fiona Tweedie. 2007. "Talkin' Jockney'? Variation and change in Glaswegian accent. *Journal of Sociolinguistics* 11(2). 221–260.

Stuart-Smith, Jane, Claire Timmins, & Alan Wrench. 2003. Sex and gender differences in Glaswegian /s/. In Maria-Josep, Daniel Recasens, & Joaquín Romero (eds.), *Proceedings of the 15th International Congress of Phonetic Sciences*, 3–9. Barcelona.

Zimman, Lal. 2012. *Voices in transition: Testosterone, transmasculinity, and the gendered voice among female-to-male transgender people*. Boulder: University of Colorado dissertation.

Zimman, Lal. 2013. Hegemonic masculinity and the variability of gay-sounding speech: The perceived sexuality of transgender men. *Journal of Language and Sexuality* 2(1). 1–39.

10

Kathoey and the Linguistic Construction of Gender Identity in Thailand

Pavadee Saisuwan

This study investigates the linguistic construction of gender identity among *kathoey*, male-to-female transgender individuals, in Thailand. I based the analyses on a comparison of *kathoey*'s use of first-person personal reference terms with that of Thai women. The goal of the study is to identify how *kathoey* use personal reference terms to position themselves within the Thai sex/gender inventory, and, in so doing, to describe how language participates in the indexation of gender identity in Thailand more broadly. Specifically, the study seeks to resolve two main questions: (1) What is the overall pattern of the use of self-reference terms among *kathoey* and women within the corpus examined? and (2) what are the social meanings of the self-reference terms for *kathoey* and woman participants? This chapter begins with a general introduction to the relationship between self-reference terms and gender identity. I then provide background information about *kathoey* and Thai first-person personal pronouns before turning to a presentation of the methods and results of the present study.

Personal Pronouns and Gender Identity

In her foundational work on indexicality, Ochs (1992) argues that the relationship between a linguistic variable and an associated social group or identity can be either direct or indirect. In the more common indirect indexicality, variants are linked to various social stances, acts, or activities that are themselves then ideologically associated with social identity categories. Ochs cites, for example, the use of the sentence-final *wa* particle in Japanese, which is considered typical of "Japanese women's language" (Uyeno 1971; Seki 1986). She argues that the reason *wa* has come to take on a gendered meaning in Japanese is because it serves to index a form of "delicate" or "gentle" intensity (as opposed to the more "coarse" intensity of sentence-final *ze*) and gender norms in Japan associate delicate or gentle speech with women. In other words, the indexical link between the linguistic feature *wa* and the category *Japanese woman* is not a direct one but is, rather, mediated by an intervening indexical layer. In direct indexicality, in contrast, no such intervening layer exists. Instead, variants are directly associated with the social group who uses them. Ochs states that a canonical example of such direct indexicality is the use of gender personal pronouns, which she argues serve to straightforwardly index the gender of the speaker.

More recent work on the use of pronouns and other self-reference terms, however, has shown that their use may in fact not always be a product of a direct indexical relationship. Rather, numerous studies have demonstrated the existence of a nonexclusive relation between personal pronoun use and speaker gender. Research on Japanese, for example, has found substantial evidence of pronominal "gender-crossing" in a variety of different social contexts. Sunaoshi (2004) describes how farm women in the Ibaraki Prefecture make frequent use of the first-person pronoun *ore* (which is normatively not available to women because of its association with vulgarity) in their discussions of agricultural product development. Similarly, Abe (2004) discusses how female workers at a lesbian bar in Tokyo use the first-person pronoun *jibun*, which is typically reserved for men in sports and military groups. Finally, Miyazaki (2002, 2004) found that Japanese high school girls also do not use first-person pronouns as prescribed in Japanese language ideology. The girls in Miyazaki's study report perceiving feminine forms as too formal and so make use of various masculine forms instead. The girls, moreover, use masculine pronouns strategically in particular interactional contexts, such as when being resistant to their teachers or to school rules. In all three of these cases, then, pronoun choice does not solely depend on the gender of the speaker. Instead, we find variation among different groups of Japanese women in the choice of so-called gendered pronouns. Nor is it the case that this variation is governed solely by a desire to index relative levels of masculinity or femininity. It seems instead that pronouns are used by Japanese speakers to help negotiate their own group memberships and their relationships with others. In other words, pronouns provide Japanese women with a means to index particular stances (Bucholtz 2009; Jaffe 2009) through which they align (or disalign) themselves with different social positions and categories.

Gendered speech, including self-referencing, is used among non-normatively gendered individuals for identity-linked purposes and also as a tool for indicating the relationship between speaker and interlocutor. Hall & O'Donovan (1996) found that Hindi-speaking *hijras*, transgender individuals in India, shift their gender positions from masculinity to femininity through the use of feminine speech, which they acquire as part of a process of fully becoming a *hijra* when joining a *hijra* community, along with other feminine behaviors such as appearance and social roles. Feminine marking shows their alignment with nonmasculinity and also solidarity with their interlocutors, as feminine speech is associated with familiarity. Masculine marking, on the other hand, is used to indicate distance between interlocutors and sometimes used for displaying affect, such as showing emphasis and anger.

In this chapter, I examine the extent to which *kathoey* in Thailand engage in similar behavior, and use gendered first-person reference terms in an effort to construct and position social identities. I pursue the hypothesis that, rather than just directly indexing a speaker's already existing social identity or position, first-person personal pronouns and other self-reference terms in Thai are linguistic resources that Thai speakers strategically deploy as part of their gendered presentations of self. In making this claim, I build on the work conducted on Japanese and Hindi, cited earlier, as well as on research by Kongtrakool (1996), who investigated the use of first-person pronouns in the speech of different groups of male, female, and effeminate male speakers in Thailand. She found that effeminate male speakers generally prefer masculine pronouns, as a result of disapproving attitudes in Thai society toward effeminate males, while switching to feminine and non–gender-specific pronouns when speaking to parents or intimates.

Kathoey

In contemporary Thai society, *kathoey* refers to male-to-female transgender individuals. Born in male bodies, *kathoey* at some point in their lives adopt certain traditionally female roles, practices, or characteristics, though the extent of adopting and expressing femininity varies greatly. *Kathoey* is a historical and cultural category in Thai society. According to traditional Thai Buddhist beliefs (*Pathamamulamuli*), *kathoey* is one of the sexes within a tripartite system of *phuchai* 'male', *phuying* 'female', and *kathoey* 'transvestite/transsexual/hermaphrodite' (Morris 1994). Etymologically, the term *kathoey* was once an umbrella term used to refer to all kinds of non-normative genders, such that a person who was not completely either a man or a woman was categorized as *kathoey*. Even though the term *kathoey* is now used in a narrower sense to refer only to male-to-female transgenders, the tripartite system of man-woman-*kathoey* remains valid as non-normative genders are often collectively categorized as *phet thi sam* 'third sex/gender' or people with *khwam laklai thang phet* 'sexual/gender diversity'. Normally translated into English as *ladyboy*, *kathoey* are also referred to as *sao praphet song* 'the second type of woman'. Yet despite this appellation, *kathoey* are viewed in Thailand as "a variety of male, not female" rather than "a genuine intermediate category" (Jackson 1997: 171).

According to Jackson (1997), *kathoey* occupy "a marginal but recognized position in Thai society" (173). *Kathoey* tend to be viewed negatively by the general public, and are often criticized for being "loud-mouthed, aggressive or lewd" (Jackson 1999: 230). Perhaps because of these stereotypical perceptions, *kathoey* have limited possibilities for employment, with available jobs primarily limited to the fields of beauty and entertainment (Beech 2008). In spite of this, *kathoey* are relatively well-tolerated when compared to their non-normative gender counterparts in other societies, such as *travesti* in Brazil (whose employment prospects are often limited to prostitution and who are frequently subject to violence from the police; Kulick 1998). Many *kathoey* are well-known celebrities or prominent figures throughout the country, and a number of films have been created with *kathoey* as main characters. In addition, two leading *kathoey* cabaret theatres are very popular tourist attractions in Pattaya, and each holds annual *kathoey* beauty contests, which receive attention nationwide. Finally, organizations such as the Thai Transgender Alliance and the TransFemale Association of Thailand have been established to support *kathoey*, and certain changes, such as the creation of separate *kathoey* toilet facilities at the Lummahachaichumpol Temple in Rayong, have further served to enfranchise the *kathoey* population.

This generally tolerant atmosphere in Thailand is arguably due to the influence of Buddhism in Thai society (Morris 1994; Taywaditep, Coleman, & Dumronggittigule 1997–2001; Jackson 1998; Totman 2003). According to Buddhist beliefs, *kathoey* are "the products of immorality" (Jackson 1998: 83) where being born *kathoey* is viewed as a result of one's karmic debts from previous lives. Since in this conceptualization being *kathoey* is predetermined and inevitable, *kathoey* should be treated with sympathy, compassion, and tolerance. However, Totman (2003) claims that Thai society's attitude toward *kathoey* is now changing in an opposite direction to that in Western societies. Thailand, highly influenced by international business and tourism, is currently trying to westernize itself toward (an imagined) modernity and cosmopolitanism. While Western societies tend to be more tolerant toward transgendered people, *kathoey*, particularly those who work in the sex industry, are more marginalized in Thai society since they are seen as incompatible with the new image of the country as modern and cosmopolitan, and thus are undesirable. Totman (2003) argues that *kathoey* are actually part of the country's cultural heritage, but they are not valued and even seen as an embarrassment. They are seen as the unclean part of the country which should be suppressed in order to achieve the new image of a modern country.

While the experiences of and beliefs about *kathoey* have been studied from a variety of disciplinary perspectives, no work to date has examined the issue of language use among *kathoey*. This present study therefore seeks to investigate how language participates in *kathoey*'s construction and presentation of self. In fact, some scholars (e.g., Winter 2003) have argued that language is not a good indicator of *kathoey* identity as *kathoey* are thought to always use feminine pronouns and particles. This study aims to investigate this anecdotal claim with regard to self-reference terms, and to compare *kathoey*'s linguistic practices with those of non-*kathoey* Thai women. The reason why *kathoey*'s practices were compared with those of Thai women and not with those of Thai men is due to *kathoey*'s general tendency to adopt and present feminine traits. Having feminine practices as their model, *kathoey* are generally expected to move away from masculine traits. This is expected to include abandoning or decreasing the use of masculine linguistic forms and adopting more of feminine ones. Therefore, it is interesting to see how *kathoey* employ the terms as compared to women, who also make use of a more or less similar set of feminine self-reference terms.

Thai First-Person Personal Pronouns

Thai has a highly articulated first-person singular pronominal system. According to Palakornkul (1972), in addition to speaker gender there are seven social factors that underlie the choice of which first-person singular pronouns to use in any given interactional context: status, age, kinship, friendship, ethnic-religious affiliation, occupation, and genealogical distance. In addition to these social factors, pronoun choice also depends on nine aspects of role relationships of the interlocutors involved. These aspects include intimacy, respect, solidarity, formality, presence of children, presence of non-acquaintances and persons with status, length of time of acquaintance, condescension, and emotional manifestations in talk. Tables 10.1 and 10.2 schematically represent this very complex system. In these tables, the sixteen different determining factors of pronoun choice have been mapped onto a simpler system based on Brown & Levinson's (1978) dimensions of Power, Distance, and Formality (see also Irvine 1979). Power here refers to differences of status between interlocutors, while Distance refers to speakers' degree of acquaintance. Formality is a property of the speech context itself. Table 10.1 presents the system for feminine

TABLE 10.1
Thai feminine first-person pronouns

		POWER		
		Reciprocal		Nonreciprocal
FORMALITY	Formal	/dĭchăn/ (/dĭchán/, /dían/, /dán/)		/nŭ:/
		DISTANCE		/ʔĭchăn/
		Intimate	Non-intimate	Impolite	(/ʔĭchán/)
	Informal	/khăw/	/chăn/	/kū:/	
		(/kháw/)	(/chán/)		
			/rāw/		

pronouns, while the system for masculine pronouns is in Table 10.2. Forms in parentheses are phonological variants of the more standard forms, and pronouns that appear in boldface type are those that are commonly used as epicene pronouns.

We see in Tables 10.1 and 10.2 that Power, Distance, and Formality frame how both feminine and masculine pronouns are used. These three dimensions, however, do not function in the same manner across the two systems. For feminine pronouns, the first consideration is whether or not the balance of power between interlocutors is reciprocal. In situations where it is not reciprocal, /nǔ:/ is used to signify a speaker's humbleness, younger age, and lower seniority or social ranking. A second pronoun, /ʔìchǎn/, can also be used in these instances, though it is much less common. /ʔìchǎn/ is viewed as old-fashioned and normally only heard among elderly speakers. If, in contrast, the balance of power between speakers is reciprocal, pronoun choice for the feminine system then depends on the formality of the context. In formal situations, /dìchǎn/, or one of its phonological variants, is the only option. In terms of variants, /dìchǎn/ can be realized as /dìchán/, or as the phonologically reduced forms /dían/ and /dán/. The two phonologically reduced forms are particularly marked among Thai speakers and are stereotypically associated with high social class. Finally, in cases where the balance of power between interlocutors is reciprocal and the situation is informal, social distance between speakers comes into play for feminine pronouns. When the level of intimacy between interlocutors is very high (e.g., as between romantic partners), /khǎw/, which can also be realized as /kháw/, can be chosen. In non-intimate situations, /chǎn/, /chán/, or /rāw/ can be used. Finally, to be impolite (including to engage in ritual insult and teasing with close friends), /kū:/ can be used. The system for masculine pronouns (Table 10.2) is much more straightforward. If there is a nonreciprocal relation of power between interlocutors, if the interlocutors are not intimately acquainted with one another, or if a situation is formal, /phǒm/ is used (Chirasombutti & Diller 1999). In other instances, the choice is among /chǎn/, /rāw/, and /kū:/ forms, which are all also available in the system for feminine pronouns (though the situations which allow any of these pronouns to be used are more restricted).

Tables 10.1 and 10.2 do not provide an exhaustive list of the first-person pronouns available in Thai. Rather, the tables include those that are most

TABLE 10.2

Thai masculine first-person pronouns

+ POWER or + DISTANCE or + FORMALITY	NONE
/phǒm/	/chǎn/ (/chán/)
	/rāw/
	/kū:/

commonly found in everyday conversation, and they do not list those pronouns that are rarely used or exclusively used in written language. It is important to note, moreover, that Tables 10.1 and 10.2 depict general patterns rather than definitive rules, and that Thai speakers have a fair amount of leeway in choosing which first-person pronouns to use. In addition, apart from personal pronouns, there are many other types of personal reference terms available in Thai, such as personal names, occupational titles, and kin terms (Iwasaki & Ingkaphirom 2005). Unlike in languages such as English, it is perfectly common in Thai for speakers to refer to themselves in the third person using their name or occupational title, rather than a first-person pronoun (e.g., *Phrae mai kin ahan thale* 'I/Phrae don't eat seafood'; *khao bok khru wa khao mai sabai* 'He told me/teacher that he was sick').[1]

Methodology

We drew the data analyzed in this study from posts to three different online webboards: Thai LadyBoYz.net, Jeban, and Pantip. The web postings are in a casual or informal speech style, corresponding to the "informal" context in Tables 10.1 and 10.2. As a written format, the web postings provide various written versions of the pronouns listed previously. Different spellings of a pronoun, particularly nonstandard spellings, illustrate its phonological variants in actual conversational use. For example, /ʔìchǎn/ and /dìchǎn/ can be realized with tonal change, becoming /ʔìchán/ and /dìchán/, respectively, in actual speech. The other two variants of /dìchǎn/—/dían/ and /dán/—are also shown in different nonstandard spellings.

Thai LadyBoYz.net: Transgender community in Thailand or TLBz (http://timecapsule.tlbz.me/tlbznet/webboard/index.php) is an online community for *kathoey* and the first webboard for transgender individuals in Thailand. The webboard is divided into twenty-one sections based on different topics. In this chapter, I consider language use in five sections where the most recent activity had taken place—Armchair Si Thao 'gray armchair' (life stories), Take Ya 'take medicine' (feminization medicine), Suay Duay Phaet 'beautified by doctor' (surgery), Beauty Lady (Boyz) (beauty and health), and Sofa Si Fa 'blue sofa' (other general topics). When we extracted the data (June 2011), there were 4,587 members and 548,779 posts in total. We collected a sample of twenty of the most recent posts from each of the five sections for a total of 100 posts overall. These 100 posts are composed of 75,870 words, with 758.7 words on average per post and 392 different people involved.

We used the other two webboards to obtain a sample of language use by non-*kathoey* women. Unlike TLBz, these two sources are not women's online communities as such. However, the topics of interest are limited to makeup and beauty, and so tend to attract primarily women. *Jeban.com: Makeup Is*

Magic! (http://www.jeban.com/board_all.php) is a website that collects news, trends, and tips about hair and makeup. The posts are categorized into six different types: How to, Reviews, New stuff, Question-answer, Salon de Jeban, and Off topic. For this study, we extracted the seventy-five most recent posts to the webboard in June 2011. These seventy-five posts are composed of 42,652 words, with 568.69 words on average per post and 398 different people involved. Finally, we extracted a further seventy-five posts from the *To Khrueang Paeng* section of *Pantip* (http://www.pantip.com/cafe/woman/), which is one of the most popular online communities in Thailand. The *To Khrueang Paeng* 'dressing table' section focuses on the topics of beauty, nutrition, and fashion. The seventy-five posts extracted from Pantip are composed of 59,904 words, with 798.72 words average per post.

In addition to examining the actual use of pronouns and other self-reference terms in the online dataset, we also distributed a questionnaire in an effort to elicit informants' perceptions of the social meanings of particular self-reference terms found in the online dataset. We asked the respondents which terms among /phǒm/, /dìchǎn/, /dían/, /dán/, /ʔìchǎn/, and /nǔː/ they use to refer to themselves most often, with whom they use the terms, and why. They were also asked to explain why they use the other terms less often or do not use them at all, and what they think of speakers who use those terms. Seventeen *kathoey* and nineteen women make up the respondent population, with an average age of twenty-eight and twenty-five years old, respectively. We solicited respondents from within my own personal network, and otherwise through a friend-of-a-friend methodology. Respondents were all aware that we were using their answers for research purposes and were informed broadly about the general aims of the project.

The Use of First-Person Pronouns in the Online Corpora Data

As shown in Table 10.3, the self-reference terms found in the data can be divided into five categories: personal pronouns, personal names, kin terms, the combination of kin term and personal name, and the fixed phrase *chaokhong krathu* 'the post owner.' In both TLBz and Jeban/Pantip, the most frequently used category of self-reference terms is personal pronouns, with 1,267 instances (74.35%) in TLBz and 1,465 instances (87.78%) in Jeban/Pantip. The pronouns used can then be further divided into masculine, feminine, and epicene forms. Table 10.4 shows all of the pronouns found in the data along with their frequency of use.

In Table 10.4, we see that of the 2,732 first-person pronouns in the dataset, 52 are the masculine form /phǒm/. This finding is somewhat anomalous, since men are not expected to post on any of the webboards considered, and the masculine pronoun /phǒm/ is not one that is used by either *kathoey* or women. In fact, closer inspection of the fifty-two tokens of /phǒm/ indicates that these are

TABLE 10.3

Overall frequency of self-reference terms

	Personal pronouns	Personal names	Kin terms	Kin term + name	"The post owner"	Total
TLBz	1267 (74.35%)	253 (14.85%)	168 (9.86%)	16 (0.94%)	0 (0%)	1704
Jeban/Pantip	1465 (87.78%)	118 (7.07%)	73 (4.37%)	2 (0.12%)	11 (0.66%)	1669

TABLE 10.4

Frequency of all first-person pronouns

		TLBz	Jeban/Pantip
Masculine	/phŏm/	27	25
Feminine	/nŭ:/	151	30
	/ʔǐchăn/[a]	14	2
	/dǐchăn/[b]	142	7
	/khăw/[c]	21	6
Epicene	/chăn/[d]	29	16
	/rāw/	883	1,374
	/kū:/	0	5
Total		1,267	1,465

[a] This category includes the variants /ʔǐchăn/ and /ʔǐchán/.

[b] This category includes the variants /dǐchăn/, /dǐchán/, /dían/, and /dán/.

[c] This category includes the variants /khăw/ and /kháw/.

[d] This category includes the variants /chăn/ and /chán/.

used by the few men who do in fact visit and post in the online communities. On Jeban/Pantip, for example, men at times posted questions about what beauty and fashion products to buy for their girlfriends or wives. In these instances they used the /phŏm/ form. Similarly, on TLBz, men asked for advice on surgery for their girlfriends using /phŏm/. Given this, I exclude from further consideration instances of the /phŏm/ pronoun in my discussion here, and focus exclusively on the use of feminine and epicene pronouns in the dataset.

As shown in Table 10.5, there is a correlation between webboard and the types of pronouns used on TLBz and Jeban/Pantip, showing a significant difference in their overall pattern. While both *kathoey* and women use epicene pronouns most of the time, feminine pronouns are favored to a much greater extent by *kathoey* on TLBz (26.45% of their tokens) than they are by women posting on Jeban/Pantip (3.13% of their tokens). What this indicates is that while epicene pronouns are the most common for both groups overall, there is a significant difference in the amount of feminine pronouns deployed. Figure 10.1 clearly represents this difference.

TABLE 10.5

Chi square of the feminine and epicene pronouns

	TLBz	Jeban/Pantip
Feminine pronouns	328	45
Epicene pronouns	912	1395

$\chi^2 = 302.60$, p < 0.0001, df = 1

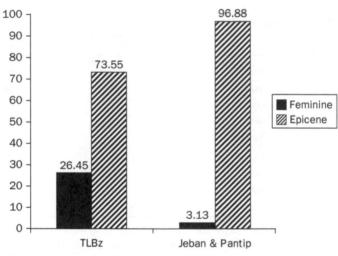

FIGURE 10.1 The percentage of feminine and epicene first-person pronouns

First-Person Feminine Pronouns, Stance-taking, and Habitual Use

Both women and *kathoey* use feminine pronouns in the dataset. However, they do not use them to the same extent or to fulfill the same goal. Of all the feminine pronouns used, women are limited to mostly /nǔ:/ (66.67%), while /dìchǎn/ (15.56%) and /khǎw/ (1.33%) are used much less. Closer analysis shows that women use each of these pronouns for taking different kinds of stances.

(1)   *nu* phueng cha tha Retin-A mueaki T-T tha pen *nu* khrai thak *nu* baep ni *nu* cha ao Retin-A bip sai pak loei! Huem!

'I've just used Retin-A T-T. If this happened to *me*, someone talked to *me* like this, *I* would put Retin-A in his/her mouth! Grrr!' (Pantip)

(2)   an ni khue namya lang praeng khong Beauty Buffet . . . tonni kam-lang lot rakha luea 205 baht (chak 295 baht) dan lang Background nankhue kong thit chu... thi *rao* chai chet praeng thi *rao* lang . . . poet

ma an raek ko Beauty Buffet ik laeo... phuean phuean at cha kamlang songsai wa inang mae mo man pen aria kap braen ni mak mai~?!! Review khrao thilaeo ko Facial Mask khong yiho ni.. 5555[2] mae ... ao na ao na ko *nu* chop ni na *Nok* wa khong khao di na kha 555 ^_^

'This is the brush cleaner from Beauty Buffet ... now it's on sale, down to 205 baht (from 295 baht). In the background is a pile of tissue paper ... that *I* used with the brush *I* cleaned ... The first one is from Beauty Buffet, again ... You might be wondering, why is this person so crazy about this brand~?!! Last time is also the review of facial mask from this brand.. 5555 well ... come on, *I* like it. *I* think their products are good 555 ^_^'
(Jeban)

(3)   si khong sao sukkhaphap di tong Anna Sui 400 yuenyan kha tae tong khoi khoi pat na kha mai ngan cha daeng pai taekon blat on khong *dichan* tong Anna Sui lae Nars thaonan tae pho dai long blat MMU laeo tong plianchai kha thuk kwa yoe si ko mi hai lueak yoe mak taela si suai thukchai thangnan naenam MMU ching ching na kha tha sanuk duai phro mi si hai lueak yoe mak mai siadai tang loei pen item thuk lae di

'The color for healthy women must be Anna Sui 400 only, I confirm that. But you have to put it on gradually; otherwise it will be too red. In the past, *my* blusher [blusher of *me*] had to be Anna Sui and Nars only. But since I tried the MMU blusher, I've changed my mind. It's a lot cheaper. There's a wide range of colors available, each of them is very nice. I really recommend MMU. It's fun to use with so many colors to choose from. It's worth paying. A cheap and good item.'
(Pantip)

(4)   *rao* tham thang 2 yang phrom phrom kan doen thang sai klang kha ngoen ko tong borihan hai pen khwam suai ko tong dulae nang nap ngoen tae nata mai mi rasi *dichan* wa man mai chai!!!

'*I* do 2 things at the same time. Keep the balance. Manage money and maintain the beauty. Counting money but having a bad-looking face, *I* think it's not right!!!'
(Pantip)

Among women, /nǔ:/ is used both on its own and along with other self-reference terms, including the gender-shared pronoun /rāw/ and nickname. In extract (1), the poster uses /nǔ:/ exclusively and consistently throughout the reply. The poster in (2) refers to herself with /rāw/ and her nickname *Nok* throughout her reply while using /nǔ:/ only once. Similarly, /dìchǎn/

(including /dìchǎn/ and /dìchán/) occurs as the only first-person pronoun in a reply and along with the gender-shared pronoun /rāw/. /dìchǎn/ is the only self-reference term used in the reply in (3) while the poster in (4) uses /dìchǎn/ and /rāw/ in her reply. However, with only a few tokens in the dataset, /dìchǎn/ is not found to be used consistently in a single reply.

Women employ /nǔ:/ women to take either an affective stance or an intimate one. An affective stance expressed by /nǔ:/ is, for example, the earlier extract in (2), in which the poster writes a review of the products she has just bought. Before moving to the actual review, she explains why she is writing a review of the product from the same brand as the one she wrote about before. She uses the gender-shared singular pronoun /rāw/ alongside her nickname *Nok* from the beginning of her post. She switches her self-reference term to /nǔ:/ when saying that she likes this brand, which is the reason why she writes about the brand again. Then, she switches back to her nickname *Nok* in the next sentence. /nǔ:/ is used only once for the purpose of expressing the poster's strong preference for the brand. Her use of this pronoun contrasts with /rāw/ and her nickname *Nok*, making her affective stance become more evident. The affect is also supported by the use of the laughing sound and the exclamation phrase *mae . . . ao na ao na* 'well . . . come on.'

(5)   phi[3] Cherry mi yoe a kho *nu* bang di

'You have so much stuff. Can *I* have some?'
(Pantip)

/nǔ:/ can also be used to take an intimate stance. Most instances of such use of /nǔ:/ occur when the poster addresses someone in particular. In (5), the poster addresses another individual who is a regular poster to the webboard and well-known among webboard members. In this post from which (5) is extracted, the post owner called Cherry displays things she bought as part of her monthly shopping. The poster in (5) mentions the name of the addressee to show that she knows her. Then the poster uses /nǔ:/ to signify intimacy, taking a stance of someone who knows and is familiar with the addressee. The difference between the use of /nǔ:/ to index affect and intimacy is the power relationship between the poster who uses the pronoun and the audience or addressee. As illustrated in Table 10.1, /nǔ:/ is used when there is a nonreciprocal power between the speaker and the listener. However, when taking an affective stance such as in (2), /nǔ:/ is chosen to highlight the expression of the poster in contrast with other self-reference terms used. The poster is not necessarily younger or in a lower social rank than the potential audience. /nǔ:/ does not signify nonreciprocal power but serves instead to signal affect. In contrast, when used for an intimate stance such as in (1) and (5), the poster uses /nǔ:/ not only to show intimacy but also to position herself as younger or less senior than the addressee.

The use of /dìchǎn/ is infrequent among the women. As illustrated in Table 10.1, /dìchǎn/ is usually associated with femininity and formality. It has a very restrictive use in formal situations. The context of the webboards, however, is informal. Seeing the use of /dìchǎn/ as indexing formality would make it pragmatically incompatible with the context. In the dataset, women do not employ /dìchǎn/ to signify formality as such. The use of /dìchǎn/ contrasts with the informality of the context and other nonformal self-reference terms. The association of /dìchǎn/ with formality allows women to express their seriousness and to take an emphatic stance, a standpoint where they express their assertiveness and confidence about something. /dìchǎn/ makes them become interactionally more forceful and convincing.

(6)   taekon *rao* mi panha rueang sio ut tan kha pen thang na loei aksep thi nueng ni thing roi daeng lae lum wai talot ko raksa duai tua-eng ma rueai rueai khrai wa tua nai di *dichan* long ma mot tae sio man muean mi phatthana tua man pai rueai rueai praman wa *rao* roem cha ao man yu laeo tae man ko plian pen sio baep mai pai choei loei a

'*I* used to have a pimple problem. I had pimples all over my face. When they're inflamed, they always left red marks and holes on my face. I kept dealing with them myself. Which kinds of medicine were said to be good, *I* tried them all. But the pimples seemed to keep developing themselves. Like when *I* started to be able to control them, they transformed themselves into a new kind of pimples.'
(Pantip)

The poster in (6) creates a post concerning her pimple problem. She starts the post using the gender-shared pronoun /rāw/. She changes her self-reference term to /dìchǎn/ when explaining how much she has been trying to cope with her problem (/dìchǎn/ is used only once). Later, she switches from /dìchǎn/ to /rāw/ and maintains her use of /rāw/ in the rest of her replies in the post. The association of /dìchǎn/ with formality is significant in this context. It is contrasted with the unmarked use of /rāw/ and conveys the assertiveness of the poster. /dìchǎn/ is more marked because of its juxtaposition with /rāw/, highlighting an emphatic stance taken by the poster. The poster in (4), shown earlier, similarly expresses her opinion about the importance of both money and beauty. She replies only once in the post. At first, she uses the gender-shared pronoun /rāw/ as a self-reference term. In the end, she switches to /dìchǎn/ to emphasize her point that both money and beauty are important, not only one of them.

(7)   nokchak ya thak phuean na pen sio laeo karuna ya thak khon kha yai duai na kha *nu* yak cha krittttttttt khue wa *rao* pen khon nong yai! ton kha mai yai thaorai tae nong ni si—' hen laeo khriat 55555 khoei mi phuean thak wa kha kae ni te chan salop dai loei na nia yai kwa

nakfutbon ik *chan* loei suan man klap pai yang wai wa yak don te pak mai la? ngiap loei -_- laeoko nong sao *rao* pen khon uap tae nata suai phro pen lukkhrueng (nong mai thae tae sanit kan) phuean phuean thi rongrian wa kha yai bang arai bang khoei pai khaet ngan khrang nueng phi thi ruchak kan bok wa ui hun baep ni ko khong cha dai ngan rok kha *dichan* krot thaen nong ching ching kha moho mak tong phut kan khanat ni loei ro? TT siachai thaen

'Apart from not remarking on your friends' pimples, please also don't remark on one's big calves. *I* want to screammmmmmmmm *I* have big calves. My thighs are not so big but my calves—They make me feel sick. 55555 My friend once said, your legs can kick me to death; they are even bigger than those of soccer players. *I* then said promptly, does your mouth want to be kicked? He/she's quiet -_- *My* younger sister [younger sister of *me*], she's plump but has a beautiful face because she's mixed-race (we're sisters of the half blood but we're close to each other). Her school friends make fun of her big legs. She once went to cast recruitment. One of our acquaintances said, oh dear, with your figure, I don't think you'll get the job. *I* was so angry for my sister, really angry. Why did she have to say such thing? TT I'm sorry for my sister.'
(Pantip)

The extract in (7) is the only example of the use of /nǔ:/ and /dìchǎn/ in the same reply found in the dataset. The poster is about to tell a story of herself being made fun of for having big calves. She introduces her story using /nǔ:/, which she uses only once. The affective stance expressed by /nǔ:/ fits with the ways she writes the word "scream" with repeated final letters, a common strategy for Thai speakers to express emphasis in writing. The pronoun /nǔ:/ is used to show her highly uncomfortable feelings toward the situation making her expression of emotion stronger. Then she moves on to her actual story using /rāw/ and /chǎn/, which are both gender-shared pronouns. Later she refers to herself with /dìchǎn/ when explaining how angry she is and how sorry for her sister. Using /dìchǎn/, the poster takes an emphatic stance, expressing her strong dissatisfaction with what her acquaintance said to her sister.

Turning to *kathoey*, we find that their use of feminine pronouns is evenly split between /nǔ:/ (46.04%) and /dìchǎn/ (43.29%). The pattern of distribution of /nǔ:/ among *kathoey* is rather similar to the pattern found among women. Among *kathoey*, /nǔ:/ is used both on its own and along with the gender-shared pronoun /rāw/.

(8)   kon uen kho kroen thueng khwam rak kon na kha *dichan* phop kap faen phro phromlikhit ching ching kha rao khopha duchai kan lae tatsinchai mi arai kan nai wela thi mai nan nak lae *dichan* kodai tam

khao ma yu thi ban khao kha (nong nong ya ao yiangyang na kha
mai di kha) chuang raek raek ko muean promochan rak thua thua
pai nanlae kha tae langchaknan mai nan lai tang tang khao ko roem
ok thang rueang thiao phuying thi *dichan* khoei lao pai laeo na kha
man thamhai *dichan* chep thaep ba pai loeithidiao kha

'Let me first tell you my love story. *I* met my boyfriend truly because
of destiny. We started seeing each other and decided to have sex not
so long afterwards. And then *I* moved to his house (don't behave like
I did, it's not good). At first it was great like other typical relationships. Soon after that, he started to show his dark side. He went out
with other women, as *I*'ve talked about earlier. It hurt *me* so much
that I almost went crazy.'
(TLBz)

/dìchǎn/ is used the mostly consistently within replies by *kathoey*. The
pronoun is used exclusively as the only first-person pronoun in a reply as
shown, for example, in the extract in (8). Some posters are not only consistent
within a reply but also use /dìchǎn/ as the only feminine pronoun when participating in the webboard. They use /dìchǎn/ across all replies and posts they
participate in.

(9)　tha *rao* mai bok khao khao ko khong mai rangkiat *rao* rok kha rue
tha man chon mum laeo hetkan nan man bipbangkhap *rao* ko ching
bok loek khao loei kha doithi mai tong bok wa *rao* pen arai laeo ha
hetphon uen uen thi cha ma bok loek ka khao phromkap ha khon
mai thi khao rap *rao* dai pai duai nai wela diaokan sueng tonni
dichan ko patibat baep ni kha khon thi *dichan* khui kan ma khrueng
pi khao mai ru wa *rao* pen kathoey lae tua phuchai ko khonkhang
klua kathoey duai tae *rao* ko rak khao na khao ko rak *rao* mak tae
rao rak tuarao eng mak kwa pho thueng wela thi nat choe kan *dichan*
ching ni loei kha ha khon mai pai duai

'If *we* don't tell them [men], they won't mind *us*. Or if there's no way
out and such situation pressures *us*, just break up. We don't have to
tell them what's wrong with *us*. Find other reasons to break up with
them while at the same time looking for a new guy who can accept
who *we* are. This is what *I*'m doing now. The guy *I* was seeing for
half a year didn't know *I*'m a kathoey, and he's also rather afraid of
kathoey. But *I* loved him. He loved *me* so much, too. But *I* love myself
more. On a date, *I* got away. I'm looking for a new guy as well.'
(TLBz)

Very occasionally, /dìchǎn/ is used along with /rāw/ in a reply. In the
dataset, there is only one poster, as shown in (9), who uses /dìchǎn/ and

/rāw/ together in the same reply. She participates only in the post where the extract in (9) is taken from. She mixes /dìchǎn/ and /rāw/ in most of her replies. Similar to when /nǔː/ and /rāw/ are mixed in one reply, some instances of /rāw/ carry an inclusive feature. In (9), those translated to 'we' or 'us' are the instances of /rāw/ where the poster includes the addressee and potentially the audience in general. Also, as shown in (10), the poster uses both /nǔː/ and /dìchǎn/—the only instance in the dataset in which the webboard poster switches back and forth between these pronouns throughout her reply.

(10)   lasut wan kon *nu* ao pai hai phuean khon chin du kha (khao phut thai dai kha khae maikhoi chat na kha i i) pho *nu* ao pai hai pup khao tham ya arai ni *dichan* bok pai wa yakhum chin [. . .] tae khao tokchai mak kha wa *dichan* sue ma tang phaeng 250 baht khao bok wa thi chin khai khae 5 yuan eng na nu sarup laeo *nu* loei mai than na kha phrowa klua wa cha koet phon khangkhiang rue plao (samai kon khoei phae yakhum bang tua na kha thamhai thang achian thang puatthong na kha) kwa cha kla kin yakhum dai loei tatsin-chai sue Diane ma than na kha yang noi noi *dichan* ko khoei than Diane ma lai pi na kha

'The other day *I* showed the pills to my Chinese friend (he/she can speak Thai, not very clearly though, hehe) When *I* showed him/her the pills, he/she asked me, what kind of medicine are they. *I* said they're Chinese birth-control pills. [...] But he's very shocked because *I* bought a pack for 250 baht. He said in China it costs only 5 yuan. So in the end *I* don't take the pills as I'm afraid of potential side-effects (I used to be allergic to some birth-control pills, which caused me to throw up and have stomach ache). It took me a while to be brave enough to take the pills. So I've decided to buy Diane. At least, *I* used to take Diane for many years.'
(TLBz)

Among *kathoey*, /nǔː/ does not seem to index affect as it does among (non-*kathoey*) women. Its consistent use throughout replies contributes to the fact that it is one of the most common feminine pronouns among *kathoey*. With the consistent use, /nǔː/ does not serve to particularly highlight the poster's expression in the same way it does among women. Instead, using /nǔː/, the poster aligns herself with femininity and younger age or lower seniority, the characteristics associated with the pronoun. In (11) and (12), the posters talk about their romantic relationships which ended because of their being *kathoey*. Seeking comfort and advice, the poster uses /nǔː/ in order to index her status as younger, and a potentially less experienced *kathoey*, as compared to other webboard members.

(11)   phi khao bok wa phi khao phit eng *nu* mai phit phi khao mong mai
        ok eng tae *nu* wa *nu* nia lae phit ruyu kae chai tae mai bok khao yang
        di thi khao pen khon arom yen khao ayu 20 rian pi 2

> 'He said he himself was wrong, *I* wasn't. He was the one who didn't
> recognize me. But *I* thought *I* was wrong. I know who I am but
> didn't tell him. Lucky that he's a calm person. He's 20 years old,
> second year in college.'
> (TLBz)

(12)   khopkhun thi hai khamnaenam na kha *nu* buea *nu* seng mai ru wa
        phuchai khao chop kathoey baep nai baep nian ni rue kathoey baep
        thammada thi du laeo ru wa pen phuchai bang khon ma khui kap
        nu nu ko mai dai bok wa pen sao song tae pho ma ru thilang ko ha
        wa *rao* kohok lok luang *nu* mai ru wa *rao* phit mai lae phuchai bang
        khon thi *rao* tatsinchai bok wa pen sao song thi raek ko bok wa *rao*
        kohok mai chuea tae pho ma ru ik thi wa pen ching ko ni hai thang
        thang thi *rao* ko mai dai phit arai khwamching ko bok pai mot thuk
        yang tangtae raek laeo

> 'Thank you for your advice. *I'm* bored. *I'm* sick of it. I don't know
> what kind of kathoey men like, a woman-like one or an ordinary
> kathoey who you can identify. Some men approached *me* and *I* didn't
> tell them I'm a kathoey. When they discovered that later, they accused
> *me* of lying. *I* don't know if *I'm* wrong. And some men who *I* decided
> to tell I'm a kathoey, they at first said *I* lied. They didn't believe me.
> When they realized that it's true, they disappeared, even though *I*
> wasn't wrong. I've already told them the truth since the beginning.'
> (TLBz)

While women make use of /dìchǎn/'s association with formality in taking an emphatic stance, *kathoey* do not do the same thing. /dìchǎn/ is used by
kathoey very consistently and becomes an unmarked form among *kathoey*—a
form that does not index formality anymore. I argue that *kathoeys'* frequent
and repetitive use of /dìchǎn/ in various contexts makes the form become part
of their habitual use. As a result, /dìchǎn/ becomes less associated with formality. Such an association fades away while the association with femininity
is repeated through the process of stance-taking. /dìchǎn/ is then realized as
expressing femininity rather than formality. In other words, *kathoey* renegoti-
ate the meaning of /dìchǎn/. They make use of /dìchǎn/ for gender purposes,
in effect transforming it into their informal feminine pronoun. However,
unlike /nǔ:/, /dìchǎn/ is used when there is no power difference between the
interlocutors.

Apart from /nǔ:/ and /dìchǎn/, other feminine pronouns are used among
women and *kathoey*, though with a significantly lower frequency. The uses of /

dían/, /dán/, /ʔìchǎn/, and /khǎw/ among the two groups of speakers are similar to each other. Among the variants of /dìchǎn/, there are three instances of /dían/ among women, one instance of /dían/, and one instance of /dán/ among *kathoey*. /dían/ and /dán/ are very marked variants of /dìchǎn/. The pronouns are stereotypically associated with people from high social class and are frequently the linguistic means for mocking these people. In the dataset, women and *kathoey* do not use the variants to refer to the high social class. They make use of the two pronouns for humorous purposes when taking an affective stance.

(13)   khran cha khao pai thi King Power maechao ko mai khai hai *dian* phro mai mi Boarding-pass wen kam!! mi satang khrai wa tham dai thuk yang

'Even though I go to King Power, they won't sell it to *me* because I don't have a boarding pass. Oh my goodness!! Who says money can buy everything?'
(Pantip)

(14)   it ni khon nian nian nian a *dan* doen ma 5 met ko ru la wa kathoey

'I'm jealous at those who look really woman-like. *I*'m five meters away and you can tell I'm a kathoey.'
(TLBz)

In (13), the poster complains that she cannot find the perfume she wants and that she cannot buy it at the duty free shop called King Power as she does not have a boarding pass. She mocks herself and the situation she is facing. Similarly, in (14), the poster makes fun of her own appearance, which is not woman-like. Using /dían/ and /dán/ as a mocking tool, the posters make their situations sound dramatic and humorous at the same time.

(15)   phuean phuean thuk khon kha ya phoeng buea thi cha an thi *ichan* khian na kha ao wai pen korani sueksa la kan . . .

'Guys, don't get fed up with what *I* write. Let's take it as a case study . . .'
(TLBz)

(16)   dan lang ni ngam ngot tae ya dai hanna ma chiao *ichan* na ban pen dokhet mak 55555555

'The back is very beautiful but don't let me show you the front. *I* have a very big face, like mushrooms 55555555'
(Pantip)

(17)   sawatdi chao kha thuk khon kon uen tong kho-aphai duai na kha thi ma top cha phodi muea wan tang krathu set sami loek ngan phodi loei ma chikhua *ichan* klapban oei! rap klapban

'Hello everyone. First of all, I have to apologize for replying late. Yesterday after creating this post, my husband just finished his work. So he forced *me* to go back home. Oops! He picked me up then we went back home.'

(TLBz)

/ʔìchǎn/ is an old-fashioned pronoun typically associated with older speakers who are lower in social ranking than the addressee. It is used in the dataset as a way of expressing inferiority or humbleness. In (15), the poster writes about her relationship. Her story is long and she responds in many replies. So she asks other webboard members to bear with her. The use of /ʔìchǎn/ emphasizes her act of begging by putting herself in a lower position than others making her sound humble. The extracts in (16) and (17) show how women use /ʔìchǎn/ for an affective stance, similar to their use of /dían/ and /dán/. Using /ʔìchǎn/, the posters do not identify themselves as elderly speakers or as being socially inferior. The association of the form with certain groups of speaker, its infrequent use, and its being seen as old-fashioned make the form marked and unexpected in the context, leading to a perception of affect and humor. The poster in (16) talks about her new haircut, which she thinks makes her face look very big. The use of /ʔìchǎn/ makes her story sound entertaining and humorous. The humor also lies in the comparison of her face with a mushroom. The poster in (17) explains that the reason why she is responding late is because she had to go home with her husband and was too busy to respond to the post immediately. Similar to the poster in (16), she makes use of /ʔìchǎn/ to create affect and humor. The pronoun makes her explanation sound playful rather than serious.

(18)   thang widi-o *khao* mi yang diao khue lip 5555555

'Of everything shown in the video, *I* only have one which is the lipstick 5555555'
(Jeban)

(19)   *khao* cha pai tat khai laeo na khong ik lai wan cha ma khao bot khit-thueng thuk khon na

'*I*'m having my testicle taken out. It's gonna be many days until I come back to the webboard. Miss you everyone.'
(TLBz)

/khǎw/ is usually used in informal situations indicating intimacy between interlocutors. In the dataset, both women and *kathoey* use the pronoun to take a stance of being girlish. In (18), the poster refers to the video of the post owner who demonstrates how she cleans her face. The poster in (19) says good-bye to other webboard members as she is going for an operation and will be away from the webboard for a long time. Using /khǎw/, the posters position themselves like a "cute, adorable girl."

To summarize, there are both similarities and differences between the use of feminine pronouns among women and *kathoey*. Comparing the use of /nǔ:/ and /dìchǎn/ among women and *kathoey*, the occurrence of the two pronouns is quite similar. Both /nǔ:/ and /dìchǎn/ are used on their own and combined with the gender-shared pronoun /rāw/. *Kathoeys'* use of the two pronouns is generally more consistent within a reply as compared to women, who use the pronouns less often and tend to mix them with /rāw/ or other self-reference terms. /nǔ:/ is used by women to express affect and intimacy, while /dìchǎn/ is used to indicate emphasis. *Kathoey*, on the other hand, have a much more consistent use of /nǔ:/ and /dìchǎn/. They use /nǔ:/ to index femininity and lower seniority while /dìchǎn/ is reinterpreted as an informal and unmarked feminine pronoun, becoming part of *kathoey*'s habitual pronoun. /dían/, /dán/, and /ʔìchǎn/ are used by both women and *kathoey* for the purpose of taking an affective stance and for creating humor. Women and *kathoey* share the use of /khǎw/ for taking a stance of girlishness.

Perceived Social Meanings of First-Person Feminine Pronouns

We designed a questionnaire to elicit responses on *kathoey* and women's perceptions of the social meanings of particular self-reference terms found in the online dataset. Women and *kathoey* report their perceptions relatively similarly. The responses obtained from the questionnaire agree with the use and meanings of feminine pronouns found in the Internet dataset.

(20)   *nu* chai kap phuyai thi khonkhang sanit chen achan phomae rue yat phuyai hetphon thi chai khue sadaeng khwam nopnom to phuyai lae mai pen thangkan

'*Nu* is used with my elders who I'm quite close to such as teachers, parents or senior relatives. The reason why I use it is to show respect to my elders and it's not formal.' (women)

(21)   *nu* chai riak thaen tua-eng muea khui kap phufang thi mi ayu mak kwa lueak chai phro pen phasa phut sadaeng thueng kan hai kiat lae khaorop phufang sueng mi ayu mak kwa

'*Nu* refers to myself when speaking to people who are older than me. I choose it because it's colloquial showing honor and respect to addressees who are older.'
(women)

(22) *nu*—chai kap phu thi mi ayu mak kwa thi sanit phro sadaeng khwam pen kan-eng baep onnom thom ton

'*Nu*—is used with my intimate elders because it shows friendliness and humbleness.'
(*kathoey*)

(23) *nu* maikhoi dai chai tha cha chai ko khong nai okat khui kap run phi thi pen krathoey

'I rarely use *nu*. I may use it when talking to my seniors who are kathoey.'
(*kathoey*)

As shown, for example, in (20)–(23), women and *kathoey* agree on the use of /nǔ:/ to refer to oneself as a speaker who is younger than the addressee. The pronoun is a way of showing respect to the addressee and making the speaker sound humble and "adorable" while not being formal. /nǔ:/ can also indicate intimacy between speaker and addressee. Additionally, some *kathoey* respondents mention the use of /nǔ:/ particularly with *kathoey* who are more senior. The pronoun, however, is rarely referred to as a feminine pronoun by either women or *kathoey*.

(24) *dichan* chai kap khon mai sanit korani top khamtham yang pen thangkan phro khit wa pen kan sadaeng rayahang lae hai kiat

'*Dichan* is used with people I'm not close to when answering questions formally because I think it shows distance and honor.'
(women)

(25) *dichan* chai thaen tua-eng nai korani tongkan khwam pen thangkan chen kan nam sanoe phonngan nai kan prachum kan banyai thang wichakan

'*Dichan* is used to refer to myself to show formality such as in conference presentations and academic lectures.'
(women)

(26) *dichan* pen laksana khong kham thaen ton thi mi laksana pen thangkan lae mak chai nai kan titto suesan thi pen kan pen ngan lae tongkan khwam suphap khonkhang mak

'*Dichan* is a self-reference term which is formal and usually used for serious communication which requires quite a high level of politeness.'
(women)

(27)   *dichan* pen kham sapphanam thaen tua-eng samrap phuying phu
phut na cha chai nai korani thi pen kan sonthana thi pen thangkan
thuapai

'*Dichan* is a first-person pronoun for women. The speaker tends to
use it in formal conversations.'
(*kathoey*)

(28)   kham wa *dichan* lae anuphan pen kham khong phuying mai dai
taeng ying lae mai yak sadaeng-ok mak pai kwa ni

'The term *dichan* and its derivatives are for women. I don't dress
femininely and don't want to express myself more than I do now.'
(*kathoey*)

(29)   "*dichan*" thaen tua phet ying rue kathoey thi du ying mak mak rue
plaeng phet laeo chai laeo khong mai khoe khoen

'"*Dichan*" is a self-reference term for female or kathoey who look
very feminine or have their sex changed. That won't be awkward.'
(*kathoey*)

The responses in (24)–(29) are examples from women's and *kathoeys'*
self-reports. /dìchăn/ is used in formal situations such as academic lectures,
conference presentations, and meetings. It makes the speaker look confident
and professional while being polite and respectful. /dìchăn/ is also used to indicate the distance between speaker and addressee. /dìchăn/ is rarely mentioned
as a feminine form by women. Many *kathoey* respondents, however, report that
/dìchăn/ is a term for women and that it is used by *kathoey* who have feminine
appearance or have undergone sex reassignment surgery. Using or not using
/dìchăn/ therefore indicates *kathoey's* level of feminine presentation in public.

The questionnaire responses illustrate that among women and *kathoey*,
/nŭ:/ strongly connotes power. They report their choice of the pronoun when
talking to their elders in order to show respect and humbleness, rather than
femininity. This, especially among *kathoey* who report their use of the pronoun with their senior *kathoey*, corresponds to the way women and *kathoey* use
/nŭ:/ to index their younger and less experienced self in the online dataset. /nŭ:/
positions the speaker as a younger, "adorable" and less formal individual, which
also allows women to seem more emotional and do affect in the online dataset.
The fact that women report using /nŭ:/ with their intimate elders also explains
the way that women use the pronoun in the online dataset to express intimacy.

/dìchăn/, on the other hand, strongly connotes formality among both
women and *kathoey*. Women associate the pronoun firmly with formality. They
report the form to be used in formal situations to show respect and politeness
while attending notably less to the femininity aspect of the pronoun. Their strong
association of the pronoun with formality enables them to make use of /dìchăn/

to index emphasis, as seen in the online dataset since the pronoun is exceptionally formal and has a very restrictive and specific use among women. Based on the questionnaire responses, *kathoey* explicitly mention the femininity aspect of /dìchăn/ more than women do. They are well aware of the pronoun "belonging" to women. /dìchăn/ seems to be strictly feminine for *kathoey* allowing them to use it to present their femininity, as identified in the online dataset.

Women and *kathoey* also perceive the meanings of /dían/, /dán/, and /ʔìchăn/ similarly. Their responses agree with the use of the three pronouns found in the online dataset. /dían/ and /dán/ are reported by women and *kathoey* to be associated with high social class. They are used for speaking in an affected style. Some respondents also perceive /dán/ to be more affected than /dían/. /ʔìchăn/ is reported to be an old-fashioned form used by older people when speaking to someone higher in terms of social ranking. It is used for affect as well. The three pronouns are also reported to be commonly found in television series and used for humorous purpose.

Discussion

Kathoey and women share access to the same set of Thai first-person feminine pronouns. They also share certain ideas or perceptions of how the feminine pronouns should be used and interpreted. The similarities are shown in the questionnaire responses where they report the use and meanings of feminine pronouns found in the online dataset in a similar way. In the online dataset, *kathoey* and women share similarities in their use of certain pronouns (i.e., /dían/, /dán/, /ʔìchăn/, and /khăw/). However, using the same pronouns does not always mean that the two groups of speakers do the same thing with the pronouns.

Women and *kathoey* have their own way of using and interpreting the pronouns. In the online dataset, women use the two feminine pronouns /nŭ:/ and /dìchăn/ for stance-taking purposes. Women select particular meanings associated with the pronouns, such as formality associated with /dìchăn/, and employ such meanings to take an emphatic stance. While women make use of these gendered forms for nongendered purposes, *kathoey* use the gendered pronouns in identifying with femininity. *Kathoey* use /nŭ:/ and /dìchăn/ frequently and the two pronouns function as part of *kathoey*'s habitual pronoun use. /dìchăn/ is reinterpreted as an informal feminine pronoun among *kathoey*, who use it for their own purpose of presenting femininity.

Through the use of feminine pronouns, *kathoey* negotiate a position for themselves in the Thai sex/gender inventory by aligning themselves with femininity. Thai society in general expects a male-bodied person to be masculine and a female-bodied to be feminine. This expectation leaves *kathoey* in an in-between position as those with a male body behaving in a feminine fashion. *Kathoey* adopt feminine personal reference terms in an effort to position themselves within the binary of masculinity and femininity. They select certain feminine forms and reanalyze those forms for their own use. In other words, they strategically use first-person personal reference terms for gender presentation by choosing particular forms to do femininity.

Thai does not show the gender of speaker morphologically in the language. The primary way of identifying one's gender is through the use of personal reference terms and polite final particles. Gender presentation through language is limited to only these linguistic tools and only at the pragmatic level rather than the morphological one. However, with a limited set of linguistic tools, language can still play an important role in indexing gender in Thai. The results of this study are evidence that language participates in the indexation of gender identity in Thailand in a subtle way. *Kathoey* do not simply use feminine forms in order to sound like women. They share a limited set of linguistic forms with women, but are not necessarily restricted to the way women use the forms. They make their own linguistic choices by selecting particular forms to be used in a particular way. Language is thus one of the resources *kathoey* use to feminize themselves (along with other means such as wearing feminine clothes, taking hormones and undergoing surgery). Linguistic choice is another tool *kathoey* can make use of to construct their femininity.

Acknowledgments

The research upon which this chapter is based was funded by Chulalongkorn University Doctoral Scholarship Programme and H.M. King Bhumibol Adulyadej's 72nd Birthday Scholarship. I am grateful to Lauren Hall-Lew and Erez Levon for their helpful comments and detailed suggestions on earlier versions of this chapter.

Notes

1. Apart from the various choices of self-reference terms available, Thai is also a pro-drop language (e.g., Hoonchamlong 1991; Phimsawat 2011). Pronouns or other self-reference terms can be omitted in any context where the identity of the speaker can be retrieved pragmatically. Pro-drop is not the focus of the present study. However, it could be interesting in future research to investigate the relationship, if any, between the uses of overt versus dropped pronouns and speaker gender.

2. The word *five* in Thai is /hâː/. The pronunciation is similar to the laughing sound. The figure "5" is commonly used to represent this laughing sound in informal writing, especially on the Internet.

3. *Phi* is a kin term meaning 'older sibling.'

References

Abe, Hideko. 2004. Lesbian bar talk in Shinjuku, Tokyo. In Shigeko Okamoto & Janet S. Shibamoto Smith (eds.), *Japanese language, gender, and ideology: Cultural models and real people*, 205–221. Oxford: Oxford University Press.

Beech, Hannah. 2008. Where the "ladyboys" are, http://www.time.com/time/world/article/0,8599,1820633,00.html. (July 25, 2011.)

Brown, Penelope & Stephen Levinson. 1978. Universals in language usage: Politeness phenomena. In Esther N. Goody (ed.), *Questions and politeness: Strategies in social interaction*, 56–311. Cambridge: Cambridge University Press.

Bucholtz, Mary. 2009. From stance to style: Gender, interaction, and indexicality in Mexican immigrant youth slang. In Alexandra Jaffe (ed.), *Stance: Sociolinguistic perspectives*, 46–70. Oxford: Oxford University Press.

Chirasombutti, Voravudhi & Anthony Diller. 1999. Who am "I" in Thai?—The Thai first person: Self-reference or gendered self? In Peter A. Jackson & Nerida M. Cook (eds.), *Genders & sexualities in modern Thailand*, 114–133. Chiang Mai: Silkworm Books.

Hall, Kira & Veronica O'Donovan. 1996. Shifting gender positions among Hindi speaking hijras. In Victoria L. Bergvall, Janet M. Bing, & Alice F. Freed (eds.), *Rethinking language and gender research: Theory and practice*, 228–266. London: Longman.

Hoonchamlong, Yuphaphann. 1991. *Some issues in Thai anaphora: A government and binding approach*. Madison: University of Wisconsin dissertation.

Irvine, Judith T. 1979. Formality and informality in communicative events. *American Anthropologist* 81(4). 773–790.

Iwasaki, Shoichi & Preeya Ingkaphirom. 2005. *A reference grammar of Thai*. Cambridge: Cambridge University Press.

Jackson, Peter A. 1997. Kathoey >< gay >< man: The historical emergence of gay male identity in Thailand. In Lenore Manderson & Margaret Jolly (eds.), *Sites of desire, economies of pleasure: Sexualities in Asia and the Pacific*, 166–190. Chicago: University of Chicago Press.

Jackson, Peter A. 1998. From *kamma* to unnatural vice: Male homosexuality and transgenderism in the Thai Buddhist tradition. In Winston Leyland (ed.), *Queer dharma: Voices of gay Buddhists*, Vol. 1, 55–89. San Francisco, CA: Gay Sunshine Press.

Jackson, Peter A. 1999. Tolerant but unaccepting: The myth of a Thai "gay paradise." In Peter A. Jackson & Nerida M. Cook (eds.), *Genders and sexualities in modern Thailand*, 226–242. Chiang Mai: Silkworm Books.

Jaffe, Alexandra. 2009. Introduction: The sociolinguistics of stance. In Alexandra Jaffe (ed.), *Stance: Sociolinguistic perspectives*, 1–28. Oxford: Oxford University Press.

Kongtrakool, Sompittaya. 1996. *Sex differentiation in the use of first person personal pronouns and polite final particles by Chulalongkorn University Arts students*. Bangkok: Chulalongkorn University MA thesis. (In Thai.)

Kulick, Don. 1998. *Travesti: Sex, gender and culture among Brazilian transgendered prostitutes*. Chicago: University of Chicago Press.

Miyazaki, Ayumi. 2002. Relational shift: Japanese girls' nontraditional first person pronouns. In Sarah Benor, Mary Rose, Devyani Sharma, Julie Sweetland, & Qing Zhang (eds.), *Gendered practices in languages*, 355–374. Stanford, CA: CSLI.

Miyazaki, Ayumi. 2004. Japanese junior high school girls' and boys' first-person pronoun use and their social world. In Shigeko Okamoto & Janet S. Shibamoto Smith (eds.),

Japanese language, gender, and ideology: Cultural models and real people, 256–274. New York & Oxford: Oxford University Press.

Morris, Rosalind C. 1994. Three sexes and four sexualities: Redressing the discourses on gender and sexuality in contemporary Thailand. *Positions* 2(1). 15–43.

Ochs, Elinor. 1992. Indexing gender. In Alessandro Duranti & Charles Goodwin (eds.), *Rethinking context*, 336–346. Cambridge: Cambridge University Press.

Palakornkul, Angkab. 1972. *A socio-linguistic study of pronominal strategy in spoken Bangkok Thai*. Austin: University of Texas dissertation.

Phimsawat, On-Usa. 2011. *The syntax of pro-drop in Thai*. Newcastle, UK: Newcastle University dissertation.

Seki, Minako. 1986. *Gender particles and linguistic/non-linguistic context*. Los Angeles: University of Southern California manuscript.

Sunaoshi, Yukako. 2004. Farm women's professional discourse in Ibaraki. In Shigeko Okamoto & Janet S. Shibamoto Smith (eds.), *Japanese language, gender, and ideology: Cultural models and real people*, 187–204. New York & Oxford: Oxford University Press.

Taywaditep, Kittiwut Jod, Eli Coleman, & Pacharin Dumronggittigule. 1997–2001. Thailand (Muang Thai). In Robert T. Francoeur (ed.), *The international encyclopedia of sexuality*, http://www2.hu-berlin.de/sexology/IES/index.html. (February 23, 2012.)

Totman, Richard. 2003. *The third sex: Kathoey—Thailand's ladyboys*. London: Souvenir Press Ltd.

Uyeno, Tazuko Y. 1971. *A study of Japanese modality: A performative analysis of sentence particles*. Ann Arbor: University of Michigan dissertation.

Winter, Sam. 2003. *Language and identity in transgender: Gender wars and the case of the Thai kathoey*. Paper presented at the Hawaii conference on social sciences, Waikiki. http://web.hku.hk/~sjwinter/TransgenderASIA/paper_language_and_identity.htm. (February 23, 2012.)

11

Conflicted Selves

LANGUAGE, RELIGION, AND SAME-SEX DESIRE IN ISRAEL

Erez Levon

I'm in the closet. Completely. Even though in reality there's no such thing since every time you go out and you want to meet people, you're exposing yourself whether you want to or not.

This quote comes from an interview I conducted in Jerusalem with "Igal," a forty-year-old Orthodox Jewish man who is married, has children, and also engages in sexual and romantic relationships with other men.[1] The quote provides one example of a series of conflicts Igal describes between his sexual desires (*to go out and meet people*) and the religious valuative framework of Orthodox Judaism within which he organizes his life—a framework that requires that his sexual desires not be *exposed*. Igal's comments in this regard resonate with much previous research on the intersection of religion and sexuality. Yip (1999, 2002), for example, discusses how nonheterosexual Catholics often experience an "intractable opposition" between their sexualities and normative articulations of their Christian faith (see also, e.g., Yarhouse 2001). Despite this opposition, however, Yip (2002) argues that the majority of the individuals he studied managed to reconcile these conflicting identifications by "harmoniously incorporating" both their sexual and religious identifications into a unified conceptualization of self (203). According to Yip, this incorporation is made possible by his informants' reinterpretations of religious doctrinal strictures in light of their own understandings of self. In other words, rather than giving up on their faith altogether, Yip's informants transform what it means for them to be Catholic, such that their religious and sexual identifications are rendered compatible.

The process of transformation and integration that Yip describes is a clear example of what developmental psychologists term *identity synthesis*, or the incorporation of multiple constitutive aspects of self into an internally consistent whole (e.g., Erikson 1968; Syed 2012). For many writers in both the scholarly and popular literature, synthesis of this kind has been considered a necessary precursor to psychic health given the self's assumed abhorrence of internal dissonance and its inability to accommodate inconsistency. Yet, more recent research in psychology on identificational conflict has argued that synthesis is not the only option available. Halbertal & Koren (2006), for example, draw on alternative models of identity formation (e.g., Hermans, Kempen, & Van Loon 1992; Côté 1996) to argue that the lesbian and gay Orthodox Jews they study do not work to assimilate their sexual and religious identifications or to resolve the opposition between them but instead develop multidimensional understandings of self that allow these conflicting identifications to coexist. According to Halbertal & Koren (2006), this is because, despite identifying as lesbian or gay, the individuals in their study also "*internally* identify with the antigay valuative framework" of Orthodox Judaism (56; emphasis in the original). What this means is that externalizing or abandoning any aspect of Jewish law or tradition is not an option, even when that law explicitly repudiates homosexuality. In this situation, a multidimensional understanding of self is what emerges, in which there are multiple *I positions* such that the "*I* in one position can agree, disagree, understand, misunderstand, oppose, contradict, question and even ridicule the *I* in another position" (Hermans, Kempen, & Van Loon 1992: 29).

In this chapter, I build on Halbertal & Koren's research to examine the role that linguistic variation plays in the construction of these sorts of multidimensional understandings of self. I draw my data from a case study of Igal, the Orthodox Jewish man I mentioned previously. I focus in my discussion on Igal's use of creaky voice throughout the interview I conducted with him. I argue that Igal uses creaky voice as a means to negotiate his conflicting sexual and religious identifications, and so construct the kind of multidimensional understanding of self that Halbertal & Koren describe. Crucially, I do not argue that Igal uses creak in an effort to present a distinct "gay" or "religious" self. Rather, I suggest that creaky voice serves as a way for Igal to adopt a particular deontic stance (Shoaps 2004) through which he reaffirms his commitment to Jewish laws and customs despite the transgression of these laws that his identification with same-sex desire represents. In using creaky voice to take this stance, I argue that Igal is able to orient himself to homosexuality while simultaneously signaling an awareness of the impossibility of this orientation. It is through this linguistic process then that Igal succeeds in materializing a multidimensional self of which both homosexuality and Orthodox Judaism are an integral part.

Language and the Disunity of Identity

Unlike in psychology, research in linguistics has long recognized the ability of individuals to hold multiple and conflicting understandings of self. Rather than assuming identificational consistency and closure, research has instead been devoted to investigating the ways in which speakers use language in an effort to construct the semblance of subjective coherence (e.g., Linde 1993; Ochs & Capps 2001). Work in this paradigm has been heavily influenced by Goffman's (1974) theory of production formats, and particularly the idea that speakers can "animate" different selves over the course of an interaction through the strategic deployment of socially salient voices. For Goffman, it is this act of *lamination* (the layering of multiple voices in the mouth of a single speaker) that demonstrates that the self need not be singular. Instead, it can be viewed as a "loosely compacted person" (Peirce 1955: 258) potentially comprised of several distinct "individuals" (see also Singer 1980, 1984).

Goffman's arguments in this regard are in many ways similar to Bakhtin's (1981) theory of the emergence of subjectivity (what he calls *consciousness*) in discourse, though Bakhtin is more explicit than Goffman about the relationship between the self and broader social structures and ideologies. According to Bakhtin (1981), the formation of consciousness requires negotiating the heteroglossia that is present among any community of speakers. This heteroglossia is characterized by the coexistence of a multiplicity of "languages" (i.e., ways of speaking), each one linked to particular "ideological systems and approaches to the world" (296). Adopting a language also entails adopting its associated ideological system, and so, according to Bakhtin, serves to position a "self" in the heteroglossic universe. In other words, the formation of consciousness for Bakhtin is essentially a process of orienting one's self to an ideological system by adopting the language with which that system is affiliated. Bakhtin views this process (which he terms *voicing*) as an active one, and, like Goffman, he allows for the possibility that individuals can "voice" multiple and contradictory selves over the course of an interaction. Similar to the psychological theories of the multidimensional self noted previously, Bakhtin maintains that there can be multiple "I"s in discourse, with each "I" corresponding to a different social or moral positioning yet all of them ultimately referring to the same individual.

Both Bakhtin's theory of voicing and Goffman's concept of self-lamination have been fruitfully applied to the study of the emergence of multidimensional selves in spoken interaction. Hill (1995), for example, describes how Don Gabriel, a Mexican peasant, deploys multiple voices in narrating the story of his son's murder by business partners who were envious of the son's financial successes. The voices, which are distinguished by such features as code choice (i.e., Mexicano vs. Spanish), pitch, voice quality, and intonational contour, include both participants and bystanders to the action as well as multiple laminations of Don Gabriel himself. Hill argues that Don Gabriel uses these voices to identify and juxtapose two competing moral universes: a peasant ideology of solidarity and communal reciprocity and a capitalist one of individualism and "business-for-profit." While Don Gabriel mostly associates capitalism with voices external to himself (through the use of reported speech and the construction of different "figures" in the story; Goffman 1974), he is nevertheless occasionally required to assimilate capitalist beliefs into his own narrative voice, despite the fact that these beliefs are antithetical to the peasant values Don Gabriel holds dear. Hill demonstrates how Don Gabriel accomplishes this via a series of self-laminations, in effect creating a distinct voice of "neutral narrator" that, while still his own, he contrasts with a more morally central voice that rejects capitalism and everything it stands for. For Hill, this interplay of self-laminations in Don Gabriel's story indicates that subjectivity is by no means unitary. Rather, she claims that it is comprised of a "kaleidoscope" of selves, each with a foot planted in a distinct moral universe.

While Hill's account posits the existence of multiple selves, it nevertheless maintains that there is a central or primary "authorial" self that can be taken to represent the essence of individual consciousness. More recently, however, research has questioned whether we need to posit the existence of such a unified inner core, or whether the authorial self itself can instead be comprised of multiple and conflicting identifications and orientations (e.g., Cameron & Kulick 2003; Kulick 2005). This is an issue addressed, for example, in McIntosh's (2009) examination of white Kenyan narratives about the African occult. According to McIntosh, the subject of the occult is particularly fraught for white Kenyans because it brings to the fore a potential subjective conflict in white Kenyans' experiences as being descendants of European Christian missionaries who simultaneously view themselves as "native" Africans. Distancing themselves from occult beliefs and practices allows white Kenyans to orient to the European (and Christian) values of their families and communities. At the same time, they must also orient (at least partially) to occult mythology or risk losing their claim to authentic "African-ness." In short then, white Kenyan subjectivity (or *consciousness*, to use Bakhtin's term) requires a simultaneous orientation to two mutually incompatible belief systems.

In her work, McIntosh examines how white Kenyans accomplish these conflicting positionings of self through language. She grounds her analysis in a theory of stance, or the linguistic strategies speakers use to construct orientations to the content of their talk and to the more durable identities and activities indexed through that talk (Du Bois 2007; Jaffe 2009). In contrast to concepts such as *voice* or *persona*, which presume a somewhat more durable and holistic positioning, stances are by definition necessarily fleeting—they are orientations speakers adopt in specific moments of interaction. This is not to say that stances cannot become habitual or that they are not linked to more static identity frames. Research on stance accretion has demonstrated the ways in which speakers engage in repeated acts of stance-taking in order to construct durable personae that exceed the confines of a single interaction (e.g., Ochs 1992; Rauniomaa 2003; Bucholtz 2009; Damari 2010). But stance itself crucially refers to a momentary orientation that speakers adopt in a specific interactional context. It is this inherent dynamism of stance that makes it a useful tool for examining the kind of subjective conflict experienced by white Kenyans. As McIntosh (2009) puts it, "stance-taking may raise contradictions, but it does not always require a final declaration or resolution on the part of the stance-taker" (74).

McIntosh focuses on a variety of different stance-taking strategies that white Kenyans adopt to simultaneously distance themselves from and orient to the African occult. These include, for example, the use of certain entextualized utterances to materialize a social stance away from the occult while explicitly adopting an ontological stance of belief in occult powers. McIntosh argues that these acts of stance-taking serve as self-laminations, allowing white Kenyans to construct contradictory images of self with correspondingly contradictory footings toward "native" African beliefs. In contrast, however, to Don Gabriel, these contradictory footings are not distributed among external others or set in opposition to a "true" inner self. They are instead integral and constitutive aspects of her informants' subjectivities. That said, McIntosh also describes how her informants work to discursively privilege certain footings over others. The result of this is the appearance of a hierarchy of selves, in which particular orientations are rendered more prominent and presented as more important than others. Crucially, McIntosh views this privileging of selves as a discursive accomplishment, as something that is done through language and not something that simply reflects an already existing distinction between more core and more peripheral aspects of self. In other words, McIntosh argues that white Kenyans privilege certain selves over others for specific social and interactional reasons, not because the development of such a hierarchy is inherent to the formation of subjectivity itself (cf. Billig 1997, 1999; Cameron & Kulick 2005).

In my discussion, I follow McIntosh's lead by examining the ways in which Igal uses stance to adopt contradictory footings to both Orthodox Judaism and same-sex desire. I document how, for Igal, these footings are not treated as belonging to entirely distinct selves or personae but are instead presented as conflicting aspects of a multidimensional subjectivity. I argue, moreover, that Igal enacts this multidimensionality via the strategic use of creaky voice throughout his interview. I therefore turn to a brief discussion of treatments of creaky voice in the sociolinguistic literature on stance, before going on to the main body of my analysis.

Stance and Creaky Voice

Of the various linguistic strategies available for stance-taking, manipulation of voice quality is arguably one of the most salient and the most prevalent. In an early discussion of the topic, Sapir (1927) observes that variation in voice quality is a social phenomenon, a "symbolic index of personality" (896) that is akin to gesture in its ability to express thought or emotion. Since this initial observation, a substantial body of research has been devoted to identifying the various social and interactional meanings of voice quality, and, in particular, of creaky voice (see, e.g., Laver 1968; Couper-Kuhlen 2003; Sicoli 2010 for reviews).

The term *creaky voice* refers to a range of articulatory configurations, all of them characterized by high levels of adductive tension of the vocal folds (Ladefoged 1971; Gordon & Ladefoged 2001).[2] This tension diminishes the ability of air to flow through the glottis, resulting in low frequency and often aperiodic vocal fold vibration. Acoustically, this corresponds to a low pitch and discernible glottal tapping in the voice, or, in the words of Sicoli (2010) a voice that sounds like "an old hinge needing oil" (523). Given these perceptual characteristics, it perhaps not surprising that creaky voice has historically been found to predominate in the speech of men (e.g., Esling 1978; Henton & Bladon 1988; Stuart-Smith 1999), and has been argued to be iconically related to notions of hegemonic masculinity. More recent research, however, has also shown creaky voice to be prevalent in the speech of women, especially in the United States. Lefkowitz & Sicoli (2007), for example, identified frequent use of creak among university-age women in Virginia, while Podesva (2013) reports that women in a stratified sample of Washington, DC speakers use creaky voice more than three times as much as men. Similarly, Yuasa (2010) argues that creaky voice has come to be associated with an "upwardly mobile professional woman" persona in northern California.

These more recent studies indicate that the social meanings of creaky voice extend beyond simple one-to-one mappings between voice quality and gender and are instead situated within a more complex indexical field (Eckert 2008; Podesva 2013). Returning to the example of Lefkowitz & Sicoli's (2007) examination of creaky voice in Virginia, not only do they demonstrate that the young women in their sample use creaky voice frequently, they also show that they do so as a way of taking authoritative stances through speech. This argument resonates with research on the functions of creaky voice in talk-in-interaction more broadly. Laver (1994), for example, reports that, in British English, creaky voice signals a lack of interest in the topic of conversation and a "bored resignation" to the prospect of continuing to discuss it. Similarly, in their examination of the use of creaky voice and turn-final *yeah* in US English, Grivičić & Nilep (2004) argue that creak in this position serves to indicate a dispreference to continue with the current topic of conversation and/or a disalignment with the current speaker. In other words, Grivičić & Nilep claim that creaky voice allows speakers to establish interactional distance from the immediate context. Both of these meanings—bored resignation and interactional distance—are also apparent in how the Latina gang girls described by Mendoza-Denton use the feature (Jannedy & Mendoza-Denton 1998; Mendoza-Denton 2008, 2011). Part of a broader symbolic economy of affect, creaky voice is deployed by the girls at particular interactional moments as a means of constructing a persona centered on the values of "being silent, being hard of heart (hardcore), and being toughened through experience" (Mendoza-Denton 2011: 269). Whereas many popular conceptualizations of what it means to be a "man" share these values of silence and affective restraint, Mendoza-Denton clearly demonstrates that the girls do not use creaky voice to index masculinity. Rather, creak provides the girls with a mechanism for signaling *control*, both emotional and interactional, and, in doing so, to materialize a locally relevant "hardcore" persona (see also Bolinger 1982).

In what follows, I examine the extent to which my informant Igal recruits the meanings of "authority," "distance," and "emotional restraint" that have been associated with creaky voice in his own use of the feature. As described earlier, I do so in an effort to understand how Igal negotiates the subjective contradiction that exists between his Orthodox Judaism and his same-sex desire. I begin by investigating the quantitative distribution of creaky voice across my conversation with Igal. This helps me to demonstrate creak's socioindexical relevance in the interview and to pinpoint locations for subsequent qualitative analysis. I then turn to a close examination of those instances where Igal uses creak to illustrate how it serves as a tool for stance-taking and, ultimately, for the construction of a multidimensional self.

Distributional Analysis

My interview with Igal occurred in the context of a larger sociolinguistic ethnography of sexuality in Israel (Levon 2010). Unlike with the other participants in that study, the interview was the first and only time that I met or spoke to Igal at length.[3] The interview took place in 2005 in a small café in West Jerusalem and lasted for just over an hour. The interview was semistructured in format and began with Igal providing a chronological narrative of his life story, followed by a discussion of his views on both Israeli politics generally and lesbian and gay politics in Israel more specifically (for further details of the basic interview structure, see Levon 2009, 2010). Because in this chapter I focus on language use in a single interview with one speaker, the analysis I provide is grounded in a framework of language style, and particularly stylistic variation by speech topic (Bell 1984, 2001). While an admittedly somewhat blunt instrument for examining speakers' sociolinguistic moves in interaction, topic has nevertheless been shown to be a robust heuristic for tracking speakers' shifting orientations through talk (e.g., Schilling-Estes 2004; Levon 2009).

For the purposes of quantitative analysis, I divide Igal's speech into five topic categories: Personal Biography, Gay Life, Sexuality and Religion, Israeli Politics, and Mechanics. Personal Biography covers Igal's retelling of past events in his life, including his childhood and schooling, his military service, and his present occupation. Gay Life refers to Igal's description of his realization of his same-sex desires, his erotic and romantic experiences with men, and his opinions regarding configurations of gayness and "the gay community" in Israel. Sexuality and Religion is comprised of Igal's explicit discussions of the intersection of these two constructs, including a narrative about his marriage (to a woman). Israeli Politics refers to instances where Igal provided his opinions about then-current events taking place in the Israeli sociopolitical sphere. Finally, Mechanics is talk about the interview itself (e.g., *ask whatever you like*) or about goings-on in the immediate context (e.g., *can we move to another table?*). Topic was coded at the level of the intonational phrase (IP) in order to allow me to capture turn-internal topic shifts.

The presence or absence of creaky voice was coded auditorily as a binary factor on a syllable-by-syllable basis. In other words, for each syllable in Igal's speech, I coded for whether creaky voice was impressionistically present or not. Waveforms were inspected to verify the presence of creak in auditorily ambiguous cases. In addition to topic, I also coded for four other factors that can potentially constrain the appearance of creaky voice. Research has shown that creaky voice is common at the end of IPs, as a result of a regular process of declination (whereby fundamental frequencies decrease over the course of an utterance) and speakers' overall diminished capacity to sustain the airflow required for modal voicing as an IP reaches its end (Henton & Bladon 1988). Creaked tokens were therefore coded as being in either final or nonfinal position.[4] Additionally, Dilley, Shattuck-Hufnagel, & Ostendorf (1996) and Podesva (2007) note that creaky voice is more common in syllables containing other glottal elements (such as glottal stops or glottalized plosives). Creaked syllables were therefore also coded as to whether other glottal elements occurred within the same syllable. Podesva (2007) further states that creaky voice can be an articulatory by-product of the elasticity of the vocal folds as they move from some other nonmodal phonation (like falsetto) back to modal voice. The idea here is that the release of a phonatory setting like falsetto (where the vocal folds are stretched longitudinally) to the more neutral modal position can cause the vocal folds to "snap" into the medially compressed position that gives rise to creaky voice. All syllables were therefore coded for the other phonation types that occurred in the same IP (modal, creaky, breathy, falsetto, or some combination thereof). Finally, all syllables were also coded for whether they occurred during constructed dialogue as opposed to direct speech, based on earlier work (e.g., Podesva 2013) showing that shifts in production format are often accompanied by a change in voice quality.

In total, there were 8,123 syllables in Igal's speech across the interview. Of these, 365 (or 4.5%) contained creaky voice. To test whether any of the independent factors described earlier influence the appearance of creak, I built a binomial logistic regression (in R) that modeled the prevalence of creak in Igal's speech according to speech topic, the presence or absence of constructed dialogue, and the other phonation types present in the IP. I examined position in the IP (final or nonfinal) and the existence of other glottal segments in the syllable via contingency tables for creaked tokens only.

Results of the regression analysis indicate that topic is the only significant constraint on the appearance of creaky voice among the factors considered ($p = 0.000$). Neither "type of speech" (i.e., constructed dialogue vs. direct speech) nor "other phonation types present in the IP" were selected as having a significant effect. Figure 11.1 provides a representation of the distribution of creaked syllables across topic categories. In that figure we see that talk in the Sexuality & Religion category has the highest proportion of creaky voice (9.1% creaked syllables), followed by Personal Biography (6.7%), Gay Life (5.4%), Israeli Politics (3.9%), and Mechanics (2.9%). Post-hoc pairwise comparisons among these topic categories further indicate that the only significant difference within the group is between Sexuality & Religion and all other topic categories (which are not themselves significantly differentiated from one another). Overall, then, the regression analysis demonstrates that Igal creaks significantly more when talking about sexuality and religion than on any other topic, and that these other topics are not distinguished from one another in terms of frequencies of creak observed.

The importance of topic in constraining the appearance of creaky voice is further demonstrated by significant interactions between topic

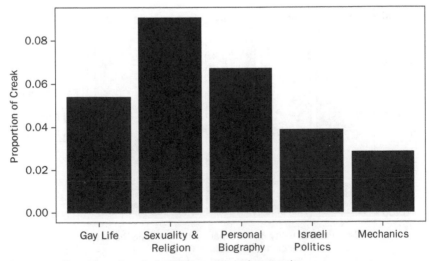

FIGURE 11.1 Proportion of creaked syllables across topic categories

and both IP position and the presence of other glottal segments in the syllable. Recall from earlier that creaky voice is normally more likely to occur in IP-final position, due to the regular process of declination across utterances, as well as in syllables containing other glottal(ized) segments. Figures 11.2 and 11.3, however, illustrate that, for Igal, topic serves to at least partially override both of these linguistically driven patterns. In Figure 11.2, we find that tokens of creak in both the Gay Life and Sexuality & Religion categories occur predominantly in nonfinal position (the grey portions of the bars). While it is true that in Igal's speech creak occurs more frequently in nonfinal positions in all categories, the ratio of creak in nonfinal versus final position is significantly greater for talk on Gay Life and Sexuality & Religion than it is for talk on Personal Biography, Israeli Politics, or Mechanics (which are not significantly differentiated from one another; p = 0.041). Similarly, Figure 11.3 shows that when talking on topics related to Gay Life, Sexuality & Religion, and Mechanics, Igal uses creaky voice in syllables that do not contain other glottal elements (the black portions of the bars) proportionally more often than he does when speaking on Personal Biography or Israeli Politics (*p* = 0.024). In both Figure 11.2 and Figure 11.3, then, we find that speech in the Gay Life and the Sexuality & Religion categories is "creakier" than the linguistic factors would lead us to expect. This, taken together with the fact that creaky voice is significantly more frequent on Sexuality & Religion topics overall, provides us with initial evidence that Igal uses creak strategically as a way of achieving some stylistic or interactional goal when speaking about sexuality and religion.

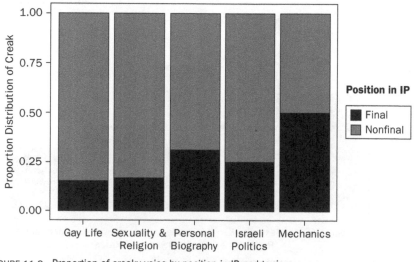

FIGURE 11.2   Proportion of creaky voice by position in IP and topic

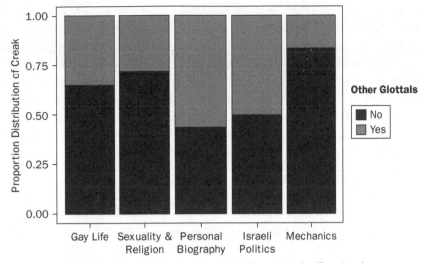

FIGURE 11.3 Proportion of creaky voice by other glottal elements in the IP and topic

Creak in Context

The distributional analysis of creaky voice in the preceding section provides two important pieces of information about Igal's use of the feature. First, it indicates that creaky voice carries social and/or interactional meaning for Igal. This is demonstrated by the fact that Igal's use of creak cannot be modeled by internal linguistic factors alone. Rather, the variation we find in the use of creak across topic categories can be taken as evidence that creak has a specific socioindexical value for Igal in this conversation. The second piece of information that the distributional analysis provides is that this socioindexical value is in some way related to Igal's understanding of the intersection of sexuality and religion. This is apparent in that talk on this topic features proportionally more creaky voice overall and more creak in linguistically unexpected contexts (i.e., IP nonfinally and without other glottal elements in the syllable) than talk on other topics does. What the distributional analysis cannot tell us, however, is what precisely the socioindexical value of creaky voice is, or what sociolinguistic move Igal is using it to make. Answering these questions requires a close qualitative analysis of creaky voice "in action," which is what I aim to do in this section.

As I have already noted, the stylistic distribution of creaky voice across the interview indicates that the feature carries particular meaning for Igal in discussions of the intersection of sexuality and religion. I therefore begin my examination by looking at the orientations that Igal adopts with respect to Orthodox Judaism and same-sex desire separately, before turning to discussions of how the two interact. Aside from a couple of very brief introductory comments about how he "grew up in an Orthodox household" and "went to an Orthodox primary school," Igal never explicitly describes his faith or his relationship with Judaism in the interview. His orientation to religion is nevertheless implicit in his discussion of other major events in his life, most notably the story of his marriage to his wife of seventeen years. This story, which appears in (1), was volunteered by Igal toward the beginning of the interview in the course of providing a chronological history of his life and was not offered in response to any specific question on my part. Boldface and underlined text represent best approximations in the English translation of where creaky voice occurs in the original Hebrew.[5]

(1) "time to get married"

> Igal: A:::nd I finished my BA. And I decided that it's necessary, that the time had come to get married. So I started going out with women. People introduced me to women. Friends. Family. From here from there. Would go out with women (Heb. *haja jotse im baxurot*). Sometimes I didn't like her sometimes she didn't like me. Once it's one thing, the next time it's another. e:m I have no idea how many women I went out with. And I hated it. I hated that whole period. You need to show yourself off and to sell yourself. e::::
>
> EL: When was this? When you were in=
>
> Igal: =24. I was 24. I finished my BA and said OK I have some time now to do this. e:m in the end I met- also there never really was this feeling of (1) yes this will work or no this won't work. You you (.) it's like with a man that you (.) you weigh all sorts of things. He looks good, he's smart, intelligent, he's interesting. He's serious. **e:: if there's** a chance or there isn't a **chance**. **A::nd** fine so at the end of the day I met **someone** (Heb. *mišehi*) **and**. We went out for three months **and then** we got engaged. And three months later we got married. **And a year** after that the eldest son was born, who's already 15 years old **now**. **e:** a year and a half after him the second son was born. **A::nd** (.) that's it.

Igal introduces the topic of marriage by describing it as a necessary step in the progression of his life (*the time had come to get married*). He goes on to recount in a straightforward and generally affectless fashion how, after obtaining his undergraduate degree, he therefore began to go out with women to whom he was introduced by his friends and family. Igal's description of these events is succinct and told in a detached narrative voice. He summarizes this period of his life with the phrase *haja jotse im baxurot* ('would go out with women'), employing the third-person singular past habitual form *haja jotse* ('he would go out') rather than the first person *hajiti jotse* ('I would go out'), in effect positioning himself as an external character in the story. He goes on to describe the transactional nature of these meetings, where you *weigh all sorts of things . . .* [to see] *if there's a chance or there isn't a chance.* Interestingly, he explains the terms of these transactions through analogy to romantic encounters with men, where a generic "you" determines whether the man in question matches the various criteria that have been set. Igal finishes the story by stating that, in the end, he met a woman (using the feminine form of the Hebrew word for "someone"), and moved quickly through dating to engagement to marriage to children. *And that's it.*

Save the passing analogy to same-sex romance, Igal's story is a fairly standard description of courtship and marriage within Orthodox Jewish communities, where marriage is something that is entered into relatively quickly, normally as early as possible and with the help of parents and friends who act as formal (or semiformal) matchmakers, and with the express purpose of having children very soon thereafter (Safir 1991; Lavee & Katz 2003). Igal does not, however, present his own story as a specifically Orthodox one or contrast it to other possible life trajectories. The analogy that he makes with same-sex romance (*it's like with a man*) can actually be seen as a way to try to normalize his own experiences and render them comparable with the experiences of others (including, perhaps, me, the non-Orthodox gay man he was talking to). In the end, the events surrounding Igal's marriage are presented as necessary and inevitable—things that had to happen once he had the time for them. I would argue that by backgrounding Orthodox conceptualizations of marriage and family in this way, Igal's telling of this story serves to express an implicit orientation to the valuative framework of Orthodox Judaism. I suggest, moreover, that this orientation is characterized by a resigned acceptance of the expectations and obligations incumbent in Orthodox life, including, notably, those associated with marriage and family. Given my argument in this regard, it is perhaps interesting to note that there are eighteen tokens of creaky voice, which Laver (1994) has argued can serve to signal a stance of "bored resignation," clustered toward the end of Igal's story. It is unclear, however, whether these tokens function as acts of interactional stance-taking given that they all occur either IP-finally or in syllables that (in Hebrew) contain other glottal segments. It could therefore be the case that the appearance of creaky voice here is entirely determined by linguistic factors, and that the co-occurrence of creak with what I argue is a more general stance of "resigned acceptance" is coincidental. This possibility notwithstanding, the story in (1) is nevertheless useful in illustrating Igal's alignment to the principles and practices of Orthodox Judaism, an alignment that engenders no emotion or affect on Igal's part and is instead presented as an unquestioned and fundamental component of his subjectivity.

Immediately following this story, Igal segues into a new narrative about his first experience of same-sex desire. This narrative is presented in (2).

(2) "apparently I'm in love with him"
   I:: (1) all this time nothing was clear to me about **e** (1) who I am or what I want **or or** (.) what it even means to be gay. **e:::: and there**

wasn't any way to check it out or t- to ask anybody. u::m **but e** around around age thirty**::** (2) there were two things. I went to **to** (.) abroad **to** (.) I went to study a language **and and** (.) there I met a man. We became really good friends. There was never anything between us. And only on the last day the day before the last day ((in English)) *it dawned on me* that that (.) that apparently I was in love with him. And and **that there was something more there**. And then uh I was already lying in bed, I couldn't fall asleep, I called him to me and (1) for an hour tentatively and circling around it and here and there **tell me are you are you** (.) straight o:r (.) not? So he said he didn't know a:nd. And that he had had experiences with men. And that's it, it ended at that. e he was the first person I had ever even talked to about it.

Igal begins by stating that throughout his engagement and the first five years of his marriage, he did not know *who I am or what I want or or (.) what it even means to be gay*. He continues by describing how this all changed when he went abroad, where he met a man and soon after discovered that he was in love with him. Unlike the story of his marriage, Igal provides a detailed recounting of the specific events in question, describing lying in bed unable to sleep until he finally musters the courage to ask the man directly whether he is *straight o:r (.) not*. And while nothing physical or romantic comes out of this exchange, it is clear from Igal's telling that this was a turning point in his life, the first time that he had *ever even talked about it*.

In comparison with the unproblematic and inevitable character of the events in (1), the story in (2) reveals a much more personal and conflicted relationship with same-sex desire. From the very start, Igal expresses ignorance about what it means to be gay, implicitly indicating an orientation to that category without necessarily knowing what that orientation entails. This ignorance is juxtaposed with Igal's subsequent realization that he was in love, and that *there was something more there*. This "something" is presented as both deeply subjective and demanding to be shared (*I couldn't sleep, I called him to me*), in stark contrast with his realization six years prior that *the time had come to get married*. What I would argue emerges from the story in (2), then, is an orientation to same-sex desire that is much more affectively loaded than the orientation to Orthodox Judaism was in (1). It is, for example, telling that the concept of love appears nowhere in Igal's description of his married family life, whereas it is through being in love that Igal's orientation to gayness is realized. That said, it is I think equally important that Igal's realization of same-sex desire does not actually involve his engaging in any same-sex acts, sexual or otherwise. In his story, Igal never tells his friend that he is in love with him, and clearly states that after asking his friend whether he was straight or not, *it ended at that*. In other words, Igal's portrays his sexuality in a way that does not explicitly conflict with his commitment to Orthodox Judaism, allowing him to express affiliations with both of these otherwise contradictory identifications simultaneously.

From a linguistic perspective, the story in (2) is the first time that we encounter instances of creaky voice in Igal's speech that cannot be accounted for by properties of the linguistic context. Both of these occurrences (*that there was something more there*, when Igal realizes that he is in love with a man, and *tell me are you are you*, when he voices his former self uttering those words to the man in question) are located at moments in the narrative when Igal's personal affiliation with same-sex desire is the most heightened and, conversely, his orientation to Orthodox Judaism the most threatened. Crucially, it is not the case that we find creak appearing whenever Igal expresses an identification with homosexuality. The beginning of the narrative, for example, is the first (and only) time that Igal explicitly orients to the category *gay*, and yet there is no evidence that he is using creaky voice stylistically there. Instead, we only find stylistic creak employed when the conflict between same-sex desire and Orthodox Judaism is emphasized, and Igal's affiliation with the former threatens to contravene his obligations to the latter. I would argue, therefore, that in these instances creaky voice functions as a stance-taking device. Specifically, I suggest that Igal uses creaky voice to adopt a *deontic stance* (Shoaps 2004, 2009), through which he acknowledges his moral responsibilities to the values of Orthodox Judaism despite his orientation to same-sex desire. According to Shoaps, acts of deontic stance-taking provide speakers with a mechanism for positioning themselves with respect to a set of moral rules and obligations and, from that position, to evaluate the people and activities described in speech. Here, I claim that Igal uses creak to adopt a deontic stance that positions himself within the valuative system of Orthodox Judaism and therefore to evaluate with ambivalence his expressed identification with same-sex desire. I believe that it is through this act of stance-taking that Igal manages to contain his affective connection with homosexuality in favor of a discursively privileged identification with Orthodox Judaism (cf. McIntosh 2009).

Further support for my assertion that creaky voice functions as a deontic stance-taking device can be found at points in the interview where Igal explicitly alludes to the conflict between his religion and his sexuality. In the extract in (3), Igal recounts a somewhat lengthy narrative about meeting the man who he describes as the biggest love of his life. This extract appears as one of a sequence of short narratives about the different sexual and romantic relationships that Igal had had over the past ten years.

(3) "the biggest love of my life"
     And then e:: someone approached me who had already approached
     me a year earlier and I had said no no (.) that I wasn't interested.
     e:: because (1) I didn't even know who he was and he wasn't

attractive and. I told him that he was embarrassing me and that was the end of the story. A year later he tried again. And somehow we got into a conversation. **And** even though we were (.) complete opposites. He came a few times to Jerusalem and we talked and we talked and we talked and we talked. **A:::nd** that's it. And then I went to him in Tel Aviv. And we slept together. And slowly something that he thought would just be this fun summer romance for him (.) e: turned into love that for me was the biggest love of my life. **I never loved like I loved him**. I guess I'd never truly loved anyone until I loved him. **And also for him it was** (2) things got a lot more complicated than he thought they would be. e:: **uh u:::h** I don't know how t- t- to **explain it**. I was really in love. **And and** (.) I I (.) for him I was ready e (1) I fought with my wife and (.) I would go stay at his sometimes and stay over the night and come back the next day. Which I had never done before. e::: but from his point of view after a few months it became intolerable. Because he **wanted, he said that he couldn't be satisfied with once a week**. And with all the patience, with all of that. **And and** he wanted me to come and live with him. And I said that there's no chance. We both knew the restrictions on our relationship from the beginning. And that I had no intention of breaking up my marriage for something unknown. e:: (1) that's it. it it. He said let's stop then and I said no I don't want to stop I love you and and. No it'll be harder later, I said what do you care? I'm a big boy. And I want to stay, if it'll hurt more then it'll hurt more but as long as I can stay with you I want to stay with you. So we had about two arguments like that. **And each time we stayed together** a bit longer. And in the end we were together for seven months. e it was exactly at the end of de- December two years ago that we split up. e **and I was** ((in English)) *devastated*.

There are four clearly stylistic uses of creaky voice in (3). The first occurs when Igal states that he had never loved anyone like he loved the man in the story. In the context of the rest of the interview, this statement is unusual for its transparent emotional honesty. It also contrasts with Igal's descriptions of his feelings toward other men he had been with, which are always portrayed sardonically and dismissively. Here, though, Igal expresses a deeply held affective commitment to this man, a commitment we are given to understand he has never felt before (including, presumably, for his wife). The second instance of creaky voice then occurs when Igal reports that the other man felt the same way about him. Again, this statement is unique in the context of the rest of the interview as it is the only time that Igal describes reciprocal feelings of love and affection. Finally, the last two stylistic uses of creaky voice appear when Igal describes the eventual dissolution of the relationship. This dissolution is brought about the fact that the other man *couldn't be satisfied with once a week*, essentially disrupting the balance that Igal had achieved between his sexual and familial (i.e., Jewish) identifications. Yet despite the potential hazard that the relationship posed to Igal's family life (exemplified most concretely by his arguing with his wife), the two manage to *stay together a bit longer* until, eventually, the relationship ends. These four instances of creak, then, occur at four pivotal moments in the story, moments when Igal's same-sex desires threaten to exceed the space that he has allotted for them in his life. Elsewhere, this space is characterized by a lack of deep emotion and a set of very specific rules about what is possible (e.g., sex and fun) and what is not (e.g., spending the night). I therefore argue that, once again, Igal uses creaky voice at these moments as a way of (re)grounding himself within an Orthodox Jewish frame, from which he evaluates with ambivalence the acts and emotions he describes.

Finally, there are two instances in the interview in which Igal explicitly discusses the conflict between sexuality and religion, both of which contain telling examples of creaky voice. The first, extracted in (4), comes at the end of a lengthy discussion about lesbian and gay rights in Israel, during which Igal expresses the view popular among many Israelis (see Levon 2010) that there have been huge advances in this area over the past ten to fifteen years such that lesbians and gays are almost fully enfranchised in the Israeli context.

(4) "I also pay a heavy price"
but **e:: absurdly** this makes things harder for people **who who who are in a situation like m-** (.) my situation. e: I don't envy a a person who (.) who is married today and who needs to decide (.) a religious guy and he needs to decide what to do. **e::** let's say that he decides that he **wants to live with a man or for the moment to live like a gay man** (Heb. *ki homo*). And he ruins his life because becau:::se. e he goes into a place that there's no coming back from afterwards. It's really hard to disconnect from this later and (.) and e (.) to to to build a family and to get married and all that. So I'm happy that I got into it (.) e without knowing and and and I'm not alone. I also **pay a heavy price but** but e:. I think that it's worth it.

In the extract in (4), Igal describes how, in his opinion, the more generalized acceptance of lesbians and gays in Israeli society today makes life more difficult for people who are *in a situation like m- (.) my situation*. Though not explicitly articulated as such, I would argue that (4) can be taken as an example of what Ochs & Capps (2001) term *side-shadowing*, or narrative episodes in which narrators present a hypothetical series of events that could have happened had some earlier decision been made differently. For Igal, I suggest that what he is doing in (4) is describing the kind of life he could have led had he been born at a later time or made different choices. In terms of creaky voice, we find that it occurs in three places. The first is when Igal describes his own "situation," directly admitting that it is a conflicted one. The second then occurs when he articulates the source of that conflict, namely, a desire to *live with a man or for the moment to live like a gay man*. The final instance of creak appears when Igal states that he *pay[s] a heavy price* for the choices he has made. In all three occurrences, the use of creaky voice coincides with an ambivalent self-positioning on Igal's part, an evaluation of his own same-sex desires as something that cause significant strain but that he is nevertheless unwilling to give up. I would thus argue that, as before, creaky voice allows Igal to adopt a deontic stance of upholding Orthodox Jewish values even as he acknowledges an affiliation with same-sex desire that contradicts those same values.

The final extract I consider occurred immediately after Igal's comments in (4). Responding to his statements regarding how difficult it would be to be accepted in an Orthodox context after having lived a "gay life" previously, I wanted to ask Igal about whether there are any overt discussions of homosexuality within Orthodox communities. Igal, however, interprets the beginning of my question differently, and interrupts me to comment on how men in his position negotiate the biblical prohibition on same-sex sex (i.e., *Leviticus*, ch. 18).

(5) "nowhere is it written"
      EL: I wanted to ask a few questions about within the Orthodox
            community, e like=
      Igal: = look (.) in the beginning (2) it's it really bothered me. Later
            you come to understand **that** (1) **e** (.) **as long as you don't get
            into having anal relations** e (.) then you haven't really done
            anything worse **than than masturbation**. And that's fine.
            You've done it before, **you'll do it again**. If you find someone
            that you're happy with, fine. Nowhere is it written that you're
            not allowed **to love a man or to hug him or to kiss him or to
            caress him**. (1) e:: the the the: the other issue is much more
            problematic **and**. So some of the **religious people** (Heb.
            ha-dati'im) e (.) stop here. **And say that I'm not going to do**.
            And some of them (1) e everyone has (.) some some kind of
            different excuse some kind of **different** story (.) gets over it
            and says. OK. e: I don't care so **I'll I'll get my punishment** in
            the next world or I'll deal with it or it's not relevant to me **and
            so on and so on and so on**. And and this too passes.

Compared to standard Orthodox interpretations of Jewish law (Heb. *halaxa*), Igal's comments in (5) about what is and what is not permissible are relatively progressive (see Halbertal & Koren 2006). Igal, for example, argues that as long as individuals do not engage in anal sex, no biblical proscriptions have been breached. This contrasts with most Orthodox rabbinic commentary on the subject, which claims that all forms of sexual contact between men (including masturbation) are forbidden. Similarly, Igal argues that nowhere in the Bible is it written that men are not allowed to love one another, or to hug, kiss, or caress one another. While this is technically true, both traditional and modern interpretations of *halaxa* consider all these acts to be nonpermissible. Finally, when discussing engaging in behavior (like anal sex) that is clearly disallowed by Jewish law, Igal suggests that there are ways to *get over it*, by, for example, accepting the fact that a punishment will be forthcoming in the after-life. The sort of personal and transactional relationship with God and divine law described by Igal here (i.e., "I'll pay for it later") stands in stark opposition to standard Orthodox beliefs about the necessity of "integrating biblical and rabbinic imperatives with internal experience" (Halbertal & Koren 2006: 44), such that one's commitment to Judaism is expressed not (only) by individual faith but by daily obedience to communally shared commandments (Heb. *mitsvot*).When looking at the distribution of creaky voice across Igal's comments in (5), we find that creak appears whenever Igal offers a reinterpretation of normative Orthodox beliefs. Creak is used, for example, when Igal claims that loving and hugging and kissing a man are permissible, and it is also used when he suggests that even if one engages in anal sex, punishment for that act can be postponed. As I have argued earlier, I therefore suggest that Igal's use of creak in (5) is an act of deontic stance-taking through which he reaffirms his positioning within the valuative framework of Orthodox Judaism even while the content of his talk troubles that positioning.

Discussion

My primary goal in this chapter has been to examine how Igal negotiates his conflicting identifications with both Orthodox Judaism and homosexuality. To that end, I examine Igal's use of creaky voice in the interview I conducted with him. A quantitative distributional analysis of creak demonstrates that Igal uses this feature significantly more frequently and in more unexpected linguistic contexts when talking about the intersection of sexuality and religion than when talking on other topics. I argue that this finding indicates that Igal is using creaky voice stylistically and in order to achieve some social and/or interactional goal related to his sexual and religious identifications. A qualitative analysis of creak in context then reveals that Igal deploys the feature whenever he expresses an affective alignment with same-sex desire that threatens to disrupt his simultaneous alignment with Orthodox Judaism. In other words, it is not the case that creak coincides with all instances of Igal orienting to homosexuality. There are many examples of Igal describing same-sex desires and experiences that contain no stylistic creak whatsoever. Rather, creak only occurs when the specific orientation to homosexuality that Igal adopts potentially undermines his positioning as an Orthodox Jew (because, for example, that orientation is too affective or personal, or because it involves engaging in explicitly forbidden acts).

For this reason, I argue that creaky voice serves as a deontic stance-marker for Igal, through which he signals his continued commitment to the valuative framework of Orthodox Judaism. In essence, I suggest that with creaky voice Igal laminates a deontic stance of Orthodox positionality onto a simultaneous expression of orientation to same-sex desire. This has the effect of discursively containing his identification with homosexuality and relegating it to a hier- archically lower position than his identification with Orthodox Judaism. Put another way, creaky voice allows Igal to layer an identificationally privileged commitment to religion onto a simultaneous commitment to same-sex desire. Crucially, I argue that simultaneity here does not imply a harmonious recon- ciliation of these two conflicting identifications (cf. Yip 2002) but, rather, a state in which the contradiction remains in stable tension.

I believe that this argument has several important ramifications. First, my analysis supports the claim that linguistic practice can result from the exis- tence of multiple and conflicting identifications (Cameron & Kulick 2003; Kulick 2005). Essentially, I argue that creaky voice is a materialization of the subjective conflict that Igal experiences between his sexual and religious iden- tifications. What I mean by this is that we find creaky voice precisely at those moments when Igal aligns himself with a potentially threatening articulation of homosexuality (e.g., homosexuality as reciprocal love or as engaging in for- bidden sexual acts). I suggest that creaky voice provides Igal with a mechanism for laminating a strategic and partial disalignment with these articulations of homosexuality at the very same time that he is also aligning with them. In other words, I argue that at these moments Igal simultaneously orients to and away from particular conceptualizations of same-sex desire, and that it is creaky voice that allows him to adopt this internally contradictory positioning. What this means is that neither Igal's identification with homosexuality nor his identification with Judaism can account for the observed patterns of language use. Rather, it is the combination (and contradiction) of the two that does.

The second ramification of this analysis, then, is that it highlights the importance of a theory of stance to our understandings of the social meaning of variation. I argue that it is not the case that Igal deploys creaky voice in an effort to actively construct a "gay" or "Orthodox" or even "gay Orthodox" per- sona. While I acknowledge that such a persona may emerge from Igal's speech (Podesva 2007), I maintain that a close analysis of Igal's use of creaky voice demonstrates that it functions as a means for Igal to adopt a deontic stance and so position himself with respect to both his sexual and religious identifica- tions. Given this, I would argue that the primary meaning of creaky voice in the interview is not (as a simple correlational analysis might assume) "gayness" or "masculinity" or "religion." Rather, I propose that the reason Igal uses creak to take a deontic stance is because of the feature's association with "contained" or "suppressed" emotion, what Bolinger (1982) calls "tension under control." I believe that Igal recruits this meaning as a way of limiting or, perhaps more

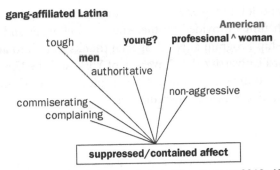

FIGURE 11.4   An indexical field for creaky voice (adapted from Podesva 2013: 436)

appropriately, *managing* his affective and personal orientation to "trouble-some" articulations of same-sex desire. Ultimately, I argue that managing his affective orientation toward homosexuality via creaky voice is the means through which Igal adopts a deontic stance that positions him firmly within the valuative framework of Orthodox Judaism. In this sense, then, the meaning of creaky voice for Igal is not so much about "identity" or "personae" as it is about the stances that he takes with respect to his identifications.

To conclude, I would note that this proposed meaning of "suppressed or contained affect" for creaky voice also applies to all of the previous analyses of creak mentioned at the beginning of this chapter. Creak's association with men and masculinity, for example, could result from the normative linking of "manliness" with rational and affect-free behavior (e.g., Sattel 1983). Similarly, the use of creak by young women in the United States to take stances of "authority" or to portray "upwardly-mobile professional" personae could also be based on a belief that professionalism and authority entail suppressing one's emotions. And, finally, Mendoza-Denton (2011) explicitly links the "tough" and "hard-core" meaning of creaky voice among Latina gang girls with emotional distance and being "hard of heart." It therefore appears that all the uses of creak that have been identified previously in the literature can be seen as ideological elaborations of a fundamental (and perhaps iconic) association between creaky voice and suppressed affect. I would therefore propose that "suppression/containment of affect" is the core meaning that anchors the indexical field of creaky voice (see Figure 11.4), making the feature available for a variety of related social and interactional purposes, including, in the case of Igal, negotiating the subjective conflict between Orthodox Judaism and same-sex desire.

Acknowledgments

The research that the data for this chapter are drawn from would not have been possible without the guidance of Renée Blake, Rudi Gaudio, Greg Guy,

Don Kulick, and John Singler and the support of the Social Science Research Council (with funds provided by the Andrew Mellon Foundation) and the Torch Fellowship Program at NYU. Special thanks as well to audience members at Stanford University, the University of York, and the University of Cape Town for their comments on the work presented here. I, of course, am alone responsible for all errors and shortcomings.

Notes

1. Igal is a pseudonym. My interview with Igal took place entirely in Hebrew, though in the interest of space I only provide English translations here. The translation of this quote, like all other translations in the chapter, is my own.

2. For the purposes of my discussion here, I abstract away from the difference between *creak* (sometimes also called glottal fry), characterized by maximal adduction of the vocal folds, and *creaky voice*, a compound phonation type derived from the combination of *creak* and *modal* voicing (see Laver 1980, 1994). While there are important phonetic differences between the two, they are tangential to my arguments here and so I use the terms *creaky voice* and *creak* interchangeably.

3. I had originally hoped to solicit participation from a network of Orthodox Jewish women and men who engage in same-sex practice, but this ultimately proved to be impossible. My interview with Igal can thus serve as no more than a case study of individuals in that situation.

4. If an instance of creak began in a nonfinal syllable and continued to final position (in a multisyllabic word, for example), all syllables were coded as "final."

5. Transcription conventions are as follows:

.?, Intonation contour
::: Vowel lengthening
(.) Short pause (less than 0.5 seconds)
(1) Numbers of seconds of pause
= latching (no audible break between speakers)
- speaker abruptly stopping
(()) transcriber comments
word Speech in English

References

Bakhtin, Mikhail. 1981. *The dialogic imagination: Four essays* (ed. Michael Holquist). Austin: University of Texas Press.

Bell, Allan. 1984. Language style as audience design. *Language in Society* 13. 145–204.

Bell, Allan. 2001. Back in style: Reworking audience design. In Penelope Eckert & John R. Rickford (eds.), *Style and sociolinguistic variation*, 139–169. New York: Cambridge University Press.

Billig, Michael. 1997. The dialogic unconscious: Psychoanalysis, discursive psychology and the nature of repression. *British Journal of Social Psychology* 36. 139–159.

Billig, Michael. 1999. *Freudian repression: Conversation creating the unconscious.* Cambridge: Cambridge University Press.

Bolinger, Dwight. 1982. Intonation and its parts. *Language* 58. 505–533.

Bucholtz, Mary. 2009. From stance to style: Gender, interaction and indexicality in mexican immigrant youth slang. In Alexandra Jaffe (ed.), *Stance: Sociolinguistic perspectives*, 146–170. Oxford: Oxford University Press.

Cameron, Deborah & Don Kulick. 2003. *Language and sexuality.* Cambridge: Cambridge University Press.

Cameron, Deborah & Don Kulick. 2005. Identity crisis? *Language and Communication* 25. 107–125.

Côté, James. 1996. Identity: A multidimensional analysis. In Gerald Adams, Raymond Montemayor, & Thomas Gullota (eds.), *Psychosocial development during adolescence*, 130–180. London: Sage.

Couper-Kuhlen, Elizabeth. 2003. Intonation and discourse: Current views from within. In Deborah Schiffrin, Deborah Tanner, & Heidi Hamilton (eds.), *The handbook of discourse analysis*, 13–34. Oxford: Blackwell.

Damari, Rebecca. 2010. Intertextual stancetaking and the local negotiation of cultural identities by a binational couple. *Journal of Sociolinguistics* 14. 609–629.

Dilley, Laura, Stefanie Shattuck-Hufnagel, & Mari Ostendorf. 1996. Glottalization of word-initial vowels as a function of prosodic structure. *Journal of Phonetics* 24. 423–444.

Du Bois, John. 2007. The stance triangle. In Robert Englebretson (ed.), *Stancetaking in discourse*, 139–182. Amsterdam: John Benjamins.

Eckert, Penelope. 2008. Variation and the indexical field. *Journal of Sociolinguistics* 12. 453–476.

Erikson, Erik. 1968. *Identity: Youth and crisis.* New York: Norton.

Esling, John. 1978. The identification of features of voice quality in social groups. *Journal of the International Phonetic Association* 8. 18–23.

Goffman, Erving. 1974. *Frame analysis.* Cambridge, MA: Harper & Row.

Gordon, Matthew & Peter Ladefoged. 2001. Phonation types: A cross-linguistic overview. *Journal of Phonetics* 29. 383–406.

Grivičić, Tamara & Chad Nilep. 2004. When phonation matters: The use and function of *yeah* and creaky voice. *Colorado Research in Linguistics* 17. 1–11.

Halbertal, Tova & Irit Koren. 2006. Between "being" and "doing": Conflict and coherence in the identity formation of gay and lesbian Orthodox Jews. In Dan McAdams, Ruthellen Josselson, & Amia Lieblich (eds.), *Identity and story: Creating self in narrative*, 37–61. Washington, DC: American Psychological Association.

Henton, Caroline & Anthony Bladon. 1988. Creak as a sociophonetic marker. In Larry Hyman & Charles Li (eds.), *Language, speech and mind: Studies in honor of Victoria A. Fromkin*, 3–29. London: Routledge.

Hermans, Hubert, Harry Kempen, & Rens Van Loon. 1992. The dialogial self: Beyond individualism and rationalism. *American Psychologist* 47. 23–33.

Hill, Jane. 1995. The voices of Don Gabriel: Responsibility and self in a modern Mexicano narrative. In Dennis Tedlock & Bruce Mannheim (eds.), *The dialogic emergence of culture*, 97–147. Urbana, IL: Univeristy of Illinois Press.

Jaffe, Alexandra. 2009. Introduction: The sociolinguistics of stance. In Alexandra Jaffe (ed.), *Stance: Sociolinguistic perspectives*, 3–28. Oxford: Oxford University Press.

Jannedy, Stefanie & Norma Mendoza-Denton. 1998. *Low pitch in the linguistic performance of Latina gang girls.* Paper presented at the Perceiving and Performing Gender Conference, University of Kiel, Germany.

Kulick, Don. 2005. The importance of what gets left out. *Discourse & Society* 7. 615–624.

Ladefoged, Peter. 1971. *Preliminaries to linguistic phonetics.* Chicago: University of Chicago Press.

Lavee, Yoav & Ruth Katz. 2003. The family in Israel: Between tradition and modernity. *Marriage and Family Review* 35. 193–217.

Laver, John. 1968. Voice quality and indexical information. *International Journal of Language and Communication Disorders* 3. 43–54.

Laver, John. 1980. *The phonetic description of voice quality.* Cambridge: Cambridge University Press.

Laver, John. 1994. *Principles of phonetics.* Cambridge: Cambridge University Press.

Lefkowitz, Daniel & Mark Sicoli. 2007. *Creaky voice: Constructions of gender and authority in American English.* Paper presented at the annual meeting of the Anthropological Association of America, Washington, DC.

Levon, Erez. 2009. Dimensions of style: Context, politics and motivation in gay Israeli speech. *Journal of Sociolinguistics* 13. 29–58.

Levon, Erez. 2010. *Language and the politics of sexuality: Lesbians and gays in Israel.* Basingstoke, UK: Palgrave.

Linde, Charlotte. 1993. *Life stories: The creation of coherence.* Oxford: Oxford University Press.

McIntosh, Janet. 2009. Stance and distance: Social boundaries, self-lamination and metalinguistic anxiety in White Kenyan narratives about the African occult. In Alexandra Jaffe (ed.), *Stance: Sociolinguistic perspectives*, 72–91. Oxford: Oxford University Press.

Mendoza-Denton, Norma. 2008. *Homegirls: Language and cultural practice among Latina youth gangs.* Oxford: Blackwell.

Mendoza-Denton, Norma. 2011. The semiotic hitchhiker's guide to creaky voice: Circulation and gendered hardcore in a Chicana/o gang persona. *Journal of Linguistic Anthropology* 21. 261–280.

Ochs, Elinor. 1992. Indexing gender. In Alessandro Duranti & Charles Goodwin (eds.), *Rethinking context: Language as an interactive phenomenon*, 335–358. New York: Cambridge University Press.

Ochs, Elinor & Lisa Capps. 2001. *Living narrative: Creating lives in everyday storytelling.* Cambridge: Harvard University Press.

Peirce, Charles Sanders. 1955. *Philosophical writings of Peirce* (ed. Justus Buchler). New York: Dover Publications.

Podesva, Robert. 2007. Phonation type as a stylistic variable: The use of falsetto in constructing a persona. *Journal of Sociolinguistics* 11. 478–504.

Podesva, Robert. 2013. Gender and the social meaning of non-modal phonation types. *Proceedings of the Annual Meeting of the Berkeley Linguistics Society* 37. 427–448.

Rauniomaa, Mirka. 2003. Stance accretion: Some initial observations. Santa Barbara: University of California Santa Barbara, unpublished manuscript.

Safir, Marilyn. 1991. Religion, tradition and public policy give family first priority. In Barbara Swirski & Marilyn Safir (eds.), *Calling the equality bluff: Women in Israel*, 57–65. New York: Pergamon.

Sapir, Edward. 1927. Speech as a personality trait. *American Journal of Sociology* 32. 892–905.

Sattel, Jack. 1983. Men, inexpressiveness and power. In Barrie Thorne, Cheris Kramarae, & Nancy Henley (eds.), *Language, gender and society*, 118–124. Rowley, MA: Newbury House.

Schilling-Estes, Natalie. 2004. Constructing ethnicity in interaction. *Journal of Sociolinguistics* 8. 163–195.

Shoaps, Robin. 2004. Morality in grammar and discourse: Stance-taking and the negotiation of moral personhood in Sakapultek wedding counsels. Santa Barbara: Department of Linguistics, University of California Santa Barbara, unpublished PhD dissertation.

Shoaps, Robin. 2009. Moral irony and moral personhood in Sakapultek discourse and culture. In Alexandra Jaffe (ed.), *Stance: Sociolinguistic perspectives*, 92–118. Oxford: Oxford University Press.

Sicoli, Mark. 2010. Shifting voices with participant roles: Voice qualities and speech registers in Mesoamerica. *Language in Society* 39. 521–553.

Singer, Milton. 1980. Signs of the self: An exploration in semiotic anthropology. *American Anthropologist* 82. 485–507.

Singer, Milton. 1984. *Man's glassy essence: Explorations in semiotic anthropology*. Bloomington: Indiana University Press.

Stuart-Smith, Jane. 1999. Glasgow: Accent and voice quality. In Paul Foulkes & Gerard Docherty (eds.), *Urban voices: Accent studies in the British Isles*, 203–222. London: Edward Arnold.

Syed, Moin. 2012. The past, present and future of Eriksonian identity research. *Identity: An International Journal of Theory and Research* 12. 1–7.

Yarhouse, Mark. 2001. Sexual identity development: The influence of valuative frameworks on identity synthesis. *Psychotherapy* 28. 331–341.

Yip, Andrew. 1999. The politics of counter-rejection: Gay Christians and the church. *Journal of Homosexuality* 37. 47–61.

Yip, Andrew. 2002. The persistence of faith among non-heterosexual Christians: Evidence for the nonsecularization thesis of religious transformation. *Journal for the Scientific Study of Religion* 41. 199–212.

Yuasa, Ikuko. 2010. Creaky voice: A new feminine voice quality for young urban-oriented upwardly mobile American women? *American Speech* 85. 315–337.

INDEX

241